Universality, Ethics and International Relations

'A sophisticated and refreshing argument against the metaphysical seductions of universalism in IR theory. Pin-Fat's Wittgensteinian 'grammatical reading' takes theories of international ethics back to the rough ground in ways that challenge realist, cosmopolitan and communitarian approaches.'

Kimberly Hutchings *London School of Economics, UK*

'Central to critical discourses in international relations are questions related to what constitutes the 'universal', how it is used in political thought, and the ways in which it relates to operations of power in global politics. Véronique Pin-Fat's 'grammatical' reading is one of the most original interventions on the relationship between ethics, universality, and international politics, bringing not only Wittgenstein, but her own voice to our deliberations. This is one of the most challenging contributions to international relations theory in general and to critical thought in particular.'

Vivienne Jabri *Kings College London, UK*

Universality, Ethics and International Relations introduces students to the key debates about ethics in international relations theory. This book explores the reasons why grappling with universality and ethics seems to be a profound endeavour and where we end up when we do.

By offering a new way of thinking about ethics in international relations, Pin-Fat shows that there are several varieties of universality which are offered as *the* answer to ethics in global politics; the divine universality of Hans Morgenthau, the ideal universality of Charles R. Beitz and the binary universality of Michael Walzer. Taking the reader on a grammatical odyssey through each, the book concludes that profound searches for the foundations of universality can't fulfil our deepest desires for an answer to ethics in global politics. Pin-Fat suggests that the failure of these searches reveals the ethical desirability of defending universality as (im)possible.

An ideal text for use in a wide variety of courses, including ethics in international relations, international relations theory, and international political theory, this work provides a valuable new contribution to this rapidly developing field of research.

Véronique Pin-Fat is Senior Lecturer in International Relations in the Centre for International Politics at the University of Manchester. She is co-editor of *Sovereign Lives: Power in Global Politics* (2004) with Jenny Edkins and Michael J. Shapiro.

Interventions
Edited by Jenny Edkins, Aberystwyth University, and
Nick Vaughan-Williams, University of Exeter

'As Michel Foucault has famously stated, "knowledge is not made for understanding; it is made for cutting." In this spirit, The Edkins–Vaughan-Williams
Interventions series solicits cutting edge, critical works that challenge mainstream
understandings in international relations. It is the best place to contribute post
disciplinary works that think rather than merely recognize and affirm the world
recycled in IR's traditional geopolitical imaginary.'
Michael J. Shapiro, University of Hawai'i at Mānoa, USA

The series aims to advance understanding of the key areas in which scholars
working within broad critical post-structural and post-colonial traditions
have chosen to make their interventions, and to present innovative analyses
of important topics.

Titles in the series engage with critical thinkers in philosophy, sociology,
politics and other disciplines and provide situated historical, empirical and
textual studies in international politics.

Critical Theorists and International Relations
Edited by Jenny Edkins and Nick Vaughan-Williams

Ethics as Foreign Policy
Britain, the EU and the other
Dan Bulley

Universality, Ethics and International Relations
A grammatical reading
Véronique Pin-Fat

Universality, Ethics and International Relations

A grammatical reading

Véronique Pin-Fat

Routledge
Taylor & Francis Group

LONDON AND NEW YORK

First published 2010
by Routledge
2 Park Square, Milton Park, Abingdon, Oxon OX14 4RN

Simultaneously published in the USA and Canada
by Routledge
270 Madison Ave, New York, NY 10016

Routledge is an imprint of the Taylor & Francis Group, an informa business

Typeset in Times New Roman by
Book Now Ltd, London
Printed and bound in Great Britain by
CPI Antony Rowe, Chippenham, Wiltshire

British Library Cataloguing in Publication Data
A catalogue record for this book is available from the British Library

Library of Congress Cataloging in Publication Data
Pin-Fat, Véronique, 1965–.
Universality, ethics, and international relations : a grammatical
reading / Véronique Pin-Fat.
    p. cm.—(Interventions)
Includes bibliographical references.
1. International relations—Moral and ethical aspects. I. Title.

JZ1306.P56 2009
172'.4—dc22   2009015745

ISBN10: 0–415–49205–X (hbk)
ISBN10: 0–415–49206–8 (pbk)
ISBN10: 0–203–86779–3 (ebk)

ISBN13: 978–0–415–49205–8 (hbk)
ISBN13: 978–0–415–49206–5 (pbk)
ISBN13: 978–0–203–86779–2 (ebk)

In memory of Howard Dennis Suttle
(14 May 1954–10 January 2000)
Beloved.

Contents

Acknowledgements

In conversation, this piece of work goes by the much shorter and snappier title of *Howard's Book*. I wish I could say that writing it was easy. It wasn't and because of that there are many people to acknowledge for so much more than the writing of it.

I must admit to having always enjoyed reading authors' acknowledgements. I rather like that polite tendency to wait until the end to thank those who have had to tolerate them. The reader can usually surmise that these are the very people that the author loves, is closest to, is supported by and without whom their life wouldn't be as much fun. I'm just not as polite as I should be. These people are all those things and more: Luc and Françoise Pin-Fat, Olivier Pin-Fat, Sally Berry, Judy and Barry Shaw, Angela Streblow, Cécile Treulé, Alain and Christiane Fleury, Michèle Fleury, Jean-Luc and Nelly Fleury, Dominique and Gérard Lelarge, Mee-Lin Moss, Fritz Watson, Hamish Mitchell, Rob Macgrory, Odile Vassallo, Simon and Bryony Pennington, Pamela and Leli Salvaris, Linda Burton, Wilma Burton, Jenny Edkins, Emma Macfarlane-Lewis, Ruth Beaver, Kate Bennett, Catherine Conybeare, Karen White, Sally Morris, the Milners, Dana Hanni, Rae-Lene Berubé, Connor Wood, Liz Prince, Peter Lawler, Maria Stern and Kirshen Rundle have all contributed to an ever-increasing brighter set of horizons. The person who shines brightest throughout is Jacques Suttle without whom all would have been lost and who will always be 'the best thing that ever happened' to his father and me. It's also Jacques who has tolerated me every day with great love, kindness and cuddles. I never would have made it without him.

For making the intolerable manageable, I want to thank the staff of Stewart Medical Centre in Buxton, Stepping Hill Hospital in Stockport and the staff of Toddbrook Nursery in Whaley Bridge, especially Brian Williams, William Brough, Val, Donna, Sally, Christine, Kerrie and Sue Bithell.

I enjoy going to work. In my workplace, at the University of Manchester, I have colleagues who offered me support, patience and space when I needed it most. These people, somehow, made it possible for me to continue working when my heart seemed to have lost its beat: Lucy James, Norman

Geras, Paul Cammack, Simon Bulmer, Ursula Vogel, Yoram Gorlizki, Hillel Steiner, Martin Burch and David Farrell deserve special mention. But to all in Politics at Manchester, I remain forever deeply indebted to you. To my more recent colleagues I thank you for the gentle prods (as well as the kicks up the backside) to finish this monster: Maja Zehfuss, Stuart Shields, Nicola Phillips and Cristina Masters.

I have the good fortune to teach a large number of undergraduate and postgraduate students who cheerfully allow me to try out my ideas with them, help me develop them and, generally just play along. I do so hope you will recognise your input in the final version of 'there's this long overdue book I'm working on'. You know who you are but, in particular, I thank my long-suffering PhD students for their indulgence and their insights: Phil Hutchinson, Simona Rentea, Robin Redhead, Kelly Staples, Katherine Allison, Kathryn Starnes and Andrew Slack.

How to do this bit without Jenny Edkins wanting to throttle me? There is probably none. What I will say is that one of the most remarkable things I have personally experienced is the possibility that one can encounter someone who has shaped and encouraged the development of what one holds most dear and actively facilitated its expression academically as a writing partner and personally as a friend. Nothing of value in this book would be what it is without the influence of having had such an encounter and its longevity.

On the theme of influences, I want to acknowledge Chris Brown whose book *International Relations Theory* provided me with an intellectual sweet shop to explore when ethics was still chronically marginal to the academy. He made my career possible as did my former, wonderful, supervisors Steve Smith and Tim Dunne; and the teacher who started it all, Jennie Jackson. The Economic and Social Research Council, UK, funded earlier parts of the research.

Last but not least, to the gentle man who made this so incredibly difficult and yet remains throughout: these pictures are for you.

Buxton, 2009

Permissions

The author would like to thank the following publishers for permission to reproduce parts of work previously published:

Cambridge University Press for permission to reprint: Pin-Fat, Véronique. '(Im)possible Universalism: Reading Human Rights in World Politics', *Review of International Studies* 26, no. 4 (2000): 663–74.

Pin-Fat, Véronique. 'The Metaphysics of the National Interest and the "Mysticism" of the Nation State: Reading Hans J. Morgenthau', *Review of International Studies* 31, no. 2 (2005): 217–36.

Lynne Rienner for permission to reprint: Pin-Fat, Véronique, and Maria Stern. 'The Scripting of Private Jessica Lynch: Biopolitics, Gender and the "Feminization" of the US Military', *Alternatives: Global, Local, Political* 30 (2005): 25–53.

Routledge for permission to reprint: Edkins, Jenny, and Véronique Pin-Fat. 'Life, Power, Resistance', in *Sovereign Lives: Power in Global Politics*, edited by Jenny Edkins, Véronique Pin-Fat and Michael J. Shapiro. New York: Routledge, 2004.

Sage for permission to reprint: Edkins, Jenny, and Véronique Pin-Fat. 'Through the Wire: Relations of Power and Relations of Violence', *Millennium: Journal of International Studies* 34, no. 1 (2005): 1–24.

Introduction

Were I really to write a book about universality, ethics and global politics I wouldn't write *this* one.[1] Instead, this book confines itself primarily to being a collection of grammatical remarks about universality and its relationship to ethics as it appears within the academic discipline of International Relations (IR). It may seem tangential and strange to want to make remarks about grammar. After all, universality, ethics and global politics are supposed to be serious subjects and need to be engaged with, not stepped back from as though one were outlining rules on the use of interrogatives, the definite article, adjectives, reflexive pronouns, gerunds, tenses, and adverbs, for example. This book isn't one of those kinds of grammar books but it is one about different sorts of grammars, how to read them and what happens when we do. Specifically, this book reads language games of international ethics as they appear in IR theory and the 'things' that each language game's grammar produces. The most important 'thing' that gets produced, in this context, is universality but that is not all. Related to ethics and its purported universality, as we shall see, are notions of what it is to be human,[2] what reason is and its role in a universalisable ethic[3] and last, but not least, where such an ethic can, or should, take place.[4]

Literally, universality is the biggest claim you could make about any 'thing'. In everyday usage,[5] the word 'universal' has a meaning of cosmic proportions being applicable to the entire universe.[6] On a more down-to-earth scale, it usually means of, or relating to, or typical of, or affecting all people and/or all things in the world. Broadly speaking, universal simply means applicable, or related, to all cases without exception. This book would be considerably shorter if that were all there was to say about this cosmic-sized word. The reason for there being many more pages than the one you are currently reading is because of a plethora of problems that seem to arise when claims are made that, in global politics, ethics is, or at least in principle ought to be, universal. Even in the everyday sense discussed above, universal ethical claims are asserting that ethics relates to, or is applicable to, everyone in the world. Unsurprisingly, the problems associated with universality are because of its extension and all-encompassing scope.

The thing about International Relations, of course, is that it purports to be talking about politics on a global scale. The whole world seems to lie before the IR scholar so that the urge to make universal claims is (almost) irresistible. Asking what anarchy is, what a state is, what war is, what power is, what security is, and so on, seems to require that the answer apply universally to all instances of that 'thing' in global politics without exception. The pull towards universality, one might say, is a double whammy when it comes to questions about the possibility of ethics in global politics. Not only does there appear to be a requirement that some universal 'thing' about global politics needs to be located, but that that 'thing' also needs to be an accommodating locus for a global ethic.

This collection of grammatical remarks is about these very 'things' and differs from other books on international ethics in a number of ways. First, it proposes that we read universality, ethics and International Relations grammatically.[7] Chapter 1 sets out the contours of what I call a grammatical reading and suggests that, were we to deploy it, we might find ourselves surprised at what we find as familiar landscapes are rendered unfamiliar through nothing more than 'assembling reminders for a particular purpose' (Wittgenstein 1958a: §127). It is not a chapter on methodology *per se* for, as will be seen, it can hardly be labelled a 'method' at all in a formal sense.

Subsequent chapters of the book then set about rendering the familiar unfamiliar. It's somewhat like embarking on a grammatical odyssey as we explore the grammatical contours of international ethical landscapes. The first landscape that I sketch is the one that is evoked by the use of the term 'ethics and international politics' in IR. In Chapter 2, I seek to show that the way in which the field is understood is one where 'ethics' and 'international politics' are seen as separate and, this being so, the ethical conundrum consists of how we are to put them back together again, a bit like Humpty Dumpty. The question that lies in the background is how we might build a universal bridge between them so that ethics *in* international political practice is possible and can include everyone. Needless to say, there are differing answers to what such a bridge may consist of, how it may safely be traversed and by whom. In Chapters 3 to 5, a grammatical reading is provided of three iconic answers in IR: a Realist answer as provided by Hans J. Morgenthau, a cosmopolitan answer as provided by Charles R. Beitz, and, finally, a communitarian answer provided by Michael Walzer. In these chapters we go where each theorist's grammar tells us we must, take a look around at what we can see and determine whether we've ended up where our theorist's grammar tells us we should be. At this point something already appears seriously 'wrong' with the content of this book. Surely two of these thinkers, the communitarian and the Realist, are not going to embark on a quest for a universal?

Chris Brown's seminal text *International Relations Theory: New Normative Approaches* was the first to introduce the debate between cosmopolitans and communitarians to IR (Brown 1992).[8] It provided a framework for dividing ethically universalist (cosmopolitan) and particularist (communitarian) positions and it is a framework that has been widely adopted in IR since.[9] In the many books on ethics and international politics that have subsequently been published, an obligatory discussion of Realism often appears as the odd one out: the approach to an international ethics that may be amoral at worst or morally sceptical at the very least. The second way in which this book differs from others on 'ethics and international politics', then, is that it becomes very quickly apparent that I have not adopted this way of organising such approaches. Why? Very simply, it is because this book is about *universality*, ethics and International Relations. One of the effects of having read ethics grammatically is that, for me at least, it rendered the approaches of Morgenthau, Beitz and Walzer unfamiliar. The surprise was that a grammatical reading highlighted how each was committed to a different form of universality. Thus, one of the claims that this collection of grammatical remarks is making is that theorisations of international ethics in IR are not necessarily best divided into a debate between universalists and particularists. Indeed, I am claiming that the Realist, cosmopolitan and communitarian thinkers read herein are all universalists of one sort or another.[10]

There are reasons for the pervasiveness of ethical universalism that a grammatical reading highlights, most notably, the (almost) irresistible metaphysical pull towards being seduced by the notion of universality. The central theme of this book, that runs throughout each chapter, is what I call a 'metaphysical seduction' – a desire to locate a foundation for universality so that an international ethic can, indeed, apply to everyone on a global scale. When a theorist is metaphysically seduced, they have an irresistible urge to dig, to dig beneath the surface of reality (language) in order hit upon the real nature of things and of humanity. It is an urge to seek the profound, to provide a universalist resolution to the double whammy outlined briefly above and at length, in Chapter 2.

Perhaps the seductive appeal of a need for universality in relation to ethics cannot be fully resisted, though the need for foundations and a successful resolution may. In the final chapter I present a series of grammatical remarks about universality/universalisms as they appear in IR. I conclude that each version of universality is grammatically (im)possible.[11] That is to say, each version of universality is an example of conjunctive failure. Surprisingly, perhaps, it is the grammatical necessity of universality's failure that I seek to defend as ethico-politically desirable. In the final analysis, my defence of universality is simply a plea for us to return to and stay on the surface of language. I suggest it's a less dangerous and isolating place to be. It's where we are and where we live among others; it is an ethico-political landscape of life.

1 Reading grammatically

Reading, representation and the limits of language

Grammar is the shadow of possibility cast by language on phenomena.
(Wittgenstein 1974: §329)

The aim of this chapter is to outline a way of approaching ethics in International Relations (IR) that allows us to understand the ways in which universality has been theoretically produced in the discipline. It is neither novel nor unique to point out that universality matters. One could claim, with some grounds, that the history of Western philosophy is the story of a veritable obsession it. The theorists considered in this book, and indeed its author, are no exception. By reading grammatically I hope to show that, for IR, the dominant ethical position, whether implicit or explicit, is that the location of a universal is a fundamental requirement of ethics. More to the point, regardless of what the ultimate source of universality may be, humanity must embody it. Of course, different theorists occupy this position in different ways and, sometimes, my interpretation of what they are doing may seem directly at odds with their own description of theirs. Nevertheless, a notion of universality which serves as the foundation of ethics appears for each, albeit differently configured. And, it matters. On the one hand, it matters because their understandings of universality delineate the very possibility of ethics in world politics. On the other hand, more importantly, such delineations matter ethico-politically. By its end, this book will have embarked on several grammatical odysseys as a way of climbing each rung of each language game. The point of doing this will simply be that, by reading grammatically, we can ask for a re-opening of the question of universality and ethics in world politics and change 'what we want to do in ethics' and world politics (Diamond 1995: 24). We might say that reading grammatically sets a different task.

The questions about universality, ethics and world politics that a grammatical reading poses are therefore, going to be somewhat different from the standard one. Instead of asking, and providing answers to, the question 'What is ethics in world politics?' I will be asking 'How does grammar constitute universality and thereby, delineate ethical possibility in world politics? What are the effects of this? Where do we end up?' Two reading steps are involved in order to explore this alternative. First, it suggests reading in order to locate the most salient grammatical features of each theorist and show how grammar is the constitutive dynamic that accounts not only for their specific configuration of what the problem of ethics is in IR (the question) but also their answers (which, in the final analysis, rely on a configuration of universality). And second, it also suggests reading in such a way as to notice that what theorists want may not only be where they think it can be, nor dependent upon what they think it must depend on. This second aspect of reading can help uncover the latent narrowness of the approaches considered and the surprising (albeit dangerous) effects that this has on the possibility of ethics in world politics.

The grammatical focus that is proposed, it should be emphasised, is *not* a focus on just 'words' and therefore, an avoidance of 'real-world' ethical conundrums. On the contrary, an engagement with what might count as 'reality' is itself a central ethico-political theme that motivates this book. However, the route I have chosen by way of engagement with these questions is through a consideration of what the relationship between language and reality/the world might be.

The approach of reading grammatically that is being proposed here is an applied interpretation of the implications of Ludwig Wittgenstein's thoughts on language and reality and his notion of a 'grammatical investigation' for IR theory generally, and ethics within it more specifically.[1] The result, I hope, is a particular way of reading paradigmatic contributors to IR that can be mobilised throughout subsequent chapters in order for us to appreciate the constitutive dynamics of each form of universality they propose and the consequences of their resultant delineations of ethical possibility in world politics.

So, what sort of themes can we expect a grammatical reading to involve? On the one hand, it will involve addressing some methodological questions such as: Is the role of theory to uncover the nature of international political reality and/or the nature of the ethical? Is the separation of theory and practice unavoidable? If, following Wittgenstein, the answer to these questions is a firm 'no', then we can expect a grammatical reading to offer us an alternative way of proceeding that still makes engaging with ethics in world politics possible. On the other hand, a grammatical reading will involve a number of refusals: A refusal to be seduced by metaphysics, epistemology, a search for foundations and the notion that language *represents* reality.[2] We might say that reading grammatically is an *ethos* of reading which is determined to avoid the seduction of 'digging' deep into phenomena to find 'reality' and *the* answer. On the positive side, it also involves an *ethos* that fully embraces contingency and uncertainty. While for traditional theorists this sounds far removed from a positive move, I hope to show that a return to this 'rough ground' is fruitful. I shall now address each of these themes in turn.

'Sketches of landscapes': an ethos of reading

In order to try to convey an *ethos* of reading grammatically or, what others have described as, the 'spirit' of Wittgenstein's later philosophy (Diamond 1995; Edwards 1982: 1), it is worth recounting a story about how Wittgenstein wrote his profoundly influential *Philosophical Investigations* (Wittgenstein 1958a). Doing it 'the bloody *hard* way' is how Wittgenstein summarised it. Indeed, the style in which his later philosophy was written shows the difficulties he was grappling with and how he reconciled himself to them (Binkley 1973; Staten 1985: 64). The final result was a book that 'only' consisted of 'a number of sketches of landscapes' written in the form of remarks and short paragraphs (Wittgenstein 1958a: vii). He says:

> My thoughts were soon crippled if I tried to force them on in any single direction against their natural inclination. – And this was, of course, connected with the very nature of the investigation. For this compels us to travel over a wide field of thought criss-cross[ing] in every direction. – The same or almost the same points were always being approached afresh from many different directions, and new sketches made . . . Thus this book is really only an album.
>
> (Wittgenstein 1958a: vii)

That Wittgenstein was only able to piece together an 'album' of his thoughts had nothing to do with a lack of ability to write in a linear fashion as the style of the *Tractatus Logico-Philosophicus*, the pinnacle of his early philosophy, testifies (Wittgenstein 1922). His *Tractatus* is perhaps the apotheosis of the linear model of argumentation. His unique (and often copied) complex numbering of each paragraph, sub-paragraph, sub-sub-paragraph and so on, illustrated how he had previously explored how each proposition could be broken down into its component parts, and thus reflect the structure of reality (logical positivism). The radical change in his form of writing, from linear to zigzagging, suggests something far more significant than just a matter of stylistic taste (Wittgenstein 1958a, 1958b, 1969, 1974, 1978, 1980a, 1980b, 1980c, 1980d, 1981, 1993). It marks a profound sea change in the way he sought to communicate the relationship between language and reality in his later work. This sea change is perhaps best summarised as a rejection of not only the linear model of argumentation which assumes a high degree of determinism as to what can logically follow from a premise or set of premises, but a different approach to unsettling the central idea in the history of Western metaphysics which underpins it – the impulse to find 'a "below-the-world" foundation' of reality (Finch 1995: 158). The rejection of such an impulse results in two casualties. The first casualty is a concern with epistemology understood as 'knowledge as accurate representation, made possible by special mental processes, and intelligible through a general theory of representation' (Rorty 1980: 6). Once we give up the possibility of *representing* 'reality' ('below-the-world' foundations), we also have to let go of the idea of knowledge as accurate representa*tion*. The second casualty is certainty. If we open our ears to the echo of Wittgenstein's spirit, we no longer inhabit a world where it is possible to apprehend a reality which is 'out there' (i.e. outside language) and is the object that is represented so that assessments of claims about it can be measured as accurate (true) or inaccurate (false). Without the possibility of knowledge of this kind, certainty becomes impossible because it rests upon it. It is Wittgenstein's resistance to and, refusal of, both metaphysics and epistemology that characterise the 'spirit' of his philosophy and, indeed, an *ethos* of reading grammatically.

To engage with an *ethos* of reading grammatically, then, suggests reading otherwise. It recommends letting go of the idea that accounts of ethics in world politics are accurate (or inaccurate) *representations* of reality. And it, therefore, pleads that we avoid the temptation to dig 'beneath' the surface for the foundations of reality that might serve as the true answer to our questions about ethics in world politics. This is not as easy as it sounds ('the bloody hard way'). It cannot be achieved by using traditional philosophical methods since they rely so heavily on the very assumptions that a grammatical reading leaves behind. It is unsurprising then that Wittgenstein could not write the *Investigations* by using traditional philosophical arguments and found himself with 'only' an album of sketches. These sketches are, in the main, grammatical remarks. Why 'grammatical'? As we shall see below, an *ethos* of reading grammatically means staying on the surface of language in contrast to traditional philosophical methods. This is far from superficial. Rather, taking my cue from Wittgenstein, I will argue that staying on the surface of language implies a commitment to a full engagement with reality rather than taking flight from it. Bluntly, Wittgenstein's rejection of metaphysics means there is nowhere else to go.

The limits of language: refusing the search for foundations, essences, and explanations

In this section I want to explore some of the reasons why Wittgenstein rejects the metaphysical impulse to find foundations beneath language and why this is relevant to questioning the delineation of ethical possibility in world politics. Put differently, I want to explore why the act of digging and what our spade unearths cannot satisfy our metaphysical desire for the answers we seek. I argue that, as an investigation into forms of representation, Wittgenstein's work can be applied so that it assists us in looking at how universality in international ethics is *constituted* and how to trace its effects. The move towards the constitutive aspects of universality in world politics that I am proposing parallels Wittgenstein's move away from metaphysics towards an investigation of grammar. This move requires challenging the assumptions that inform the representational view of thought and language. It will become increasingly clear that a central argument of this book is that forms of universality, and the ethical possibility of enactment that they circumscribe, are forms of representation (pictures). As such, they are open not only to some of Wittgenstein's criticisms, but more positively, his way of philosophising otherwise.

While it may seem tangential to IR to engage with philosophy of language and the torment of metaphysics, I believe that it becomes very quickly apparent why it is central. Wittgenstein held the view that philosophical puzzlement is generated by certain pictures which lie in language holding us captive. In particular,

> 'The general form of propositions is: This is how things are.' – That is the kind of proposition one repeats to oneself countless times. One thinks that one is tracing the outline of the thing's nature over and over again, and one is merely tracing round the frame through which we look at it. A *picture* held us captive. And we could not get outside it, for it lay in our language and language seemed to repeat it to us inexorably.
>
> (Wittgenstein 1958a: §§114–15)

The target of his remarks here are propositions that take the form 'This is how things are'. It does not take a massive leap of the imagination to recognise that in the area of ethics in IR, propositions like this abound: 'In understanding morality and politics . . . confusion is compounded when personal and international morality are equated' (Thompson 1985b). 'The moral dilemma of foreign policy is but a special – it is true – particularly flagrant case of the moral dilemma which faces man on all levels of social action' (Morgenthau 1962: 319). 'Ideal justice . . . comes into nonideal politics by way of the natural duty to secure just institutions where none presently exist' (Beitz 1979: 171) and 'The community is itself a good – conceivably the most important good' (Walzer 1983: 29). We could say that such propositions act as an ontological marker of 'how things are in world politics' and what is possible, ethically, as a result.

What's 'captivating' about such propositions or pictures? What captivates us into reading accounts of ethics in world politics as representations of international political reality? Primarily, it is that we think that theorists are outlining the 'thing's nature': the nature of the international, the nature of the ethical, the nature of anarchy, the nature of states, the nature of theory, and so on. According to Wittgenstein, this kind of captivity arises because traditional philosophers (and, as I will show in subsequent chapters, some IR theorists) are seduced by a metaphysical notion of what makes a philosophical or theoretical inquiry profound (deep), namely, the search for *essences* (Wittgenstein 1958a: §97). In the case of some philosophers, it is the search for the essence of language. In the case of the IR theorists that are considered in this book, it is the location of some 'thing' essential about international politics and/or ethical phenomena. What that 'thing' is, of course, varies from theorist to theorist. Nonetheless, directing theoretical inquiry towards the nature of things, however understood, is for Wittgenstein a metaphysical urge and, I am suggesting, to be resisted by an *ethos* of reading grammatically.

For Wittgenstein, we think we are outlining a 'thing's nature' and are captivated by it, because of the view that language and thought *represent* reality. In other words, that the role of language and thought is representational or a 'mirror of nature' (Rorty 1980). As Rorty puts it:

> Philosophy's central concern is to be a general theory of representation, a theory which will divide culture up into the areas which represent reality well, those which represent it less well, and those which do not represent it at all (despite their pretence of doing so).
>
> (Ibid.: 3)

The importance of this cannot be emphasised enough. Wittgenstein's philosophical 'sketches' can be construed as an investigation into the assumptions (the pictures that hold us captive) which inform the notion of language and thought as representation.

What, then, are some of the pictures that lead to the notion of language and thought as representation and the location of the nature of phenomena? One such picture is a picture of language which Wittgenstein associates with Augustine but is constructed in the widest sense to include any view where

> the individual words in language name objects – sentences are combinations of such names. – In this picture of language we find the roots of the following idea: Every word has a meaning. This meaning is correlated with the word. It is the object for which the word stands.
>
> (Wittgenstein 1958a: §1)

In this view, the relationship between language and reality comes through naming. Language can represent reality because names name objects and configurations of names depict possible configurations of objects in the world. In this way, language can represent possible states of affairs because it shares the same structure. Thus, the truth or falsity of a proposition depends on whether it agrees or disagrees with reality (Wittgenstein 1922: 2.223, 4.05). This picture of language generated the idea that there must be a *super*-order between *super*-concepts – a 'hard' connection between the order of possibilities common to both thought and world (Wittgenstein 1958a: §97).

In many ways, this view of language seems like 'common sense', after all, don't words refer to objects? Wittgenstein suggests that one of the reasons why such a picture is captivating is precisely because it does seem 'obvious'. As he says, 'The aspects of things which are most important for us are hidden because of their simplicity and familiarity' (ibid.: §129). In order to break the captivating influence of such a picture, he brings to the forefront of investigation precisely that which is so familiar and simple that we no longer notice it. In this case, it is the role of naming in language.

Wittgenstein breaks the spell by using the metaphor of games through which he introduces his famous 'language games'. The purpose of this, on the one hand, is to show that naming is only a small part of language use, and, on the other, to show that the meaning of a word does not require a naming relationship, i.e. what it refers to in the world, but instead its use within a particular context (the language game). Thus, of the representational picture of language (wherein language names objects, the objects to which words refer confer meaning and sentences are combinations of such names) Wittgenstein says:

> 'Yes, it is appropriate, but only for this narrowly circumscribed region, not for the whole of what you are claiming to describe [i.e. language].' It is as if someone were to say: 'A game consists of moving objects about on a surface according to certain rules . . . ' – and we replied: You seem to be thinking of board games, but there are others. You can make your definition correct by expressly restricting it to those games.
>
> (Ibid.: §3)

Wittgenstein's point is not to deny that naming is a use of language, but rather that it is the *whole* of it. Naming is a too narrow, and over-generalised, conception. Consequently, he points out several other different ways in which language is used. Indeed, he even says that there are 'countless' kinds of sentences which are not combinations of names (ibid.: §23). Examples would include giving orders and obeying them, reporting an event, forming and testing a hypothesis, making a joke, praying, translating one language from another, speculating about an event (ibid.: §23) and, we can add, theorising ethics in IR.[3] Noticing and taking seriously the different landscapes of language use is a simple but powerful move on his part. He is simply reminding us that language may, and often is, used otherwise. It's his enactment of his view that the task of the philosopher or theorist is much more modest than metaphysical digging. As he says 'The work of the philosopher consists in assembling reminders for a particular purpose', nothing more (ibid.: §217). Accordingly, appeals to universality in international ethics need *not* be read as a naming relationship. Universality might be doing a variety of other things or more accurately, playing a multiplicity of roles within a language game, to which we are blind because of our one-eyed focus on naming. If we agree with these insights, a space is opened that legitimately allows for a reading of universality in world politics as the delineation of possibility – that which circumscribes the limits of ethics in world politics: a sketch of a different landscape.

The metaphor of language *games* can also be used to highlight what kind of an investigation a grammatical reading is refusing as part of its *ethos*.

Language games present an insurmountable problem for any form of explanation (including explanations in IR) that rests on the 'discovery' of a property that is common to all instances of phenomena under investigation. Wittgenstein uses 'games' to illustrate his point which is worth quoting at length:

> Consider for example the proceedings we call 'games'. I mean board-games, card-games, ball-games, Olympic games and so on. What is common to them all? – Don't say: 'There *must* be something common, or they would not be called "games"' – but *look and see* whether there is anything common to all. – For if you look at them you will not see something that is common to all, but similarities, relationships, and a whole series of them at that. To repeat: don't think, but look! ... And the result of this examination is: we see a complicated network of similarities overlapping and criss-crossing: sometimes overall similarities, sometimes similarities of detail. I can think of no better expression to characterize these similarities than 'family resemblance' ... And I shall say: 'games' form a family.
>
> (Ibid.: §66)

Instead of considering 'games' in IR, we could consider, for example, 'states', 'foreign policies', 'wars', and more to the point here, 'ethics' and 'universality'. Ethics, as a term, is not captured or explained by 'discovering' an element which is common to all, purported, instances of it in world politics. The seductiveness of searching for an element common to *all* instances of phenomena is (almost) irresistible in the case of ethics because the fundamental, and dominant, idea is that ethics *must* have a universal (that can be named and located) so that it applies to *all* human beings. This is, seductively so, because the use of 'universality' is often as a classification of a rather peculiar kind: a class that necessarily includes all. On this view, it is the universal that supplies the grounds, and possibility of, ethics being relevant and applicable to everyone (all). Paraphrasing Wittgenstein, the metaphysical urge is to say 'There *must* be something common [a universal], or it could not be called "ethics"'.

This brings us to a further implication of having introduced the metaphor of language *games*. We have already noted, above, how all the activities called 'games' do not have common properties by virtue of which we apply the word 'game' to them. Thus, it is a false dogma to suppose that this criterion is necessary for the word to be meaningful. Rather what makes them all 'games' is a complicated network of similarities and relationships: a family resemblance. Language games then, are not the representation of the *super*-order of reality, nor are they representation*al* and hence metaphysical. Coping with a multiplicity (of games) is not the only problem for explanations, in IR, that seek to specify necessary and sufficient conditions for a concept-word's correct application. There is also a further problem with the determinacy that such conditions presuppose in order to have purchase as explanations. For Wittgenstein, the meaningfulness of a concept-word, e.g. universality, does not require that we be able to specify the necessary and sufficient conditions for its fulfilment, i.e. determinate boundaries. Using the metaphor of games again,

> One might say that the concept 'game' is a concept with blurred edges ... Frege compares a concept to an area and says that an area with vague boundaries cannot be called an area at all. This presumably means that we cannot do anything with it. – But is it senseless to say 'Stand roughly there'? Suppose that I were standing with someone in a city square and said that. As I say it I do not draw any kind of boundary, but perhaps point with my hand – as if I were indicating a particular *spot*. And this is just how one might explain to someone what a game is. One gives examples and intends them to be taken in a particular way ... The point is that *this* is how we play the game.
>
> (Ibid.: §71)

We might say, 'Explanations are comparable to indicating a place by pointing, not to demarcating it by drawing a boundary' (Baker and Hacker 1980: 327). Wittgenstein's position gives us an understanding of concepts where 'instead of discrete classes with a boundary of identity between them, we now have a spread of particulars varying from each other in accidental ways along a continuum until at last there has been "essential" change without a boundary of essence ever having been crossed' (Staten 1985: 96). Boundaries, or in this case, the demarcation of necessary and sufficient conditions are not written in nature. Indeed, more radically, concept-words such as 'universality' can make perfect sense even in the absence of having drawn any clear boundaries around it. A definition of universality that marks clear lines (necessary and sufficient conditions) between what universality includes and excludes is therefore not required in order to make sense and nor, therefore, is it a requirement of a grammatical reading. In the absence of such lines being drawn in nature for their sense, there is no single 'super-order' of how (for example, international) reality must be structured. This is Wittgenstein's anti-essentialism and that of the grammatical reading proposed here.

Being able to make sense of the injunction to 'stand roughly there' is a critique of ostensive definition (Glock 1996: 274; McDonald 1990). The ideal of pointing to an object and naming it (an ostensive definition), is the equivalent of 'looking' at history and saying 'this is a condition of international politics' and therefore, directly relevant to methods of explanation employed in IR. Indeed, one could say that an ostensive definition is the 'unimpeachable model of the relation between language and "reality"' (Staten 1985: 69). In the social sciences (in which one can include IR) it is, broadly speaking, an empiricist-positivist approach that 'applies scientific method to human affairs conceived as belonging to a natural order open to objective enquiry' (Hollis 1994: 41). But Wittgenstein makes us think about this otherwise, saying, 'Naming is so far not a move in the language-game – any more than putting a piece in its place on the board is a move in chess. We may say: nothing has so far been done, when a thing has been named' (Wittgenstein 1958a: §49). Pointing to an object and baptising (naming) it is a meaningless act unless '*the place is already prepared*' (Wittgenstein 1958a: §31; my italics).

There are two implications that may be drawn from this that inform a grammatical reading by approaching it from different directions. On the one hand, Wittgenstein is pointing out that objects are indeterminate in-themselves. Instead it is 'grammar which tells us what kind of object anything is' (ibid.: §370). On the other hand, he is pointing out the limita-tions of the ostensive definition model of naming which separates the name from the *practice* of naming. Wittgenstein thinks that ostensive definitions, far from working because they are grounded in a basic experience such as a Humean apprehension of a particular, work because we are already masters of other linguistic techniques. 'The ostensive definition explains the use – the meaning – of the word when the overall role of the word is in language is clear' (ibid.: §30).

So, for Wittgenstein, the meaning of a word 'would . . . depend on the circumstances – that is, on what happened before and after the pointing' (ibid.: §35). A word's meaning, whether accompanied by a gesture of pointing or not, depends on what surrounds it: its context. This way meaning cannot be fixed, since there are innumerable possibilities of what may come 'before' and 'after'. Hence, there can be no super-order of super-concepts that a commitment to metaphysics presupposes. There is no longer *an* order, but rather order*s* which are contingent upon the placing of words within 'signifying chains' (Staten 1985: 98). This in part, is why the remarks of the *Investigations* criss-cross and similar points are 'always being approached afresh from different directions' (Wittgenstein 1958a: vii). By itself, the naming of an object does not provide the meaning of the word anymore than putting the Queen on her square is a move in chess. The positivist, empirical link between reality and observer is thereby challenged given that the naming of an object as a 'fact' requires not only some familiarity in other practices, e.g. language games of natural science, but its place within such practices.

The point about ostensive definition may appear esoteric. Nevertheless, to say that pointing means being versed in the practices that surround it (the context) and that these have innumerable configurations of 'before' and 'after' challenges the very idea that the source of meaning lies outside language. It is therefore, not because words name an object outside language that they are meaningful. We can, and do, 'stand roughly there'. This being so, there is no cleavage between theory and practice. Theories are language games and language games are practices. Thus, we might say theories are practices. If we can accept this alongside the other implications that are attendant to the metaphor of games as outlined above, then we begin to be released from the captivity of the metaphysical urge to abstract and the search for essences, boundaries and foundations that it requires.

As Wittgenstein puts it, metaphysical searches are 'the problems arising through a misinterpretation of our forms of language [which] have the character of *depth*. They are deep disquietudes; their roots are as deep in us as the forms of our language' (ibid.: §111).[4] Questions such as 'What is ethics in international politics?' seem to necessitate finding 'something that lies *beneath* the surface. Something that lies within, which we see when we look *into* the thing, and which an analysis digs out' (ibid.: §92). Refusing to search here for satisfaction is not to suggest that the question is metaphysical nonsense but it does imply *where* we should be looking for an answer, or more precisely, answer*s*. For Wittgenstein, philosophical problems and indeed theoretical problems in International Relations which ask 'What is *x*?' have the form 'I don't know my way about' (ibid.: §123). Indeed, they uncover 'bumps that the understanding has got by running its head up against the limits of language' (ibid.: §119).

Although these remarks of Wittgenstein's are somewhat enigmatic, I think this much can be said: the notion of digging to find a 'below-the-world foundation' is where we run up against the limits of language. There is no below the surface of language which language represents for Wittgenstein. If this is so, then theorising or philosophising 'may in no way interfere with the actual use of language; it can in the end only describe it. For it cannot give it any foundation either. It leaves everything as it is' (ibid.: §124). In that sense, Wittgenstein is proposing that inquiring about ethics and world politics is flat. An analysis, or explanation, does not require 'digging' beneath the surface of language to uncover foundations and essences. The point is that 'reflection on language occurs not from outside but from within the scene of language' (Staten 1985: 98, 88). In this very specific sense, 'nothing is hidden' (Wittgenstein 1958a: §126). How this view leads to an engagement with practices is what will be addressed next.

Language as practice: problematising rule following

The previous section explored the seductiveness of a picture of language wherein the relationship between language and reality is one of representation through naming. However, this begs the question that if it is not the object to which a word refers which confers meaning, then what does? Some aspects of Wittgenstein's answer to this question have already been mentioned above. In this section, however, I seek to emphasise how and why reading grammatically is an engagement with practices (of world politics) and not an exercise in vocabulary. Furthermore, I seek to illustrate how an understanding of language games as practices leads to a problematic which is distinct from that which a metaphysical search implies. In the final analysis, unhinging the 'hard connection' between word and object makes rule following the central problematic of the *Investigations* and the grammatical readings proposed in this book (Staten 1985: 79). Thus the main aim of this section is concerned with highlighting how problematising rule following opens up space for a grammatical reading as an ethico-political engagement. Ultimately, this critical space allows us to pose the question (rather than answer it) of how rules appear 'natural' and a representation of 'how things are' in the absence of foundations

In order to tackle this, the ground needs to be prepared, so to speak. The first step is to look in more detail at how Wittgenstein uses the language game metaphor to emphasise both the role of practice (use) and rules in conferring meaning. Of this he says, 'When one shews someone the king in chess and says: "This is the king", this does not tell him the use of this piece – unless he already knows the rules of the game up to this last point: the shape of the king' (Wittgenstein 1958a: §31). Wittgenstein's analogy that naming the king does not tell us how to move the king in chess is constructed to bring to light the idea that one's ability to name an object is not sufficient for one to be able to claim that one has understood or grasped the meaning of a word. Rather, what is required for understanding is that one be able to use a word and, even more importantly, be able to use it correctly.

There are two aspects to this. On the one hand, meaning can come from the way in which a word is used in particular contexts ('the rest of our proceedings') and not naming. Hence the famous quotation that 'For a *large* class of cases – though not for all – in which we employ the word "meaning" it can be defined thus: the meaning of a word is its use in the language' (ibid.: §43). But equally, understanding the meaning of a word involves the ability to be able to use the word in the appropriate contexts correctly. For Wittgenstein then, understanding is associated with the capacity to do something, which is why naming cannot be a move in chess since the ability to name chess pieces does not, in itself, include the capacity to be able to *play the game* (i.e. use the pieces).

With regards to the first, it should be apparent by now that Wittgenstein's use of the word 'language' (though he often uses 'language game' in order to remind us of some of the features of language discussed above) is not confined to vocabulary and the uttering of sounds. Instead of viewing language in a narrow way as only form, or vocabulary, Wittgenstein says, 'I shall call the whole, consisting of language and the *actions* with which it is interwoven, "the language *game*"' (ibid.: §7). He also says, 'The word "language-*game*" is here meant to emphasize that the speaking of language is part of an activity or a form of life' (ibid.: §23). Language games are not just what we say but what we do. 'Words are Deeds' (Wittgenstein 1980c: 46).

Wittgenstein's own use of the metaphor of language games is multifarious, and this multiplicity of use is important. Sometimes language games are fictitious constructions in order for Wittgenstein to 'assemble reminders for a particular purpose'. And indeed, the construction of fictitious language games is an important part of his philosophical strategy against the inclination to metaphysics. The 'primitive' language game that he constructs for builders in §2 of the *Investigations* is probably the most famous. Here the language game only consists of four words: 'block', 'pillar', 'slab', and 'beam' and is constructed as a contrast to the Augustinian picture of language. Other types of language game he notes highlight linguistic activities such as swearing, giving orders, confessing a motive, talking about sense impressions, physical objects. Indeed he also talks of language games with the use of words such as, 'game', 'proposition', 'thought' (Glock 1996: 196). One might add to the list here language games of International Relations played with the use of words such as 'ethics', 'universality', 'politics', 'international', 'anarchy', and so on.

Wittgenstein also uses the term language game to signify the overall system of linguistic practices, and indeed Wittgenstein's remark of calling the language game, 'the whole and the actions with which it is interwoven', appears within this context (Glock 1996: 197). The vital point to note about Wittgenstein's uses of the term language game is that each, whether a fictitious construction or not, is meant to show the ways in which language is interwoven with practices. This undermines the very notion upon which a separation of theory and practice rests. Language is not simply what we say so that we can represent the 'beneath' of language, but is part and parcel of what we *do* in a variety of contexts. Thus, Wittgenstein's notion of language games as activities is a rejection of the picture upon which the separation of theory and practice rests.

With regards to the second aspect of meaning as use, understanding the meaning of word means being versed in the circumstances of the word's occurrence: its place in various language games and forms of life.[5] This evokes the notion that the use of language is an activity and that to understand a language is to have mastery of a technique – the ability to do something. Understanding in this sense, is not an occult, inner process of mind but more like 'know-how' or a practical skill. Thus, 'To understand a sentence means to understand a language. To understand a language means to be master of a technique' (Wittgenstein 1958a: §199). The notion of mastery of a technique evokes being able to follow a rule e.g. the rules of chess.

It is important to emphasise that rule following raises a problem. Some commentators read this requirement of being able to follow a rule as Wittgenstein's conservatism (Cladis 1994; George 1994; Thompson 1981). I want to explore the charge of conservatism in some detail as a second step to clearing the ground for the questions that a grammatical reading seeks to pose. Without this second step, a grammatical reading cannot have the critical purchase that is being proposed. Wittgenstein makes several comments about rule following which include: 'what has the expression of a rule – say a sign-post – got to do with my actions? What sort of connexion is there here? – Well, perhaps this one: I have been trained to react to this sign in a particular way, and now I do so react to it' (Wittgenstein 1958a: §198); 'To obey a rule, to make a report, to give an order, to play a game of chess, are *customs* (uses, institutions)' (ibid.: §199); and 'The application of the concept "following a rule" presupposes a custom' (Wittgenstein 1978: 322).

Some commentators take this to imply that language use is a multi-faceted set of rule-governed activities and that these rules uphold community standards of language use (Kripke 1981; Malcolm 1986). So, knowing whether one has made a mistake in the use of a word depends on the possibility of being corrected by those who have already mastered the language game. For example, if I began to use the word 'elephant' to describe the colour of this paper, anyone able to understand this book may correct me and say that I seem to have misunderstood the use of the word 'elephant'. Although most commentators agree that Wittgenstein rejected the notion of fixed essences, as described above, not all agree as to how far the implications of this stretch.

The so-called 'communitarian interpretation' of Wittgenstein's rule following, outlined above, takes him to imply that notions such as 'ethics' or 'international' must therefore be intersubjectively created by 'the sociolinguistic conventions associated with a community' (Cladis 1994: 15; Kripke 1981; Winch 1958). This means that no-one can then step outside their sociolinguistic conditioning in order to criticise the prevailing order since this would require violating community standards of language use, hence, the charges of conservatism. However, this view supposes that rules are 'static forms to be applied to experience' (McDonald 1990: 271). Although the communitarian view allows that rules may be changed by intersubjective agreement, once in place they see rules as sets of practices to be adhered to and fulfilled.

However, I want to endorse an alternative reading of Wittgenstein's rule-following which allows his philosophy to maintain the critical potential that Jim George and others believe has been compromised (Baker and Hacker 1990; Cladis 1994; George 1994; Glock 1996; McDonald 1990; Staten 1985). Wittgenstein's comments about rule following being a custom, or that 'I obey the rule *blindly*' may be understood to highlight how much language use is automatic and normalised (Wittgenstein 1958a: §219). He says, 'It is only in *normal* cases that the use of a word is clearly prescribed; we know, are in no doubt, what to say in this or that case. The more abnormal the case, the more doubtful it becomes what we are to say' (ibid.: §142). Knowing how to continue, for example a series of numbers by adding 2, 'is a view in which the idea of *normality* . . . is seen to be an idea of *naturalness*' (Cavell 1979: 122). What is implied by 'natural' is not an underlying 'natural' regularity of human behaviour that Wittgenstein is trying to locate. Rather the 'natural' tendency to understand mathematical formulas (follow the rule of '+2') in the way that we do is only 'natural' because we have been trained to use them in this way. The difference between someone who can add 2 to sequences of numbers and someone who cannot is not that one counts as an intelligible human being and the other as unintelligible. The difference is between 'one person who is already initiated into a practice and sees it as natural, and another who is not yet initiated into it. What looks natural or even automatic from the initiate's point of view may look not at all natural from the novice's' (Staten 1985: 101).

The critical potential of this understanding of rule following is what a grammatical reading seeks to emphasise. It opens space for us to ask, though not yet answer, how it is that rules appear 'natural' as a representation of 'how things are'; how 'reality' is constituted and its effects. We already know that, for Wittgenstein, the only place to go looking for answers is to stay on the surface of language and 'leave everything as it is' rather than 'bumping our heads against the limits of language'. As I hope this section has demonstrated, staying on the surface of language means engaging with practices not taking flight from them in either metaphysical searches or analyses of vocabulary. Doing so problematises rule following. Far from being the answer to our questions, the rules that are followed are where to begin reading: What are the rules of the language games of ethics in IR? How do such rules 'normalise' and 'naturalise' states of affairs so that they appear beyond question? How do rules constitute international political reality and thereby delineate the ethical possibility of universality? What role does universality play in these language games? What are the critical ramifications of rules having no foundations? How we might proceed to find answers through reading grammatically is what shall be addressed next.

'Leaving everything as it is':[6] reading grammatically

> Philosophy simply puts everything before us, and neither explains nor deduces anything. – Since everything lies open to view there is nothing to explain. For what is hidden, for example, is of no interest to us.
>
> (Wittgenstein 1958a: §126)

In the preceding sections I have argued, using Wittgenstein, that a grammatical reading of ethics in world politics is not about an analysis that 'digs' beneath language to reveal its foundations which confer meaning: the 'nature' of things. We have also seen that a grammatical reading makes no ontological separation between theory and practice and that a concern with language is not restricted to the manner rather than the content of arguments understood as linguistic practices. And we have seen how a grammatical reading is an engagement with practices that then makes rule following its central problematic thereby giving it critical purchase. Finally, having prepared the ground, we can now move towards the more positive aspects of Wittgenstein's style of philosophising and offer a way of proceeding to read ethics in world politics: A grammatical reading.

This section, then, is concerned with showing what is involved in 'leaving everything as it is' and resisting the temptation to dig 'beneath' language.

As Wittgenstein says, 'everything lies open to view', if only we could just stay on the surface of language and keep our theorising flat thereby avoiding metaphysical temptations of explanation. Wittgenstein called this a 'grammatical investigation'. However, I prefer the term 'grammatical reading' in order to emphasise that the reading of his work offered here is an applied interpretation. As pointed out before, Wittgenstein was not concerned with politics but rather the central concerns of philosophy. This being so, the applications of his thought that appear here and in subsequent chapters necessarily differ from anything he might have had to say. Nevertheless, I seek to show that his insights offer pointers for a critical reading of universality and ethics in world politics.

The central foci of a grammatical reading are pictures: forms of representation. Given that the representation of reality, understood as the representation of the *super*-order of *super*-concepts, is not possible except as an exercise in head bumping, what are we dealing with? We might ask similarly, 'What am I believing in when I believe that men have souls? What am I believing in, when I believe that this substance contains two carbon rings?' (Wittgenstein 1958a: §422). These two examples are particularly poignant in that they differ, seemingly, substantially: one is classically metaphysical 'that men have souls' and the other classically empirical 'that this substance contains two carbon rings'. However, Wittgenstein says that,

> In *both* cases there is a picture in the foreground, but the sense lies in the background; that is, *the application of the picture is not easy to survey* . . . now all I ask is to understand the expression we use. – The picture is there. And I am not disputing its validity in any particular case. – Only I also want to understand the application of the picture.
>
> (Ibid.: §422)[7]

Seeking to understand the application of pictures signals *the* most important move for a grammatical reading that makes it centrally and unavoidably engaged with understanding ethics in world politics. If we recall, for Wittgenstein, pictures are not representations of deep metaphysical facts but, nonetheless, they hold us captive. Part of the captivity lay precisely in the picture that language represents reality through naming: the view that language is representational. In stark contrast, what is being proposed by a grammatical reading is a view of language as *normative*. That is to say, staying on the surface of language entails tracing how pictures regulate not just our understanding of what shall count as 'reality' – its constitution – but our practices/what we do. Thus, while pictures may be held by their proponents to be representations of reality, they are more accurately to be understood as regulative. As will be illustrated in detail below, pictures regulate possibility and impossibility: what can and cannot be done, what is 'real' and what is not, what is 'false' and what is 'true', what 'exists' and what does not, what is 'ethical' and what is not, what counts as 'universal' and what does not, and so on. The point of focusing on pictures, and their applications, is to argue 'against the tendency to think that our "pictures" of meaning can aspire to be the simple reflection of what actually *is* . . . To argue this way is not to close but to open up the question of what a picture is for, what are the motives for its introduction and what are its actual effects' (Staten 1988: 314).

A grammatical reading, then, does not stop with identifying the rules that regulate possibility and impossibility. Were it to stop here, it would be conservative.[8] From this conservative view, one might say, as Laclau does, that, 'The social world presents itself to us, primarily, as a sedimented ensemble of social practices accepted at face value, without questioning the founding acts of their institution' (Edkins 1999: 5). But, as the preceding section argued, rule following is the central problematic; not the end of the inquiry but its beginning. Since rules do not represent possible configurations of states of affairs in 'nature' or a 'reality' outside language, they are ultimately unfounded, having no essential foundations 'beneath' language upon which they rest. The lines drawn between possibility and impossibility that pictures mark, therefore, are not givens because they are not 'written in nature' but are written in practice/language. They are grammatical. This opens up critical space to ask how they come to be 'founded' in practice; to question 'the founding acts of their institution', as Laclau puts it. This being so a grammatical reading is, unavoidably, an engagement with politics and ethics. The 'surface of language', on this interpretation of language as normative, is an ethico-political landscape. This last point will be explored in more detail in the following section. In the meantime, it remains to explore further what the ramifications are of thinking of pictures as non-representational.

For Wittgenstein and the reading being proposed here, pictures are 'A full-blown representation of our grammar. Not facts; but as it were illustrated turns of speech' (Wittgenstein 1958a: §295). Wittgenstein's own examples of grammatical pictures include: 'The picture that men have souls' (Wittgenstein 1958a: §422); 'The religious picture of the all-seeing eye of God' (Wittgenstein 1970: 71); 'The picture that thinking goes on in the head' (Wittgenstein 1958a: §427); 'The picture of the earth as a very old planet' (Wittgenstein 1981: §462), and so on. One might add various other pictures taken from ethics in International Relations: the picture of human nature as selfish, lustful for power and sinful,[9] the picture of reason as impartial,[10] the picture of political space as 'fit' between community and state government,[11] and so on. Through the 'bewitchment of our intelligence by means of language' these pictures seem to represent something deep about the world – the way things are (Wittgenstein: 1958b §109). But, the point is, they do not. Instead, pictures are 'a full-blown representation of our grammar' so that

> We feel as if we had to *penetrate* phenomena: our investigation, however, is directed not towards phenomena, but, as one might say, towards the *'possibilities'* of phenomena. We remind ourselves, that is

to say, of the *kind of statement* that we make about phenomena . . . Our investigation is therefore a grammatical one.

(Wittgenstein 1958a: §90; original italics)

'Grammar' is not to be understood as singular nor is it to be understood as purely formal in the sense of being concerned with parts of speech, verb conjugations, pluralizing nouns and so on. Rather, there are grammars of words, expressions, phrases, sentences, states, processes and indeed, philosophical problems are grammatical (Baker and Hacker 1985). Likewise, problems of ethics in International Relations and world politics can be read as grammatical. What might this mean so that an investigation of grammar is an investigation of the possibilities of phenomena?

Vitally, in a move that identifies grammar as a constitutive dynamic, Wittgenstein claims that 'grammar tells us what kind of object anything is' (Wittgenstein 1958a: §372) and also '*essence* is expressed by grammar' (ibid.: §371). The importance of this cannot be understated. In short, Wittgenstein is telling us that it is grammar that produces 'phenomena' since they do not exist independently of language. Put another way, grammar constitutes reality by delineating the possibilities of phenomena articulated as 'pictures'.

The grammar of a word includes the various uses that it has within a language game.[12] Taking a simple example first: the grammar of the word 'chair', includes not only 'to sit on a chair', but also, 'fall off a chair', 'balance a chair', 'play musical chairs', and so on. On the one hand, grammar expresses the relation between words, e.g. chair and sit. However, more importantly perhaps it also 'determin[es] the relation between an expression and what in the world that expression is used *for*' (Pitkin 1993: 118). In other words, its *applications*. Thus, for Wittgenstein it is part of our grammar that not only can one sit on a chair but also includes *how* one sits on it. For example, that the way one sits on a chair is different, grammatically, to sitting on a drawing pin, table, or dock of the bay. The point that Wittgenstein seems to be indicating is that

> Grammar . . . establishes the place of a concept in our system of concepts, and thereby in our world. It controls what other concepts, what questions and observations, are relevant to a particular concept. [Thus] knowing what 'a mistake' is depends not on mastering its distinguishing features or characteristics, but on having mastered what sorts of circumstances count as 'making a mistake', 'preventing a mistake', 'excusing a mistake', and so on. And we will make no empirical discoveries about mistakes which our grammatical categories do not allow.
>
> (Ibid.: 119)

In other words, grammar controls what is possible in the world by regulating what kinds of statements one can make about the world. In this way then, it is grammar that tells us what kind of object anything is and expresses its 'essence'. The implications of this for an investigation of universality and ethics in International Relations are radical and far-reaching. Focusing on grammar is a commitment to a specific form of anti-foundationalism because it is a claim that grammar is arbitrary. The foundations of 'ethics', 'universality' and 'international politics' are not to be found by locating the phenomenon which each word names/refers to in an extra-linguistic reality. As Wittgenstein puts it, 'Grammar is not accountable to any reality. It is grammatical rules that determine meaning (constitute it) and so they them-selves are not answerable to any meaning and to that extent are arbitrary' (Wittgenstein 1974: 184).

The arbitrariness of grammar is meant to highlight its autonomy from a postulated extra-linguistic reality. There is no *supra*-'meaning of meaning'. This point can be illustrated by considering the tendency to think that, for example, 'there are four primary colours' is made true because of the nature of colours (Baker and Hacker 1985: 329–37).

> One is tempted to justify rules of grammar by sentences like 'But there really are four primary colours.' And the saying that the rules of grammar are arbitrary is directed against the possibility of this justifica-tion, which is constructed on the model of justifying a sentence by pointing to what it verifies.
>
> (Wittgenstein 1981: §331)

Similarly, one might say that we are tempted to justify claims that the national interest is the locus of ethics in international politics by saying 'But states really do have a national interest.' The point here is that there can be no ultimate justifications (non-arbitrary foundations) for the rules of grammar outside language. Hence, grammar is not open to epistemological questions of truth and falsity for truth and falsity are themselves grammati-cally constituted. So, rather than the *nature* of international politics creating the grammar of ethics and universality in world politics, for a grammatical reading it is the reverse: Grammar tells us what kind of phenomena they are. For example, it is the grammar of the language game employed by Morgenthau that identifies the national interest as the locus of ethical possi-bility in world politics.[13] This grammar can be contrasted with Walzer's that locates community. The point is that these differences are grammatical differences. They are differences in the way in which international political reality is constituted, its ethical possibilities and the questions deemed rele-vant to 'discovering' them. Reading 'ethics' and 'universality' is about producing grammatical remarks.

The arbitrariness of grammar clarifies the open, rather than narrow, space that a grammatical reading occupies. It has already been argued that rules are the central problematic of a grammatical reading. The full extent of this claim can now be elaborated by appreciating that the rules that cannot help but be problematic are the rules of grammar. The rules of grammar are unavoidably and ceaselessly open to question because they have no ultimate justification. If there are no ultimate, non-arbitrary, justifications to the rules of grammar, what are justifications of the kind 'But states really do have a national interest'? Well, such justifications are a picture of how things must be. They are themselves 'a full-blown representation of our grammar' and therefore, questionable. Reading grammatically, we can equally ask of these justifications what their grammar is so that they regulate and delineate what shall count as a 'justification' or not, what really 'matters' and is 'relevant', and so on. Not forgetting that grammar is a practice, and more precisely, that grammars of International Relations are international political practices, we are on the 'rough ground' of the ethico-political constitution of 'international political reality'. We are free to question, rather than to accept as given, how this reality is constituted as 'reality' and its effects. In short, directing our reading towards the grammatical. constitution of possibilities can be a form of ethico-political engagement. To question the 'founding acts of [social practices] institution' is to ask questions about their grammar: How the grammar of certain social practices (in this case, international politics) regulates what counts as 'international political reality' and how this set of phenomena delineates ethical possibility. Put bluntly, it is grammar that not only delineates but also polices the very boundaries of international politics and ethics.

We can perhaps now appreciate more fully why a grammatical reading that 'leaves everything as it is' is far from passive description. This section has suggested that staying on the surface of language involves shaking our representations to their 'foundations' in order to reveal they are not written in nature but written in practice. To read grammatically, therefore, unavoidably means to question the political practices that not only determine 'reality' by constituting their foundations as 'foundations', whether 'natural', 'inevitable' or otherwise but also the possibility for ethics in world politics attendant to them.

Throwing away the ladder: mysticism, ethics and a politics of reading grammatically

At this point, it is becoming clearer what distinguishes a grammatical reading from the kind of grammatical investigation that Wittgenstein was concerned with. First, as already mentioned, the pictures that are the concern of a grammatical reading are different. A grammatical reading is concerned with the pictures that hold us captive in International Relations and world politics, not philosophy. And as such, a grammatical reading looks to trace the effects that such pictures have both in IR, ethics and world politics. In that sense, the assemblage of 'reminders for a specific purpose' is bound to be differentiated (Wittgenstein 1958a: §127). Second, and in stark contrast to Wittgenstein, a grammatical reading takes the arbitrariness of grammar to signal the moment, and the possibility, of the political. Third, the implications of Wittgenstein's mysticism, discussed in more detail below, are applied to IR theory rather than moral philosophy.

Pictures of reason, the subject and ethico-political space

With regards to the pictures that hold us captive in IR, there are three that are of particular importance for the purposes of 'assembling reminders for a specific purpose' in relation to universality, ethics and International Relations. Pictures of reason are read grammatically because they can serve to reveal each theorist's view of what is involved in how to represent the world of international politics. Put differently, a theorist's picture of reason tells us how to dig. They can help render conspicuous what the role of theory is, for each theorist, as a means to understanding or explaining ethics and world politics. As we read, we can trace how a theorist's picture of reason is grammatically constituted and applied so that it tells us what is required for how we should think about ethics in world politics (what sort of spade), and indeed where to look (dig) for things that will be recognised as answers. We can broadly say, then, that pictures of reason play an overall role within each theorist's language game of delineating which areas are relevant or irrelevant to how one is to tackle the question of ethics and its formal, theoretical requirements.

The grammatical readings offered in subsequent chapters also focus on each theorist's picture of the subject, their representations of a human being. It just so happens that each grammatical reading reveals that the subject plays a foundational role for the possibility of universality. In the end, it is 'us' who embodies universality. Pictures of the subject tell us what, supposedly, we are as human beings and more particularly, what it is about us so that we have moral value. This is important as it shows why, for the theorists concerned, ethicality in international political practice is desirable and therefore, why spaces of different kinds should be made or protected wherein ethical action is possible. None of the theorists read believe that ethics is unimportant to being human, nor do they believe that it is impossible. If, in the broadest sense, ethics is concerned with how we are to regard others (however understood), then pictures of the subject play a fundamental role in the theorists read.

Finally, the grammatical readings in this book also look at pictures of ethico-political space. I have chosen to focus on this picture because it tells us *where*, according to the theorists concerned, the possibility of universal ethical action takes place in international politics. Is the political space where ethicality can take place the nation-state, for example? Or should political space be understood differently? How is the 'nature' of such spaces represented by the three theorists? Pictures of political space are important because they demarcate the boundaries of the area in which questions of ethics and international politics, purportedly, arise, hence I have called them *ethico*-political. They tell us what the 'world' of international political reality is and what it is like in relation to its hostility, or otherwise, to the accommodation of ethics in world politics.

Politics and the political

With regards to the second difference between Wittgenstein's grammatical investigations and the grammatical readings offered here, it is perhaps heuristically[14] helpful to distinguish between 'politics' and 'the political' (Edkins 1999). The applied interpretation of Wittgenstein being proposed here, partly, distinguishes the former from the latter on the basis of its reading of rule following. 'Politics', for example, the rules of sovereignty, the rules of foreign policy, the rules of war, and so on, tell us 'how to proceed'. We might say that to be versed in the 'art of politics' is to have mastery of a technique that shows know-how of how 'to play the game' whether it be war, diplomacy, or foreign policy for example (Fierke 1998, 2002).[15] Broadly speaking, 'politics' therefore, consists not only of establishing what the rules are, but also maintains, legitimises and polices them. This is so because mastery of a technique involves following a rule correctly, in short, adhering to them. Continuing practices of upholding rule following serve to further reinforce, maintain and police them *as* rules. Indeed, the notion that rules are policed is meant to highlight that in politics there can be, and often are, severe penalties attached to violating the rule or rules.

What is absent from politics thus understood, is the possibility of questioning and challenging the rules themselves because it is 'politics' that regulates what shall count as a 'legitimate' challenge, or indeed what shall be acknowledged as a 'challenge' itself (Edkins, *et al.* 2004). That rules of grammar constitute reality requires an appreciation of just how far reaching rules are: All phenomena of 'politics' – 'power', 'legitimacy', 'sovereignty', 'democracy', 'representation', 'the rule of law', 'citizenship', 'revolution', 'the national interest', 'community', and so on are grammatical. The point is that such phenomena are on the surface of language regulating not only what can be said but what can be done and be. In this sense, 'politics' is inescapably normative.

However, for a grammatical reading, 'the political' consists of the problematisation of rule following: questioning their establishment and practice as 'rules'. It is the arbitrariness of grammar that is key here. Being on the surface of language grammar has no foundations. It has no ultimate justification outside or beyond language and itself. On the one hand, what this means is that when pushed all justifications of rules are self-referential. There comes a point where the justification of the rule is simply its re-articulation. For example, 'But there really *is* a national interest.' On the other hand, it also means that in the absence of any justifications outside a rule's own grammar, a grammatical reading can only concern itself with surveying how grammar produces its own justifications (foundations) and the effects that this has. In this case, such an endeavour is unavoidably 'political' as it traces how 'politics' becomes politics and the ways in which this forecloses other possibilities and challenges to its ordering and regulation of socio-political practices. The arbitrariness of grammar creates a specific form of scepticism that refuses to accept that rules are 'natural', 'given' or ultimately 'founded' in socio-political practices.[16] In so doing, such scepticism creates a space that can, fundamentally, question and challenge rule following. Rules are produced and re-produced through and in practice. Thus, a grammatical reading is unavoidably concerned with 'the political' because it looks to survey how what is unfounded (grammar) is constituted as founded through 'politics'. In short, what is at stake in focussing on the captivity and application of pictures is the production and effects of a 'nonfounded founding moment'. Thus, reading grammatically challenges the normativity of 'politics' and in so doing is itself unavoidably engaged in a normative project of its own.

This leads us nicely into a third difference between a grammatical investigation and a grammatical reading, namely, that the implications of Wittgenstein's mysticism for reading ethics in world politics are, in their scope, applied to an area that he himself was not concerned with. Nevertheless, I want to suggest that a brief examination of Wittgenstein's own, supposedly mystical, approach to ethics is centrally relevant to a grammatical reading.

Mysticism and ethics[17]

When theorising the relationship between language and reality, it is tempting, perhaps, to think that a consequence of critiquing, or exploring the limits of, a view of language as representational may mean that some things cannot be represented in language. Perhaps, language can only properly represent facts and not values (Kelly 1995). More specifically, one might be inclined to suggest that ethics is a linguistically unrepresentable thing and therefore, lies outside language and cannot be spoken. Wittgenstein, himself addressed thinking of ethics in this way, (in)famously saying both in the Preface and as the last sentence of the *Tractatus*: 'Whereof one cannot speak thereof one must be silent' (Wittgenstein 1922: 27 and 7.0). The idea that, 'There is indeed the inexpressible. This *shows* itself; it is the mystical' is the mysticism of Wittgenstein's early philosophy and is subject to enormous controversy of interpretation (ibid.: 6.522). His mysticism hinges on a distinction between saying and showing and is controversial not only because there is considerable debate as to what he meant but also because, depending on the interpretation, the continuity (or lack of) philosophical endeavour between his early and late philosophy will be differently understood. It is particularly because of the latter implication that Wittgenstein's purported mysticism is relevant to a grammatical reading, given that much of what I have emphasised thus far comes from the 'spirit' of his later work and the urge, as well as the plea, to return to the 'rough ground'.

The controversy concerns what one is to make of his conclusion in his early work, the *Tractatus Logico-Philosophicus*, that

> My propositions are elucidatory in this way: he who understands me finally recognises them as senseless, when he has climbed out through them, on them, over them. (He must so to speak throw away the ladder, after he has climbed up on it.)
>
> He must surmount these propositions; then he sees the world rightly.
>
> (Ibid.: 6.54)

In a nutshell, once we climb the rungs (the propositions of the *Tractatus*) and throw away the ladder, are we also to throw away his distinction between saying and showing that underpins the mystical? In other words, are we to discard the idea that ethics is unsayable/mystical/beyond the limits of language? Along with Cora Diamond, most notably, I want to say 'yes' (Diamond 1995). To get at what is stake here requires making clearer what Wittgenstein's mode of philosophising (both in his early and late work) is trying to convey. This is where we must return to what I had earlier, following Diamond, called the 'spirit' of his work and what, in relation to a grammatical reading, I had called its *ethos*. On the one hand, this will involve endorsing a specific, albeit controversial, interpretation of Wittgenstein's work as 'therapeutic', an interpretation sometimes referred to as the 'New Wittgenstein' (Baker 2004; Conant 1991; Crary and Read 1999; Diamond 1995; Hutchinson 2005, 2008; Mulhall 2001; Pleasants 1999). And on the other hand, it will provide the opportunity to now stress the *ethos* of a grammatical reading more strongly.

With regards to Wittgenstein's mode of philosophising being therapeutic, Diamond puts it this way, 'I see the *Tractatus* as a great first expression of an idea that is deepened in Wittgenstein's later work and never given up: of the link between misunderstandings of "the truth of logic" and our attachment to philosophy thought of as doctrines and theses and theories' (Diamond 1995: 202). The therapeutic element of Wittgenstein's thought, to put it simply, is to do philosophy otherwise; to abandon, throw away, a philosopher's attachment to philosophy as an enterprise that consists of providing doctrines, theses and theories. Primarily this involves giving up, letting go of, and turning away from, the seduction of metaphysics discussed earlier. It means giving up digging. To do so requires refusing the enterprise as one which involves not only searching for, but giving articulations of, 'this is how things must be'. The search for and articulation of 'how things must be' engender a variety of *requirements*, all of which are to be resisted. These would include distinctions, necessary and sufficient conditions, abstractions based on elements common to all, generalisations, and even principles (e.g. moral principles, including international and universal moral principles) to be applied. We might simply call this a refusal to draw lines (Edkins and Pin-Fat 2004, 2005). Let us be clear here. In my opinion, the point is not that distinctions (e.g. between possibility and impossibility), theories, and so on are not made, nor cannot be made. Rather, what Wittgenstein is objecting to is that these are taken to reflect 'how things must be', that they are seen to have metaphysical significance beyond their own, grammatically constituted, necessities. *Tractatus* 6.54 emphasises this by including all its propositions (distinctions, requirements, necessary and sufficient conditions etc.) as, in the final analysis, 'senseless' and 'must' be 'surmounted'.

This way of doing philosophy otherwise by abandoning formal, theoretical, requirements is in Wittgenstein's later work, too. In the *Philosophical Investigations* he provocatively puts it this way:

> The more narrowly we examine actual language, the sharper becomes the conflict between it and our requirement. (For the crystalline purity of logic was, of course, not *a result of investigation*: it was a requirement.) The conflict becomes intolerable; the requirement is now in danger of becoming empty. – We have got on to slippery ice where there is no friction and so in a certain sense the conditions are ideal, but also, just because of that we are unable to walk. We want to walk: so we need *friction*. Back to the rough ground!
>
> (Wittgenstein 1958a: §107)

The difficulty with alternative interpretations of Wittgenstein's work that read him as generating some sort of Wittgensteinian principles and/or a Wittgensteinian use-theory of meaning is that they have not 'thrown away the ladder'. And, indeed, in International Relations, it is only such modes of his work that have been applied thus far (Duffy *et al.* 1998; Fierke 1998, 2002; Fierke and Jorgensen 2001; Kratochwil 1989; Onuf 1989; Pin-Fat 1997a, 1997b). As Hutchinson (2005) puts it, failing to engage openly with the numerous places at which Wittgenstein explicitly rejects the goal of providing philosophical theses is to reduce these remarks to 'a stylistic tic'.

But what of ethics? Why should Wittgenstein's surmounting of his grammatically induced mysticism matter for IR? Very simply, it is because, in the main, International Relations theorists and political theorists are no less prone to the metaphysical seduction of the fantasy that 'Regardless of what things look like, if we are to have or do such-and-such, there must be so-and-so' (Diamond 1995: 29). This fantasy, I contend, is especially acute when theorists tackle universality and ethics in world politics. All of the theorists that we will grammatically read in this book are advancing theses, and they, for want of a better phrase, are internationalised moral theses at that.[18] When it comes to international ethics, exacerbated perhaps by its global scale, the seduction of advancing principles and theses is (almost) too much to resist. How, precisely, this is so and the problems that it creates, are discussed in detail in the chapters that follow. Suffice it to say at this point that the problem that concerns me the most is the universalisation of such principles as though the fantasy were real: the blindness to the bumps on our heads.

It is entirely predictable that someone might now ask what one should 'do' as an alternative to indulging in the fantasy of a universalisable international ethics and its requirements. In an attempt to assist the reader, I will preview an answer here, and simply say that 'instead', a grammatical reading insists that we (as 'theorists' of IR in this case) stop at the time and place to stop. The time for stopping is when we find ourselves bumping our heads against the limits of language and the place at which to stop is at the surface of language.[19] The 'limits of language' and 'leaving everything as it is' have already been discussed, at length, above. What I want to do now is to begin to sketch out the implications of this halting response for thinking about universality, ethics and International Relations specifically.

First, whatever my response – in the form of grammatical readings – may be, it does not and cannot amount to suggesting or proposing a different set of principles and/or a different theory. The ladder *has* been thrown away and is not to be picked up again, 'repaired' and proffered as a 'better' one (Fierke 2002). Second, my response would want to explore what is being asked of us when we are asked what we should 'do' instead? What does the question, and the person who asks it, presuppose as a satisfactory answer? Are they just asking for different requirements, but requirements nonetheless? In other words, does the question appear in a language game that requires that we just bump our heads elsewhere? Third, following Diamond, I would like to suggest that stopping, far from unproductively holding us back, 'frees us from such [metaphysical] ideas, [and] will change what we want to do in ethics' (Diamond 1995: 24). Such a change, fourth, might involve showing the theorist that 'what he wants is not where he thinks it can only be, nor dependent on what he thinks it must depend on' (ibid.: 24), showing that the theorist is on slippery ice and unable to walk. In the grammatical readings that follow, this often takes the form of the theorist being unable to find what it is that he so desperately seeks as the universal answer. And, finally, in light of all the above, a change in 'what we want to do' might also well involve an 'openness to surprise', a 'quickened sense of life to what is appreciated as having its mysteries and depths and uncertainties and dangers' (Diamond 1995: 314). In short, the task of stopping involves 'describ[ing] certain features of what moral life is like, without saying anything *at all* about what it *must* be like' (ibid.: 27). It is a spirited return to, not flight from, the 'rough ground' of ethics in world politics.

At this point, it is prudent to stop and not say much more about what these themes might look like. For this we need to go to the (not so) 'rough ground' of the theorists' landscapes through reading grammatically. Necessarily, the readings offered here can only partially cover and hint at the five themes sketched above. Nevertheless, they all appear in some limited form or other throughout. I should confess at this point what I believe are the limitations of my treatment of the fifth theme in this book. Given the book's concern with theoretical articulations of universality and ethics in International Relations, the openness to surprise is not as open as it might be. This is, mainly, I suspect because the 'rough ground' that the theorists cover and identify is far from rough enough and the task too large to reintroduce it.[20] Nevertheless, significant effort is maintained in trying to show, at a minimum, the surprise that comes from climbing the rungs of each theorist's language game. Wherever we find ourselves, it isn't where our theorists want us to be. Much of what the grammatical readings seek to emphasise is facilitated by concentrating, always, on the question of ethical possibility and impossibility and their relationship to a purported universality. Ethical possibility and impossibility matter to the endeavours of reading ethics and universality grammatically. First, because a focus on them can help locate how, why and where the limits of ethical possibility in world politics lie for each theorist. Second, they help to show how grammar *constitutes* each theorist's understanding of the very possibility of ethics and universality. Third, and most importantly, possibility and impossibility are akin to the rungs of Wittgenstein's *Tractarian* ladder. They are grammatical remarks. While the theorists themselves may hold that their requirements (of possibility and impossibility) reflect 'how things must be', they are, once read grammatically, to be kicked away. Once this is done, I contend, we can re-open the question of universality and ethics in world politics and change 'what we want to do in ethics' and, indeed, world politics. We might be surprised.

2 Universality as conjunctive solution
Ethics 'and' International Relations

> The work of the philosopher consists in assembling reminders for a particular purpose.
>
> (Wittgenstein 1958a: §127)

Not so very long ago, there was a time when if you told anybody, including students or scholars of International Relations (IR), that you were writing a book on ethics in world politics the response would quite often be something along the lines of 'That must be a very short book then!' The implication was that there was really not much to write about because, in 'reality', there was next to no ethics in international political practice to include in such a book 'almost as if international politics were inevitably – and necessarily – immoral' and/or because researching ethics was not a legitimate concern of the discipline (Bonanate 1995: 7). Nevertheless, by the 1990s, the interest in ethics within IR was being described as a 'revival' (Brown 1988: 213), 'resurgent' (Smith 1992), 'a modest boom' (Frost 1994: 111) or simply, 'once again a site of industriousness and vitality' (Walker 1993: 50). Writing now, this vitality has continued apace.[1]

In this chapter, I seek to tell a story that 'assembles reminders for a particular purpose', a story that sketches the topography of the landscape demarcated by the phrase 'Ethics and International Relations' in the academic discipline of International Relations. In particular, I hope to remind the reader where the mountains in the terrain lie, what the obstacles are that are postulated as having to be climbed so that universality may be possible and therefore, an international ethics. The reason for doing this is that there are several mountains that the majority of theorists concerned with ethics are often asked to, even compelled to, climb successfully in order to be able to address ethics with justification. We will see that for those theorists who accept this as *the* challenge they must believe that there 'ain't no mountain high enough . . . to stop them from getting to' ethics in global politics (Marvin Gaye and Tammi Terrell 1966). The acceptance of this as *the* challenge, as though it were the only one that could make ethics in global politics possible, is what this book is all about. The mountain-climbing challenge works on the assumption that this is, in reality, the terrain that needs to be explored and conquered. How such mountains are climbed and what the view is like from the summit are what a grammatical reading of universality, ethics and IR seeks to consider.

Accordingly, the way I propose to structure this chapter is by focusing on 'mountains' as disjunctions in order to show the prevalence of the idea that for ethics in global politics to be possible a conjunctive solution must be found. I do so because I will be suggesting in Chapters 3, 4 and 5, that the theorists concerned have all accepted this as *the* challenge and each has offered a form of universal ethic as a conjunctive solution to the moral dilemma of international politics. Conjunctive solutions aren't necessary if one doesn't think there is a disjunction that needs to be overcome: a mountain to be scaled.

'Ain't no mountain high enough':[2] 'and' as disjunctive

There are a variety of disjunctions attendant on approaching ethics in IR but, in the main, they are a reflection of the grammar of the word 'and' in the discipline's use of the phrase 'Ethics and International Relations'. Were there some doubt as to the prevalence of this phrase and its variants, one need only look at the plethora of book titles, journal articles and even journals that evoke it. Moreover, the grammar of this phrase is so familiar in IR that some writers do not even need to bother articulating it. Luckily for them, they are free to just get on with task of climbing the mountain or mountains they've identified as the grammar of 'and' lies in the background as assumed.

The grammar of the word 'and', as it appears in this context, assumes that 'ethics' and 'International Relations' refer to different things (objects), and, therefore, that they are identifiable as separate, distinguishable phenomena. Were one to accept this grammar as a reflection of the reality of global politics, it raises the thorny question of whether, and to what extent, they might be related to each other. This disjunctive grammatical feature of 'and' sets up the problem of ethics as one where the IR theorist becomes embroiled in examining whether or not there can be ethics *in* international political practice and/or ethics *in* IR (the academic discipline), in short, whether a conjunction is possible so that ethics can be possible. There are so many disjunctions in IR that we cannot cover them all. Instead, I shall focus on those that are most prevalent and most salient to a grammatical reading. As we shall see in subsequent chapters, many of them will also appear in attempts to find a universal international ethic.

Epistemological mountains: facts, values and IR as an academic discipline

The disjunction between fact and value is fundamental in so far as it gives rise to a form of scepticism that theorists seek to overcome in order to lay claim to the legitimacy of including ethical issues within IR. This poses an epistemological problem that, first, concerns the status of value judgements and judgements of fact, broadly speaking, and, second, concerns the legitimate scope of International Relations as an academic discipline.

With regards to the epistemological status of value and fact, strictly speaking, making a distinction between fact and value is not a position of moral scepticism that is exclusive to issues in international politics. It is a position sceptical of the cognitive status of *all* value judgments.[3] As Frost points out, 'the core of all non-cognitivist positions is that about matters of value (in sharp contrast to the position about matters of fact) there can be no truth of the matter' (Frost 1986: 46).[4] For the non-cognitivist, value judgements can neither be true nor false and consequently no objectively verifiable or falsifiable standard of assessment exists. Basically, three positions have been taken to follow from this: amoralism, subjectivism and relativism.

The amoralist position maintains that:

> If about matters of value there is no truth or falsity to be had, then an actor is warranted in ignoring traditional moral injunctions and following the dictates of self-interest or prudence or, indeed, any other imperative at all. The core of amoralism, then, is that any reasons are good reasons for action.
>
> (Ibid.: 46)

This is a view, rightly or wrongly, most often associated with Realism in International Relations and especially Machiavelli (Machiavelli 1988).[5]

The subjectivist position, on the other hand, holds that a person's reasons for ethical action derive from their own values, interests or desires and that these cannot be objectively established *via* truth conditions (verifiability) or conditions of falsity (falsifiability). In other words, the reasons for action are either self-interested in some way or an expression of preference. That moral actions in international politics are ultimately self-interested is again perhaps best known in its Realist formation and will be discussed in more detail below. On this view, the standard of morality applicable to international relations is not objective, but subjective in the sense that it refers to either the self-interest of the state, the national interest, or is an expression of preference in the form of an ideological justification.

The third position, relativism, need not necessarily be non-cognitivist since it does not always deny the existence of truth in value judgements (Nardin 1989; Spegele 1995). Rather, it arises if one accepts that what is 'true' depends on specific contexts for example, societal, cultural, historical, or discursive. 'To claim that a proposition is true is therefore to claim that it is true "for" or "relative to" a given community or conceptual scheme' (Nardin 1989: 150–1). With regards to relativism, then, the disjunction appears as a conflict between one universal truth or many, particular truths. This can lead to a form of moral scepticism in international politics as to the possibility of universal criteria transcending their cultural and social roots. And, indeed, this particular aspect of scepticism is a central theme for each of the theorists that this book reads grammatically. An expression of this form of scepticism is pithily articulated in the claim that 'most accounts of the universal values that might underlie a cosmopolitan ethic seem suspiciously like inadequately camouflaged versions of the first ten Amendments of the Constitution of the United States of America' (Brown 1988/89: 105–6).

With regards to the second epistemological aspect of problems engendered by the disjuncture of fact and value, the legitimate concerns of the discipline, we need to turn to the 'positivist bias' of IR (Frost 1986: 9). Writing in the mid-1980s, Frost characterised such bias as 'a philosophical assumption which accounts for the dearth of normative theory in the discipline of international relations' (ibid.: 9). At its heart, positivist approaches to IR (in particular the prominence of Waltz's neo-realism at the time), 'applie[d] scientific method to human affairs conceived as belonging to a natural order open to objective enquiry' (Hollis 1994: 41; Waltz 1979).[6] Positivism made it clear that the discipline should only be concerned with statements of fact and not value. Ethics, belonging to the realm of value judgements therefore had no place within a discipline committed to notions of objectivity, value-free analysis and 'real-worldism' (George 1994: 17; Tooze 1988).

Positivism's seemingly iron-like grip on IR lasted for over forty years as the discipline tried to establish, and legitimise, itself as a social *science* (Smith 1992). Thankfully, for some, this grip began to loosen as a plethora of researchers began to question the possibility of distinguishing fact from value. To a certain extent, this questioning was due to IR scholars beginning to open their enquiries to a much wider base of social sciences that were 'restructuring' themselves in ways which did not rely on the fact/value distinction (Bernstein 1979, 1989, 1991).[7] That there could be alternative approaches to positivism was captured by a number of, what became, seminal texts in IR at the time (Der Derian and Shapiro 1989; Elshtain 1987; Enloe 1989; Hollis and Smith 1991; Keohane 1986; Tickner 1992). Lapid famously dubbed this the 'third debate' (Lapid 1989).[8]

So, what were the main features of the challenges posed to the disjuncture between fact and value in the so-called 'third debate'?[9] Primarily, the challenges honed in on a much more basic, foundational, disjuncture that provided the grounds upon which the separation of fact and value rested: the disjuncture between subject and object.[10] In IR, the object was 'international political reality' and the subject the political 'scientist' as supposed independent observer.

In order to maintain that facts and values could and should be kept separate with only the former the legitimate concern of the social sciences, positivism necessarily required that the values of the social scientist should have no bearing on the 'facts' that they were observing. This meant that the theories produced by the social scientist to locate and explain facts had to be value-neutral. Value neutrality is the formal requirement that choices of empirical data as facts or between rival theories are not value-laden, that is to say, choices should not be generated by values (such as gender bias or political persuasion) held by the observer (Root 1993: 43). However, this was and continues to be, persuasively challenged by feminist scholarship, for example (Ackerly, *et al.* 2006; Stern 2005).

Elshtain described her experience of the separation of subject and object as absurdly schizophrenic wherein she 'wrote papers about the national interest and changed diapers' (Elshtain 1995: 33). Her point was simply that as a political scientist the disjuncture made her realise that 'it eliminated from theorising a variety of *human* experiences considered "private", such as mothering, sentimentality, emotions, etc. and instead concentrated only on those elements of politics which can be proclaimed as "public", "scientific knowledge"' (Elshtain 1995: 89). She famously argued that not only is the separation of public and private value-laden in that it is deeply gendered with the former associated with rationality, masculinity, politics, and knowledge (public man) and the former with sentiment, femininity, the home and opinion (private woman) but it is also value-laden in that it tells us that human experiences, moral sentiments and identity are not part of 'international political reality' nor its scientific study (Elshtain 1981, 1987). The positivist requirement of distinguishing between scientific choices of 'fact' (e.g. states) over value (e.g. the experiences of women, and men, in war) therefore, became untenable when feminists pointed out that these very choices were gendered. In short, 'at the heart of value-neutrality was a very powerful normative project, one every bit as "political" or "biased" as those approaches marginalised and delegitimised in the name of science' (Smith 1992: 490).

Challenges like Elshtain's, among many others, questioned the possibility of value-neutrality upon which the fact/value disjuncture depended. As far as wanting to 'do' ethics in IR was concerned, this threw the doors wide open. After all, if value-neutrality wasn't possible, what else were we doing in IR as an academic discipline other than ethics?!

Ontological mountains: domestic and international politics

The disjunctions between fact and value, and subject and object are not the only obstacles, or mountains, that seemingly require climbing in this disjunctive configuration of the problem of ethics 'and' international relations that dominates IR. For some, in addition to the epistemological disjunctions described above, there exists a fundamental ontological disjunction. It is ontological because it focuses on some aspect or aspects of what is purported to be the reality of world politics (the nature of its existence) that prevents either the appropriateness and/or the possibility of ethics in world politics.

The ontological disjunction that we will focus on here is the separation of domestic politics from international politics. Purportedly they are two different 'realities' that, ontologically speaking, have different features so that domestic politics is more amenable to the possibility of ethics than international politics. Predictably, if anybody wants to argue that ethics may be possible in global politics, and they are seduced by the picture of this bifurcated ontological landscape, then they are going to want to bridge the disjunction between the international and domestic in some way. In other words, they are going to want to find a conjunctive solution to how ethically accommodating features of domestic politics might be translated and, indeed, transplanted into the international realm. What possible conjunctive solutions there might be to this, and their relation to universality, is the scope of the next three chapters. In the meantime, we need to return to our sketch of the mountainous terrain to see the features of the peaks, which, we are told, we must climb in order to successfully locate a universal international ethic.

The most important features of the terrain of global politics that purport to be the foundation for the ontological disjuncture between international and domestic politics are international anarchy, the national interest, national sovereignty and cultural pluralism.

In IR, anarchy doesn't mean the same thing as the Sex Pistols' use of the word in the world's first punk single (Sex Pistols 1976). Instead, at its most simple, anarchy just means that in international politics there is an absence of world government: a global sovereign (Hobbes 1968). One of the consequences of this, so the story goes, is that only states have 'a monopoly over the legitimate use of violence in the enforcement of its order' (Weber 1971). For Realists, in particular, anarchy is what distinguishes the international from the domestic as ordered. So, it is only sovereign states that can legitimately command their own military forces, police, and so on to enforce their own domestic order. They are sovereign over themselves with no authority above them. Given the absence of a global overarching authority, then states can do what they like as long as they have the power because nothing else has the legitimacy or monopoly of physical force to stop them. This means, so the Realists often tell us, that it creates a security dilemma where states cannot trust each other not to violate their sovereignty by acts of war, for example (Booth and Wheeler 2008). This lack of trust creates an anarchic international environment where states have to ensure their own survival in the absence of a global sovereign who might do it for them. This is a form of reality where state survival is the highest value. The ethical significance of this has often been taken to be that the only appropriately responsible way to think about international politics is to concentrate on survival and not worry too much, if at all, about moral values and judgements lest they hinder political action (Machiavelli 1988).

This leads nicely on to a second ontological feature of the international and that's the national interest. Implicit in the distinction between the international and domestic, as described above, is the idea that the state's primary obligation is to look after its own survival and the security of its own citizens first and foremost. We can say that this view suggests that the frontiers of the state are the boundaries of the extension of international morality. The primacy of the national interest, state survival and security (including of its citizenry), becomes the central concern in the political relations between states. This is a highly influential view and we will examine it in closer detail in the next chapter. For the moment it suffices to only remark that the national interest, and the self-interest that it promotes due to the constraining features of anarchy, are among the mountains to be climbed should a universal international ethic be possible (Morgenthau 1964; Waltz 1959, 1979).

Portraying the international as anarchic also explicitly endorses state sovereignty broadly understood as domestic jurisdiction over one's own affairs and a right to non-intervention (territorial integrity). This is because the international is defined as anarchic because of the absence of a global sovereign. Grammatically, articulations of state sovereignty as a feature of international politics are a series of propositions on what makes the domestic 'ordered' in contrast to anarchic (Walzer 1977). Whether state sovereignty is morally defensible and can serve as a foundation for a universal international ethic is a topic for Chapter 5. Again, here we will just remark its purported existence as yet another mountain to get to grips with if ethics in global politics is to be possible.

Finally, the argument about cultural pluralism is an argument about global differences. It asserts that, unlike domestic society, the international realm suffers from a lack of moral consensus and, therefore, no universal and global agreement exists as to how states *should* act ethically. From this point of view, it elides neatly with the epistemological mountain of cultural relativism. The globe is divided into sovereign states, each of which have differences in their cultures, traditions, histories, ways of life, and truths (Walzer 1994c, 1995). In this point of view, the possibility of an international ethic is hindered by a landscape where questions of justice and/or ethics do not travel nor translate easily across the boundaries of states and where notions of right and wrong are multifarious.

Universality as a conjunctive solution

This chapter has presented what I called the 'double whammy' of international ethics in the Introduction. We've now seen that it has both an onto-logical component and an epistemological one, hence it is 'double'. But also each component, whether ontological or epistemological, has two components that require a conjunctive solution for ethics to be possible and for universality to be the very answer we seek; that's what makes international ethics appear to be the difficult 'whammy' it is to grapple with.

First, there seems to be a requirement that some universal (here meaning global) 'thing'/space in world politics needs to be located which can accommodate the possibility of ethics. Our little excursion into the topography of the terrain of the ontological disjunction between international and domestic politics has shown us why a search for such a locus is deemed necessary. It is because the international realm is understood as anarchic and, as such, ontologically problematic for the accommodation of ethics. Indeed, for some, it is so problematic that anarchy has been interpreted as a mountain that cannot be climbed and that amoralism is the only conclusion to draw. However, this is not the only conclusion one could draw, otherwise this book really would be a very short book. In the next three chapters, we will look at how three different IR theorists have tried to come up with a conjunctive solution to the disjunction between the international and domestic as a part of their universalist solution to the problem of international ethics. By reading grammatically, we can explore how they've tried to climb this ontological mountain by digging deep beneath the surface of language in order to get to the *reality* of global politics.

Second, our excursion has suggested that there is also an epistemological pull towards universality as the second aspect of the double whammy. Here there seems to be a requirement that we find a 'way' of locating some universal thing about global politics. Whatever that 'way' is and whatever 'thing' it may reveal as universal, are again the subject of the next three chapters. Regardless of the detail of the possible answers, the grammar of 'and' requires that the way is a conjunctive one, one where ethics can be a part of the reality of international politics *and* where ethics is a resolution to the issue of one universal ethic over many. In the case of all three theorists, they believe that the 'way' requires knowing how to dig beneath the surface of language/reality and it relies on having a good spade in order to do so.

The title of this book emphasises the view that, in the end, the desire to dig in order to find an *answer* to the moral dilemma of international politics, the double whammy, is so strong that we can easily find ourselves postulating a universality of one kind or another. Metaphysical seduction, in this context, is the inability to resist the urge to climb the mountains as *the* challenge that must be met in order for ethics in global politics to be possible. It sets us off on a search for universality as a doubly conjunctive solution.

3 Divine universality

Morgenthau, alchemy and the national interest

Hans J. Morgenthau is considered the father of modern classical realism. As a seminal figure, accounts of his version of political realism are a compulsory component of many an Introduction to International Relations module or introductory textbooks. And, along with his iconic status there exists a mythological Morgenthau: a caricature who appears and reappears in textbooks as *the* scholar who claimed that the study of international politics should be scientific. After all, one of his principles of political realism famously states that 'politics, like society in general, is governed by objective laws which have their roots in human nature' (Morgenthau 1964: 4). Those critical of political realism have even presented the mythological Morgenthau as a positivist 'village idiot' who, being of simple mind, unproblematically suggests that the academic discipline of International Relations can and should be understood objectively as a science.[2] Taking such a positivistic stance would lead us to understanding IR as the pursuit of facts and it would eschew all, non-objective, questions of value such as ethics. To be sure, there are some people who believe this but, whoever they are, Morgenthau certainly isn't one of them.[3] Personally, I have found that this great man's body of work is so much more interesting and problematic than these little introductions would have us believe. The first thing I noticed when I actually read Morgenthau (and not accounts of him) was that any sustained reading beyond the first few pages of subsequent editions of *Politics Among Nations*, quickly revealed that questions concerning the morality of international politics are not only addressed, but indeed, are central and constitutive of his form of political realism.[4] Accordingly, he is a central and fascinating scholar for us to explore when it comes to universality, ethics and International Relations.

Very early on in his best-known book, *Politics Among Nations*, Morgenthau warns us against what he believes to be one of the greatest dangers in the practice of international politics: a form of utopianism that cannot resist identifying 'the moral aspirations of a particular nation with the moral laws that govern the universe' (ibid.: 11). Writing in the darkness cast by the shadows of unspeakable horrors perpetrated by the Nazis during the Second World War, Morgenthau was acutely aware that 'the light-hearted equation between a particular nationalism and the counsels of Providence is morally indefensible' having himself been forced to flee Germany in the late 1930s (ibid.: 11). It is precisely this kind of equation that provided Nazism with its totalitarian ideology and that Morgenthau devoted his life and career to providing an alternative to. Totalitarianism and the Holocaust that it perpetrated are Morgenthau's living nightmare. Therefore, his greatest desire in understanding ethics and international politics couldn't accurately be described as a purely 'intellectual' endeavour. Rather, as we shall see, Morgenthau's political realism is a search for some kind of deep, existential, comfort, perhaps, some kind of reassurance that, were we to access its source and act in accordance with it, we would not find ourselves repeating the mistakes Morgenthau desperately wants us to avoid.

The previous chapters emphasised two things: digging and mountains. In Chapter 1, I introduced the notion of digging as the act of those theorists and scholars who are metaphysically seduced. There I suggested that the urge to go below the surface of language in order to find the foundations of reality and knowledge is a compulsion that arises from a misunderstanding of the relationship between language and reality. That misunderstanding is a misplaced generalisation of the idea that words name objects and that therefore, language pictures/represents reality. In that chapter, very little could be said about what that actually looks like in relation to universality, ethics and IR. At long last, starting with Morgenthau, we can begin to 'look and see' how a Realist language game of international ethics deploys such digging and what it unearths (Wittgenstein 1958a: §66). Of course, we are most interested in the kind of universality that will be revealed and how we are told to go about finding it. Equally, I hope, we will also be interested in the endeavour itself: the adventures we embark on when we think a word names some 'thing'. A grammatical reading is the act of taking up that adventure (however uncomfortable it may be sometimes), seeing where we end up and asking whether we have arrived at the destination that our language game told us we were heading for or whether, perhaps, we've ended up somewhere else. What each of the grammatical readings reveals is that it is only by fully engaging with the language games of universality, hopping on board, that we can discover that our metaphysical desire hasn't been satiated by 'the answer'. Put another way, once we have climbed the mountains according to the instructions of each theorist, we may find that the view isn't quite the one we are expecting. We may be surprised.

Mountain climbing with Morgenthau is the aim of this chapter. We will begin by exploring his grammar. We have to start here because grammar is his bedrock, where he says 'my spade is turned' (Wittgenstein 1958a: §217). What that means is that all language games must proceed as though some things are beyond question and where we need not dig any deeper. As we will see, for Morgenthau, the differing ontologies of the divine and actual are bedrock and are what allow the rest of his proceedings to get off the ground. Subsequent features of his language game are grammatically produced. Here, and in the next two chapters, we will focus on how grammar produces a configuration of what the moral dilemma of international ethics is, in other words, a language game-specific articulation and specification of the double whammy. And, we will also focus on how grammar produces pictures of the subject, reason and ethico-political space which, taken together, add up to a universalist conjunctive solution. Of all the forms of universality that we will grammatically read in this book, it is Morgenthau's which is the most metaphysical as it reaches towards the heavens for an answer yet, *via* conjunctive failure, finds itself in the jaws of the veritable hell it sought to avoid.

A grammar of transcendence and actuality

All the key elements of Morgenthau's form of political realism are produced by a grammatical separation of the transcendent and the actual which he sometimes expressed as the separation of thought and action or, synonymously, of the *vita contemplativa* and *vita activa* (Morgenthau 1940, 1946, 1959, 1962, 1971, 1972).[5] As we shall explore, the unquestioned acceptance of these features of reality and their separateness is what produces the details of the mountains Morgenthau believes we need to climb in order for ethics in international politics to be possible. And, he sees those mountains as extremely ugly, power-driven and next to insurmountable. The biggest obstacle of all on the landscape is human nature: us. We are the problem because of the 'objective laws' that determine us. It is Morgenthau's grammar that names what the source of these laws are, and in the next section, therefore grammatically it produces his picture of the subject. From the point of view of a grammatical reading, the important thing to note is that, in this chapter, we will be tracing the effects of his grammar: 'the shadow of possibility cast by language upon phenomena' (Wittgenstein 1974: §329). It is worth emphasising that were Morgenthau's grammar otherwise, we would be confronted with very different configurations of the moral dilemma of international politics, the subject, reason and ethico-political space. And accordingly, therefore, universality would be very different too. The subsequent two chapters will show us that but in the meantime, we will embark on Morgenthau's grammatical adventure and travel with someone who believes that the ontology of the world, and of us, is divided into the divine and the actual. Let's see what Morgenthau's mountains look like, how he tells us we should climb them and whether we find ourselves looking at the view that he sees. It is a theological odyssey that will find us digging deep beneath the surface of language/reality into the heart of our souls and the divine fabric of life so that we may grapple with the difficulties of a universal ethic in international politics.

In his last book, *Science: Servant or Master?* Morgenthau offers us his most explicit and systematic exegesis of the transcendental metaphysic that underpins his theorising. In a revealing elaboration of human nature, Morgenthau outlines what he believes to be the existential condition of man.[6] Drawing on Plato and Aristotle, he proposes that the condition and consciousness of man's existence is characterized by 'the shock of wonderment' (Morgenthau 1972: 25). He states:

> Wonderment is the condition in which . . . reason fails to assimilate a fragment of empirical reality because its logical processes are unable to transform sensual experience into *systematic knowledge*. Man wants to know what can be known, yet empirical reality sets limits to human understanding. His desire exceeds his ability, and thus he experiences in the limits of his knowledge also the limits of his power. Hence the shock of wonderment, from which stems his longing to overcome those limits, to close the gap between what he knows and what is to be known.
>
> (Ibid.: 25)

The 'shock of wonderment' then, is the realisation of the gap between the empirical and the philosophic, between sense-objects (particulars) and knowledge (universals), and ultimately between knowledge and action (ibid.: 29). It is the existential experience of man's limited nature. Morgenthau believes that consciousness of universal knowledge and its possible attainment through theoretical thought (the *vita contemplativa*) indicates man's connection with the divine. Consciousness of the divine is Morgenthau's original moment of wonder taken from Plato and Aristotle (ibid.: 25). He claims that 'if there were no men to carry within themselves this consciousness of the divine, man's existence on earth would have lost its meaning since man would have missed his natural calling' (ibid.: 71).

The grammatical ramifications of this are numerous. First, 'the shock of wonderment' is an ontological statement. There are two types of existence: the empirical and the transcendent. The former is characterised by contingency, particularity and limitedness (including finitude) and the latter by timelessness, objectivity and universalism. Second, related to the above is the epistemological claim that the only true objects of knowledge are transcendent. This means that knowledge is of universals and not of particulars and is therefore objective rather than particularistic. Knowledge of empirical objects gained through the senses is therefore, not sufficient for true knowledge.[7] Both these statements rely on an onto-theological[8] grammatical distinction between the transcendent (divine) and the actual. In other words, Morgenthau's grammar has laid out the contours of the double whammy he believes we *must* grapple with: the mountains. There are two to climb by digging deep into their surface to get a grip on what we are dealing with and find a resolution. First, we must somehow reconcile two kinds of existence and phenomena in time – one which is essentially eternal and one which is essentially contingent. Second, we must also reconcile different sorts of knowledge that are different precisely because each has its roots in the different ontologies outlined above. Morgenthau tells us that we must be able to separate out timeless true knowledge from mere, contingent, belief. In short, we must be able to locate the objects of universal knowledge.

It's not going to be easy as the cliché 'All western philosophy is just footnotes to Plato' so pithily captures. Nevertheless, Morgenthau is wholly committed to giving it a go and, more than that, believes we have no choice but to do so. In his picture of the subject he outlines for us what we all are, how that negatively contributes to the moral dilemma of international politics and what spaces, if any, there may be for some salvation in our ethical encounters with each other. Morgenthau's picture of reason elaborates this space in more detail as not only an intuition of transcendent, divine, value but an imperative to reintroduce it into International Relations as an academic discipline. And, finally, with his picture of ethico-political space he seeks to show us how the source of universal knowledge and ethics, identified in his pictures of the subject and reason, relates to the national-interest and can form the basic of an international ethic.

Let's move to Morgenthau's picture of the subject. It's here that we see the first and foundational product of his grammar. I say this picture is foundational because it is what Morgenthau is referring to as 'the objective laws which have their roots in human nature' and it is these laws which he says 'politics . . . is governed by' and that as realists we must understand and use to govern our own actions (Morgenthau 1964: 4). Grammatically speaking, we aren't interested in whether this picture is true or false. We are interested in how it is a grammatical product and tracing its effects. One of those effects is to be foundational and create a moral dilemma where the best that is available, ethically speaking, are not acts of doing good but only less evil.

Divine universality and the limits of human nature

Given Morgenthau's separation of the transcendent and actual rooted in the thought of Plato and Aristotle, this grammar serves as the constitutive dynamic of his picture of the subject. The *separateness* of these two elements serves as the foundation upon which he elaborates his well-known description of human nature as selfish, lustful for power and sinful. In an unpublished paper 'The Significance of Being Alone', Morgenthau characterises man's relationship with God as one of *separation* (Russell 1990: 74–80). God is distinctly apart from His creation, that is part of God's perfection. God does not need a companion in perfection and so the question of whether it is good or for Him to be alone does not arise. However, in contrast, man is not perfect but yet carries a vision of perfection ('consciousness of the divine'):[9]

> This vision encompasses both the contemplation of *eternal verities* as well as the desire for perfection and a meaning to his life that transcends the mere prerequisites of corporeal existence. The Fall, the eating from

the tree of knowledge, symbolizes man's restless search for a perfection from which he is precluded by his own nature. Subsequently, the inborn loneliness of man takes on a new significance. Able to know good from evil, man acquires a sense of tragedy and guilt by recognizing the chasm that divides what he is in contrast to what he should but can never fully become.

(Ibid.: 75; italics added)

The tragedy of human existence is that man is able to *know* good from evil yet, because of his limited nature, is unable to achieve it fully given that perfection is a characteristic only applicable to God. Man wants to join God in His perfection, yet is not God hence his 'longing for union with an infinite world'. I shall call this elaboration of 'the shock of wonderment' the imperfectability thesis. The suggestion is that the 'objective laws that have their roots in human nature', upon which he insists a theory of international politics should be predicated, are generated by this theological understanding of man's relationship with God.[10]

It is vital to note that without the grammatical separation of the transcendent and the actual characterised by the 'shock of wonderment' as the human condition, Morgenthau would not be able to generate the imperfectability thesis and nor would he be able to propose that he has access to knowledge of a moral code. The imperfectability thesis is constructed by comparing eternal truths and knowledge with what is possible empirically, contrasting the transcendent and the actual. By the standards of the perfection of God, man necessarily falls short and is imperfect both epistemologically and morally. Consequently, Morgenthau's picture of the subject (human nature) relies on the grammar outlined above and the two related assumptions that it creates: (1) the imperfectability thesis; and (2) that particular characteristics of the subject can be judged as *evil*, which is a claim to knowledge of the difference between good and evil: a moral code.

In *Scientific Man*, he offers a full elaboration of the imperfectability thesis. He begins with the proposition that 'Whatever man does or intends to do emanates from himself and refers again to himself. The person of the actor is present in all intended and consummated action' (Morgenthau 1946: 191). In other words all action is self-referential. He then adds that all action, including non-action (acts of omission), connects the self to others. Using these two premises, he then concludes that selfishness is an unavoidable, universal characteristic of human nature. By not acting, a person is selfish because his omission is necessarily a negation of the possibility of an act of moral duty (ibid.: 201). In a curious construction of a paradox that relies on his proposition that all action is self-referential, Morgenthau argues that, by acting, one is forced to be selfish because 'The attempt to do justice to the ethics of unselfishness . . . leads to the paradox of the ethical obligation to be selfish in order to be able to satisfy the moral obligation of unselfishness at least to a certain extent' (ibid.: 192). His point is that in trying to avoid sacrificing the interests of others to his own, a person is forced to preserve a certain degree of their own interests so that they are not so incapacitated by moral sacrifice that they are unable to 'contribute at least a share of unselfishness to the overwhelming demands of the world' (ibid.: 191).[11] Whether through an act or an omission, one is forced to choose oneself rather than others. Consequently, for Morgenthau, 'It is here that the inevitability of evil becomes paramount' (ibid.: 191). That human nature is selfish, for Morgenthau, provides one of the bases of struggle and conflict. He gives two reasons. First, what one wants either another has or also wants. Second, because of the ensuing competition, 'man can no longer seek the goodness of his intentions in the almost complete absence of selfishness and of the concomitant harm to others but only in the limitations which conscience puts upon the drive toward evil' (ibid.: 192). Morgenthau is denying not only the possibility of unselfish action, but also unselfish intentions. This being so, the only course open to man is to act in his own interest. Any attempts to transcend the selfish 'realities' of competing egotisms are impossible, for it would require sacrificing one's existence and, paradoxically, be an act that carries the moral culpability of an omission.

The second element of human nature, the lust for power, accounts for the 'ubiquity of evil in human action'. For Morgenthau, human nature is ruled by a universal *animus dominandi*. This universal lust for power i.e. 'the desire to maintain the range of one's own person with regard to others, to increase it, or to demonstrate it', is the ubiquitous source of conflict and competition (ibid.: 188). However, he makes an important differentiation between the lust for power and selfishness, which accounts for the ubiquity of the former. Selfishness has limits because survival can be attained and hence, satisfaction. However, 'The desire for power, . . . concerns itself not with the individual's survival but with his position among his fellows once his survival has been secured. Consequently, the selfishness of man has limits; his will to power has none' (ibid.: 193). The difference between selfishness and the lust for power then, is the possibility of reaching satisfaction. In a statement that mirrors the imperfectability thesis he says, that the 'lust for power would be satisfied only if the last man became an object of his domination, there being nobody above or beside him, that is, if he became like God' (ibid.: 193). Thus, the only end to the lust for power would be total power that only an omnipotent God can have.

The lust for power is the 'ubiquitous element' of *evil* in human action because its nature necessarily violates 'a basic tenet of Western morality: to respect man as an end in himself and not to use him as a means to an end' (Morgenthau 1962: 13). Instead, the desire for power requires that we treat others as a means to an end, the end being the maintenance or extension of our own power so that we might dominate. This is a different formulation of the imperfectability thesis that he employed in his definition of man as selfish. In the latter man is selfish because he cannot attain the ethic of altruism. In the case of the lust for power, man necessarily must do evil because he cannot act upon the ethical principle of treating others as ends in themselves because of the limitation of his nature. There is then, an 'incompatibility, in the light of our own limitations, of the demands which morality makes upon us' (Morgenthau 1946: 189–90). In short, 'Man cannot attain moral perfection in this world' (Morgenthau 1962: 375).

Such are the conclusions he draws from the imperfectability thesis. Man cannot help but do evil because of his limited nature and the axiomatic impossibility of attaining perfection. However, in *Scientific Man*, Morgenthau is silent as to what he believes is the source of the moral code by which he can judge man's limitations of action and intention as *evil*. Morgenthau seems to provide an answer in 'Christian Ethics and Political Action' and the 'Epistle to the Columbians on the Meaning of Morality' (Morgenthau 1962: 368–76).[12] In the latter, Morgenthau provides a universalist argument for a 'foundation of moral understanding'. He wishes to deny that morality is relative to either environment or circumstance. This takes the same form as his argument for objective, general truth that can be seen as a re-articulation of both Plato's and Aristotle's view that knowledge is impossible without the universal.[13] Just as objective truth is impossible unless it is universally true regardless of time and place, so it is with morality. Of the latter, Morgenthau states,

> If the disparate historic systems of morality were not erected upon a common foundation of moral understanding and valuation, impervious to the changing conditions of time and place, we could not understand any other moral system but our own, nor could any other moral system but our own have any moral relevance for us.
>
> (Ibid.: 372)

For Morgenthau, then, all instances of a moral system, if they are to be identified as 'moral', must therefore share a common foundation of identity. This means that morality is singular and that it exists independently of any time, place or socio-cultural environment. It is not made by man. It has not only 'a transcendent source' but 'requires for its fulfilment transcendent orientations' (ibid.: 373). We have already seen that 'the shock of wonderment' is man's consciousness and struggle with his 'transcendent orientations'. When related to ethics, this connection with the divine provides man with a 'born . . . moral sense' and the capacity 'by nature of making moral judgments' (ibid.: 373). It would seem that for Morgenthau, the divine is also the *source* of morality. This can be deduced from Morgenthau's understanding of the unattainability of moral standards discussed above. He believes that moral laws are perfect and that only God, not man, can live in perfection. Therefore, moral laws, if they can neither be attained and are not created by man, must be created by the divine since only He can realise them. Given that God is Creator, omnipotent and omniscient, it is impossible that moral law could have a source outside Him. Indeed, without such a belief Morgenthau could not make the association of Christian ethics with that of a moral code.

Given that Morgenthau has claimed that morality is universal and that Christian ethics count as an instance of a moral code, Christian ethics must in *essence* also be universal rather than particular. Morgenthau states that 'The conflict between the demands of Christian ethics and the way man must live is the overriding moral experience of Western civilization' (ibid.: 375). On the face of it, this seems like a contradiction. It seems that he is only talking of particulars, Christian ethics and Western civilisation. Yet we have seen that Morgenthau's definition of the condition of man in 'the shock of wonderment' is meant to be universal and apply to all men [*sic*]. *All* humans share the same nature that, in large part, is characterised by the imperfectability thesis. This apparent contradiction can be explained by Morgenthau's appropriation of Aristotle. For Aristotle, knowledge is attained by moving from experience of particulars towards the universal by means of intellectual intuition (*nous*) that is linked to the divine. In the case of Morgenthau, the 'common foundation of moral understanding . . . find[s] its meaning . . . from a transcendent source' – the divine (ibid.: 372–3). Although Christian ethics and Western civilisation count as particulars, when approached with a 'transcendent orientation', their *essence* (common foundation) can be experienced and known as a universal. The grammatical separation of the transcendent and actual thus constructs the possibility and indeed the postulation, that Christian ethics is a universal standard by which to judge all human actions and intentions.

The imperfectability thesis which played such an important role in Morgenthau's characterisation of human nature as selfish and lustful for power is then re-articulated thus:

> It is the very function of Christian ethics to call upon man to comply with a code of moral conduct with which, by virtue of his nature, he cannot comply . . . The moral function of Christian ethics is to hold up to man a code of moral conduct both unattainable and approachable. Man cannot attain moral perfection in this world; the best he is capable of is to conceive its meaning.
>
> (Ibid.: 375)

We can now fully appreciate how Morgenthau's picture of the subject is grammatically produced. The subject cannot attain moral perfection in accordance with Christian ethics; an ethic that has a transcendent source which captures timeless, universal moral truths. That means that universally, we cannot *do* good. Nevertheless, not quite all is lost, as we can know what is good and evil because of our connection with the divine and the moral sense that it provides. The tragedy is that 'as soon as we leave the realm of our thoughts and aspirations we are inevitably involved in sin and guilt' (Morgenthau 1946: 188). Thus, the transcendent is accessible in thought but unattainable in action. As such, man is necessarily evil, bound by selfishness and the lust for power. That's quite an existential whammy! How can it be possible to derive a universal international ethic from this wretched reality of human existence that his grammar has unearthed? For the answers to that, we need to look at his pictures of reason and ethico-political space as his proposed resolution of the moral dilemma of international politics.

Reason and the re-introduction of transcendent value into the world

In Morgenthau's picture of reason, more accurately described as a picturing of the limits of reason, his grammatical separation of the transcendent and actual appears as a different kind of problematic. As we will see in this section, what he offers us is his sense, his experience, of what being a theorist of international politics entails. It is, of course, more than just autobiographical. Given the universality of his picture of the subject, Morgenthau believes he is presenting us with the reality of what a theoretical digging endeavour involves. Digging to get to the essence of reality is, for Morgenthau, what the theorist must do because we must have knowledge of and access to objective laws and universal truths. Morgenthau's picture of reason will tell us that in order to do that, the theorist must dig deep within to find their soul and its connection with the divine. Nothing less could, or would, do because without such access, we would only be encountering contingent, particular aspects of reality rather than timeless, universal ones. If, as Morgenthau tells us, we are to have any hope of incorporating ethics into international politics, we must cling to the universal and not be deterred or blown off course by the contingent and particularistic. Lest we have forgotten, travelling with Morgenthau is all about locating the universal, not losing our grasp on it and then working out how, despite the limits of human nature, it may guide our actions. Our access to divine universality and its role in IR is what this section will explore. It's a journey of the soul.

Morgenthau's grammatical insistence on the radical ontological difference between the transcendent and the actual leads him to express the problem of political science in the following disjunctive way:

> Theoretical thinking and action as typical modes of human behaviour are irredeemably separated by way of their logical structure. Since politics is in its essence action, there exists with the same necessity an unbridgeable chasm, an eternal tension between politics and a theoretical science of politics.
>
> (Morgenthau 1972: 34)

Unsurprisingly, the tension between transcendent moral laws and human action that was a grammatical feature of Morgenthau's picture of the subject reappears in his understanding of political science. Morgenthau's belief, taken from Aristotle most notably, that pure theoretical thinking (First Philosophy) is 'a life . . . more than merely human; it cannot be lived as man *qua* man but only by virtue of the divine that is in him', leads him to characterise the understanding of politics as a conflict between the *vita contemplativa* (life of contemplation) and the *vita activa* (life of action).[14] The objects of contemplation in the former are the objects of knowledge that for Morgenthau, are objective truth, moral law, and transcendent universals. The *vita activa* makes 'its very opposite and negation its subject', which presumably means particulars, contingent truth and the unattainability of moral law (ibid.: 34). So, for Morgenthau, the disjunctive problem of theorising politics is that the nature of theory and politics are irredeemably separate because of their different ontological and epistemological status.

Given Morgenthau's disjunctive construction of the problem of theorising politics, how does he then attempt to conjoin the two so that a science of politics is possible? What kind of conjunctive solution does he propose? He begins by referring back to the 'shock of wonderment' and claims it is the source of theoretical thinking and that it is a form of *action*. Morgenthau proposes that 'the shock of wonderment', as a tension between the will to know and the will to live, in reality amounts to 'a creative middle' once it is fully and properly realised. What he is trying to communicate here is the notion that this experience of shock is a state of consciousness that does not misunderstand either extreme. Precisely because the shock has dug up/ struck the right thing – the creative middle – it can change empirical reality (the actual). Indeed, his famous six principles of political realism are meant to be exactly that: a creative middle that can change the practice of international politics.

The will to know forms one extreme and the will to live the other. With regards to the first, Morgenthau has in mind positivist science as an example of an extreme will to know. For Morgenthau the dominance of positivist science has contributed to the deterioration of the 'moral condition of mankind' (ibid.: 11–18). As such,

> Science has not only lost its relation to a transcendent value from which it could receive its meaning but, more importantly, it has also lost the awareness of the need for such a transcendent orientation. It is no longer aware of the need for moral distinctions to be made within the sphere accessible to human knowledge. This moral crisis of science is concomitant with the disintegration of the value systems of a religious nature. For these systems decided a priori what was important and what was not in the realm of knowledge, what was and was not worth knowing. When science was thus freed from the subjection to a heteronomous order of moral values, it established its freedom from any moral limitations whatsoever.

> (Ibid.: 13)

For Morgenthau, then, positivist science is marked by its loss of transcendent meaning and value. Furthermore, it has associated human progress with a quantitative increase in theoretical knowledge. However, in Morgenthau's language game, positivist science is generated by an *incomplete* consciousness of wonderment: a failure to be conscious of the mysteries in life. Experience, according to Morgenthau, has shown that the association of accumulated knowledge with progress is a myth since 'we have experienced an unprecedented increase in theoretical knowledge and practical ability coinciding with an equally unprecedented increase in physical danger, social disintegration, and metaphysical doubt' (ibid.: 46). In this sense, positivist science is the cause rather than the cure for the dangers that it claims to be able to prevent. As an indiscriminate accumulation of knowledge that can make no distinction between what is and what is not worth knowing, due to its loss of transcendental meaning, it is the cause of the above dangers because of its failure to understand them. Thus, contemporary positivist science as the misguided manifestation of the will to know, is unable to understand the forces of human nature and therefore to offer mastery of them. As such, positivism has contributed to the deterioration of the 'moral condition of mankind'. With echoes of Max Weber's notion of a world disenchanted,[15] Morgenthau states that positivist science results in a loss of meaningfulness.[16] Such are the results of an extreme response to the element of the will to know in the partial consciousness of the grammatical features of the 'shock of wonderment'.

The other extreme response, that the 'creative middle' avoids, is generated by a partial consciousness of the will to live: an 'unconditional activism'. In this scenario, man 'despairs of the possibility of transforming reality by understanding it in a systematic, theoretical manner and sets out to transform it through the vital force of his individuality' (ibid.: 47). This unconditional activism is not quite as meaningless as positivist science in that the actor may submit to some kind of guidance from authority that most often reflects the standards of a particular society. However, such standards do not constitute a valid replacement for the loss of transcendent meaning, since they 'draw their validity from an alien source' (ibid.: 48). It's not entirely clear what Morgenthau means by 'alien' here but it seems that he is referring to these standards as coming from a source outside the human soul. For Morgenthau, action cannot be an answer to the metaphysical shock of wonderment. This is because 'That existential shock which is induced by the conflagration between the human soul and the mystery of the universe does not yield to social action' that affects the relationships between human beings (ibid.: 48). Rather, it is only social actions that have transcendent meaning that can affect man's relation with the *universe* and therefore, provide an answer for the shock of wonderment. In short, an answer to the metaphysical shock must take place in the sphere where the issue arises, in the perplexity of the human soul.

Having elaborated the disjunction between thought and action in this way, which we must remember is a consequence of the grammatical separation of the transcendent and actual, Morgenthau offers us his conjunctive solution. His answer to the contradiction between thought and action is the 'creative middle' which amounts to a full acceptance and consciousness of this contradiction rather than its dissolution. Fabulously, he articulates this position as one of 'heroic renunciation':

> It is one of the insoluble antinomies of our existence that life in its highest manifestation as reflective consciousness cannot fulfil itself without making an end to itself. Reflective consciousness reaches its limits when it accepts in heroic renunciation this inner contradiction between vitality and reflection as the last word . . . [I]t is the only answer that is true to the limits that life imposes upon thought.
>
> (Ibid.: 57)

Genuine theoretical thought, that remains fully conscious of the contradiction between thought and action, can *change* the world. This is important because Morgenthau not only wants to show us that a science of politics is possible through (re)introducing transcendent meaning and value, but also that it has a contribution to make to the 'moral condition of mankind'. Of course, he wants to show us that. What could possibly be the point of theorising international politics otherwise? We must remember what Morgenthau devoted his academic career and life to – contributing to the avoidance of another world war and another Holocaust. Morgenthau's search is serious, profound and, ultimately, it is the story of the pursuit of a form of universality that can change 'the moral condition of mankind' and offer us salvation from the evils we do to each other.

Such a contribution, for Morgenthau, must overcome theoretical thought's limitation to only the *vita contemplativa* and show how theoretical thought (political science) can contribute to the world of political *action*. It is precisely overcoming this limitation that the 'creative middle' is supposed to supply in his language game. To this end, Morgenthau offers his view on the causes of change in the realm of the actual: empirical reality. He says that such changes are 'the effect of causes through which human consciousness moves the world' (ibid.: 59). Human consciousness is linked to the divine for Morgenthau. As such, human consciousness, in the full realisation of the 'shock of wonderment', can be a form of action because of its ability to be transformative. Because of man's links with the divine, Morgenthau's understanding of the way in which consciousness can change the world is a way of re-introducing transcendent meaning into the world so that it is ameliorative to man's moral condition because it can affect empirical reality.

Thus understood, the fundamental aim of political science is to change the consciousness of the thinker to accept the disjuncture between the will to know and the will to live in order to access the creative middle. This is absolutely essential to understanding Morgenthau's picture of reason. I think it can be said that he viewed his own task as one of bringing about a change of consciousness in this way. This is a moral imperative for him, as it is nothing less than the reintroduction of moral value through transcendent meaning. Given his notion of how consciousness can affect the world, his grammar leads him to construct a heroic notion of political change in general. He says, 'The political world exists in relations among men, and if the consciousness of one single man is changed, the political world is changed at this particular point' (ibid.: 59). For Morgenthau, such a consciousness can have not only the empirical manifestation outlined above, but also an intellectual one. Indeed, this may even be taken as Morgenthau's statement of the relevance of 'speaking truth to power'.[17] In its intellectual manifestation it sets an example for others, and even if they are not willing to act themselves, genuine political scientists who have recovered the lost transcendental meaning of science can 'confirm intellectually the action that conforms with the truth' (ibid.: 60).

Reading grammatically, we can see that political science, as an aspect of Morgenthau's picture of reason, is grammatically produced. This is because, on the one hand, his grammar generates his understanding of the problem of theorising politics as the separation of the transcendent and actual in the form of a tension between thought and action. On the other, it also normatively regulates the way in which Morgenthau attempts to overcome this bifurcation by a full, (divine) consciousness of it.

However, this is not the only aspect of Morgenthau's picture of reason. In order to understand more fully the kind of reason that Morgenthau believes should be employed by the political scientist and political actor, one needs to look at the role reason plays in his language game in relation to ethics and international politics specifically. In practice, the only way that transcendence can be reintroduced is through Morgenthau's endorsement of what, I believe, is an intuitionist position. This can be shown by looking at where he draws the limits of reason within the antinomic sphere of ethics: a sphere where conflicts of value exist and cannot be rationally resolved. For Morgenthau, the 'tragic antinomies of human existence' famously take the form of 'a tragic struggle between good and evil, reason and passion' (Morgenthau 1946: 209). He says:

> The very existence of a normative sphere, in contradistinction to the sphere of mere facts, is due to the antinomy between what men are inclined to do under utilitarian considerations and what they *feel* they ought to do according to the standards of nonutilitarian ethics. In other words, the ethical norms which men feel actually bound to follow conform by no means to the rational calculus of utility but on the contrary, endeavour to satisfy nonutilitarian aspirations.
>
> (Morgenthau 1946: 209)

This passage is interesting because it brings to attention Morgenthau's picture of the subject and the relationship between 'consciousness of the divine' and ethicality. The ability to *know* what is good and evil is not calculated for Morgenthau. Rather, it is intuited through man's existential condition as the 'shock of wonderment' and in this sense is not (deductively) rational but belongs to the realm of passions. Thus, for Morgenthau, the foundation of moral obligation lies in following one's intuitions of the divine and the knowledge of goodness that it supplies. Given this construction of the subject, which in large part is informed by a grammar that emphasises *separateness* (of thought and action, the transcendent and actual, of the divine and the human, and so on), it is hardly surprising that it is re-articulated in the normative sphere as 'tragic *struggle*' between man's deductive rationality in ethics and his passion – what he *feels* he ought to do).

The struggle between good and evil is perhaps Morgenthau's best-known antinomy that takes several guises. We saw above how Morgenthau applied the grammatical separation of the transcendent and actual to create an inevitable struggle between good and evil in his picture of the subject. Man can have knowledge of goodness in thought but because of his limitations (in particular, selfishness and the lust for power) cannot put it into practice without 'sinning'. This was what I called the imperfectability thesis. Morgenthau's picture of reason is generated by the same grammar. However, in this context, it takes the form of analysing man's *lost* connection with the moral sense that comes from consciousness of the divine rather than its unattainability.

'Rationalism' is, for Morgenthau, an extreme manifestation of the will to know. Due to the lost connection with the divine, rationalist understandings of ethics such as utilitarianism, reduce the ethical sphere to the sphere of cold calculation. In this sense, rationalism for Morgenthau is an aberrant manifestation of the *vita contemplativa*. It fails to take into account the significance of transcendent meaning and to appreciate that deductive reasoning alone cannot justify ultimate value choices since it generates a problem of first premises. Morgenthau believed such justifications were only to be found in 'Philosophy as a specific response to the metaphysical shock suffered by human consciousness [and which] is implicit in all genuine science' (Morgenthau 1972: 61). Furthermore, he argues that rationalism fails to take into account the tragedy of human existence. This is because an aspect of the experience of the *vita contemplativa* reveals the *limits* of human nature just as much as the unlimitedness of what he seeks and this is the root of tragedy and 'awareness of irresolvable discord'.

Vitally for us, the same grammar produces Mogenthau's definition of what he calls the 'moral dilemma of political action' and generates an approach to ethics which is meant to overcome the limitations of rationalism: an intuitionist revision of Weber's ethic of responsibility. Morgenthau states his position:

[T]here is no way out. The moral dilemma of foreign policy is but a special and – it is true – particularly flagrant case of the moral dilemma which faces man on all levels of social action. Man cannot help sinning when he acts in relation to his fellow men; he may be able to minimize that sinfulness of social action, but he cannot escape it. For no social action can be completely free of the taint of egotism which, as selfish-ness, pride, or self-deception, seeks for the actor more than is his due. What is true of all social action is particularly true of political action and, within the latter, of foreign policy. For man's aspiration for power over other men, which is the very essence of politics, implies the denial of what is the very core of Judeo-Christian morality – respect for man as an end in himself. The power relation is the very denial of that respect; for it seeks to use man as means to the end of another man.

(Morgenthau 1962: 319)

This is a re-statement of the imperfectability thesis that has its origins in 'the shock of wonderment'. The moral dilemma of political action is the same antinomic gap between what morality tells us to do, and what we are able to do *qua* human beings – the separation of thought and action. As action, politics is 'irremediably separate by way of [its] logical structure' from thought (Morgenthau 1972: 34). Vitally, in politics, the limited aspects of human nature become particularly compelling because it is a sphere more than any other where man's aspiration for power plays a role in dictating his actions. In this way, Morgenthau arrives at the Realist-Weberian conclusion that politics is 'above all a [power] struggle between nations, classes or indi-viduals' (Aron 1971: 85). For Weber, and indeed Morgenthau, 'When a question is said to be a "political" question . . . what is always meant is that interests in the distribution, maintenance, or transfer of power are decisive for answering the questions and determining the decision or the official's sphere of activity' (Weber 1971: 78).[18] Thus, if moral standards, such as those belonging to the Judeo-Christian tradition, have no direct link with action because of their differing logical structure, the problem of ethics in politics then becomes 'the problem of justifying and limiting the power which man has over man' (Morgenthau 1946: 168).

Morgenthau's grammatical separation of the transcendent and actual, then, produces what he believes to be the problem of ethics in international politics. As such, he cannot propose a solution in the form of an attempt to bridge the antinomic chasm that exists between absolute moral standards and political action. What he offers instead is an approach to political ethics that, unlike rationalist or utopian approaches, accepts and embodies these inherent contradictions or 'tragedies of human existence'. He accepts that it is an ethic not of doing good, but of doing less evil for '[n]either science nor ethics nor politics can resolve the conflict between power and the common good' (ibid.: 203). His approach is a re-articulation of Weber's ethic of responsibility in which ethical evaluation in international politics emerges as the assessment of consequences in terms of political effectiveness (Turner and Factor 1984). This is inextricably linked to maintaining, extending or demonstrating power. The standard of political effectiveness and, therefore, the political moral standard that Morgenthau adopts is the national interest. The ethic of responsibility is the means by which power can be justified and limited by recourse to the national interest (Morgenthau 1964: 5). We will explore the national interest and its universal role in much more detail in the next section. Here we concentrate on how Morgenthau's grammar produces a limited role for reason in ethical decision-making.

Ultimately for both Weber and Morgenthau, one has to make a choice: either to follow the rules of the political art which necessarily involve a person in doing evil by following the dictates of power and treating others as means rather than an end in themselves or to adhere to an ethic of conviction and be willing to 'pay the price of using morally dubious means or at least dangerous ones – and facing the possibility or even the probability of evil ramifications' (Weber 1971: 121). Reason cannot reconcile the two, nor provide a rational basis by which one can make one's choice. Weber and Morgenthau choose the ethic of responsibility because of their concern with the attainability of one's goals: the 'political art'.

Given that deductive reason is limited and that it alone cannot provide grounds for choice, what can Morgenthau do? Unlike Weber, Morgenthau re-presents the ancient Greek notion of wisdom as a 'gift of intuition'. Wisdom plays the role of re-introducing transcendent meaning to politics. He says:

> [I]t is the political will that dominates in the true order of things. It is a will not primarily informed by scientific theory but by wisdom. Wisdom is the gift of intuition, and political wisdom is the gift to grasp intuitively the quality of diverse interests and power in the present and future and the impact of different actions upon them. Political wisdom, understood as sound political judgment, cannot be learned; it is a gift of nature, like the gift of artistic creativity or literary style or eloquence or force of personality. As such, it can be deepened and developed by example, experience, and study. But it cannot be acquired through deliberate effort by those from whom nature has withheld it.
>
> (Morgenthau 1972: 45)

For Morgenthau, the feature that differentiates an ethic of conviction (utopianism) from an ethic of responsibility (realism) is the manner in which they evaluate know-how and feasibility;[19] the adherent of an ethic of conviction concerns himself with commitment for its own sake independent of any calculation of success and the believer in an ethic of responsibility considers the instrumental value of consequences, therefore taking into account the chances of success. Morgenthau states, '[P]olitical realism considers a rational foreign policy to be a good policy; for only a rational foreign policy minimizes risks and maximizes benefits, and, hence, complies both with the moral precept of prudence and the political requirement of success' (Morgenthau 1964: 8). However, for him, the ability to assess *which* interests and power pertain to a foreign policy that minimises risks and maximises benefits is an intuition rather than deductively reasoned. Thus, political intuition or wisdom is prior to the use of deductive reason. Deductive reason may play a role once the priorities of power and interests have been identified (in this way it can play a role in the calculation of *consequences*), but it has no role to play in the choice of *ends*. Evoking Plato's ideal of the philosopher-king, Morgenthau outlines his picture of the ideal political actor. He says:

> [P]olitical actors, ignorant of what it is that they are lacking, seek salvation in theoretical science. Plato had a truer understanding of what the political actor needs. Ideally speaking, the philosophers are the professional purveyors of wisdom, while the kings need it but do not necessarily have it. Political success will be assured, insofar as it depends on the actor, when the philosophers and the kings, the men of wisdom and the men of action, become one.
>
> (Morgenthau 1972: 45)

According to Morgenthau, the ethic of responsibility is founded upon the 'gift of intuition' which cannot be taught but only refined through experience, study and example. In this way, the political actor, if in possession of such a gift, can be the embodiment of a reconciled existential condition that re-introduces the transcendental meaning that has been lost in theoretical science. Clearly, Morgenthau believes that his approach to theorising international politics reinstates this lost meaning by focusing on the 'objective laws of human nature'. These 'objective laws' include, on the negative side, the imperfectability thesis and, on the positive side, 'consciousness of the divine' that makes knowledge, truth and morality possible. Morgenthau's picture of reason, in so far as it is both (1) a criticism of deductive reason and (2) intuitionist, relies on the grammatical separation of the transcendent and actual. For Morgenthau, the 'actual' in the sphere of ethics is characterised by the conflict and irreconcilability of antinomies which, I argued above, is a re-statement of the imperfectability thesis. In the case of the 'transcendent' as consciousness of the divine, it becomes wisdom as 'a gift of intuition' which underpins how one chooses between the ethic of conviction and the ethic of responsibility. Morgenthau chooses the latter because ultimately, his grammar determines that he must since the ethic of responsibility is the only choice that embodies his imperfectability thesis. Although the ethic of responsibility concentrates on consequences and uses deductive reason to do so, it is intuition that determines *which* interests should be pursued for political success and thereby leaves space for transcendent value.

As we have seen, the ethic of responsibility is Morgenthau's answer to the epistemological aspects of the double whammy of international ethics. What are the foundations of knowledge and truth for him? It's perfectly clear that their foundations lie in with the divine and because of this ethics is universal. How can we access moral truth? Or, if you like, what kind of spade do we need to dig such knowledge and truth up? For Morgenthau, our spade is intuition, the experience of the creative middle, or more simply, the revelation of the depths of our perplexity of soul. However, while Morgenthau has offered us his antinomic universalist solution to the epistemological aspects of international ethics, he has yet to show us whether the ontological features of his picture of international political reality can accommodate the possibility of ethical universality. We turn to Morgenthau's alchemical transmutation of the national interest into a universal form of moral dignity next.

Alchemy: the transmutation of the national interest into universal ethic

Given the mountains we have climbed with Morgenthau so far, it may seem hard to see how the personal experience of 'the shock of wonderment', and the transcendent value that it reveals, can be brought into international political practice. His picture of reason tells us that it is, actually, possible *via* the gift of intuition and that, if we are lucky, state leaders will be mobilising this intuition in their decision-making following an ethic of responsibility. That covers the who and how of international ethics, if you like. But, *where* in international political practice can this take place, if anywhere? For Morgenthau's answer to that, we need to explore the contours of his picture of ethico-political space. It is an 'ethico-political' picture because it's the political space wherein the possibility of a universal ethic is postulated to take place and where it can be best accommodated. It's the place where universality happens in the world, or so Morgenthau's grammar would have us believe.

As we shall see, for Morgenthau, the place for the realisation of a universal international ethic is the nation-state. More specifically, an international ethic that has reintroduced transcendent value, follows an ethic of responsibility and is properly universal will follow the dictates of the national interest and, indeed, see the pursuit of the national interest as one that has 'moral dignity'. Grammatically speaking, it will require some alchemy on Morgenthau's part. Much as the alchemists sought to transmute lead into gold, Morgenthau seeks to turn that which ontologically belongs to the realm of the actual into a space that can accommodate the divine. This alchemical move in the language game is Morgenthau's conjunctive solution to the ontological aspect of the double whammy. Here the whammy is how to reconcile the transcendent and the actual in international political reality (the actual). To somehow bring together the radical ontological difference that Morgenthau's grammar emphasises is going to require something special. By the end of this section and chapter, a grammatical reading of the journey that Morgenthau's grammar has embarked us on will reveal that his conjunctive solution ends in failure. Alas, lead cannot be turned into gold and, for Morgenthau, that means that his grammar will lead us exactly where he doesn't want us to be: a bloody, violent place of the sort that his divine universalism is supposed to lead us away from. The horrible, dangerous grammatical conclusion is that Morgenthau has no reliable means by which he can ensure that there is any difference, at all, between divine universality and the 'morally indefensible' kind that offers a 'light-hearted equation between a particular nationalism and the counsels of Providence' (Morgenthau 1964: 11). This dreadful view from the top of the ontological mountain is not the one Morgenthau wants us to have but yet we didn't go there alone; it's *his* grammar that took us there. It is the effect of separating the transcendent and the actual and believing that each word refers to a different deep 'thing' (ontology/reality) – it may not be possible to put them together. The impossibility of a conjunctive solution, which is only a solution that is needed *because* the grammar of Morgenthau's language game tells us so, is nothing short of disastrous. We find ourselves staring into the face of totalitarianism once more.

How does this happen? Morgenthau advocates the national interest as the fulfilment of both political morality and political success. He understood the national interest to contain two elements: one that is logically necessary and one that is 'variable and determined by circumstance' (Morgenthau 1952: 972). The necessary element is that 'all nations must necessarily refer to their survival as their minimum requirements', this includes maintaining the nation's territory, its culture and its political institutions (ibid.: 972).

The necessary element implies that the statesman's ultimate ethical responsibility lies in assuring the survival of the nation. The national interest seems to share a number of similarities with his earlier discussion of individual interests and selfishness. Self-preservation is a moral duty. This mirrors the paradox in *Scientific Man* that it is necessary for an individual to be selfish in order to be ethical. Just as selfishness has a rationality by virtue of its attainability of ends (survival), so too does the national interest. National survival as a policy is the only way to achieve a 'modicum of order' and a 'minimum of moral values' (Morgenthau 1951: 38). The minimum of moral values being the shared ethic of national interest/selfishness that is common to all nation-states.

Other variable elements also determine the content of the national interest. Primarily, '[a]ll the cross currents of personalities, public opinion, sectional interests, partisan politics, and political and moral folkways', contribute to its definition (Morgenthau 1952: 973). Vitally among all these values that make up the national interest, 'a rational order must be established' (ibid.: 976). It seems that this rational order is established by consideration of what is most vital to the nation-state's survival and proceeds hierarchically from there. A hierarchy of values is internal to the national interest and this hierarchy in turn, determines which resources, because of their limitedness, will be allocated to each.

Given that a national interest is common to all nation-states, Morgenthau believes that it can act as an ethically restraining force. This is because Morgenthau places importance on the identification of common elements as the foundations upon which not only knowledge and truth can be grounded, but also political action and ethicality. The connection between the national interest and commonality in this context provide the foundations upon which Morgenthau can universalise political moral judgment and action. Consequently,

> [I]f we look at all nations, . . . as political entities pursuing their respective interest defined in terms of power, we are able to do justice to all of them . . . We are able to judge other nations as we judge our own and, having judged them in this fashion, we are then capable of pursuing policies that respect the interests of other nations, while protecting and promoting our own. Moderation in policy cannot fail to reflect the moderation of moral judgment.
>
> (Morgenthau 1964: 11)

The national interest, unlike an abstractly formulated moral principle, can therefore act as a moral principle in the sphere of international ethics. In a critical move that allows him to give ethical status to the national interest as a guide for action, he makes a vital distinction. 'Realism maintains that universal moral principles cannot be applied to the actions of states in their abstract universal formulation, but that they must be filtered through the concrete circumstances of time and place' (ibid.: 10). Morgenthau's attempt at showing how this can be achieved, discussed below, amounts to the claim that the nation-state is the ultimate source of morality (in the realm of the actual).

According to Morgenthau, the belief that one can apply universal moral standards in their purity to politics is utopian and erroneous because it is impossible. Consequently, he says, 'The appeal to moral principles in the international sphere has no concrete meaning' (Morgenthau 1951: 35). The nation-state, however, *can* give concrete meaning to the universal principles through circumstances of time and place and in this sense can be understood as the source of morality. In other words, the nation-state can give meaning to universal moral standards by making them actual rather than leaving them in the transcendent realm of the unattainable. He expresses it thus, 'Universal moral principles, such as justice or equality, are capable of guiding political action only to the extent that they have been given concrete content and have been related to political situations by society' (ibid.: 34).

The 'concretisation', as I will call it, of universal moral principles seems to be achieved through the existence of a moral consensus that exists within a nation-state, 'society', but this consensus is lacking in the international sphere. In this way, he sees a 'profound and neglected truth' in Hobbes' dictum that the state creates morality and that it does not exist outside it (ibid.: 34). We might say that society serves as the cauldron within which Morgenthau mixes his potion to turn lead into gold. It's society that seems to make 'this worldly' transcendent moral principles, embody them in the national interest and therefore, make them accessible as a guide for international political action. In this way, the national interest embodies an ethic that concerns itself with the attainable thus setting it apart from utopianism. Furthermore, because its ends are attainable, one can pursue a policy that will be successful. He says, 'A foreign policy guided by moral abstractions, without consideration of the national interest is bound to fail; for it accepts a standard of action alien to the nature of the action itself' (ibid.: 34). The standard of action that is not alien to moral action in international politics is the consensual one within national societies. So, if the state is the source of concrete morality, then a policy that defends its interests is necessarily moral. One then arrives at Morgenthau's assertion that the national interest has 'moral dignity'. Thus, the imperfectability thesis that was used to define the character of international ethics as one of necessarily doing evil is transformed in the *vita activa*, by a process of concretisation, into an attainability thesis. Ethical action can only be attained by the concretisation of moral absolutes and this takes place within national communities. As such, ethical standards of action become tied, through the process of concretisation, to territory – specifically sovereign states – and by necessity, the national interest. According to Morgenthau, this is the only way in which morality can play a role in international politics and indeed this delineates the limits of ethics in his thought. For him, political ethical responsibility extends only as far as state boundaries since it is within these that the source of morality can be made concrete and therefore relevant. The process of concretisation makes specific (particular) a universal moral code.

The alchemical idea of 'concretisation', much like the notion of 'participation' in Plato's theory of forms, is therefore an attempt to overcome the ontological difference between universals and particulars (Plato 1961). Universals are eternal and the same regardless of time or place whereas particulars are contingent and relative to time and place; universals must exist *a priori* and particulars *a posteriori*. For there to be the possibility of both knowledge and ethicality in this schema (i.e. the avoidance of 'moral abstractions'), it is grammatically necessary to make a connection between particular *instances* of a universal (particulars) and the universal itself. This is a requirement and a problem that Morgenthau has inherited *via* his appropriation of both Aristotle and Plato. However, this reading has shown that, unlike Plato and Aristotle, Morgenthau's solution locates concretisation within the *nation-state*. The national interest is an instantiation of a universal ethic leading to a magical transformation of the nation-state into an entity that has alchemical powers of transmuting the transcendent into the actual.

There are two problems with Morgenthau's alchemy which the reading offered here brings to the fore. First, even taking Morgenthau on his own terms leads us to a terrifying conclusion. If the nation-state actualises transcendent universal moral values through the consensus of 'society', then Morgenthau has committed his own cardinal 'sin' by identifying 'the moral aspirations of a particular nation with the moral laws that govern the universe' (Morgenthau 1964: 11). That any nation, in the name of itself, can proclaim that its values are instantiations of the moral laws of the universe constitutes an extreme moral and political danger. It is precisely such proclamations that justified Nazism and which Morgenthau tried to prevent reoccurring. But herein lies the tragedy of his political realism that is produced because of his grammar. Morgenthau is committed to the view that there must be universal foundations of morality. We have seen that these have a transcendent source – the divine – but require being made 'this-worldly' to have any relevance. In the case of international politics, the only candidate Morgenthau can put forward to do this is the nation-state, so that the national interest can act as a universal (i.e. a foundation for international political morality that is shared by all states). As soon as the nation-state takes on this alchemical role, totalitarianism rears its murderous head. This is simply because the grammar of totalitarianism constitutes the same role for the nation-state whereby the ideology of the ruling political party is heralded as having universal authority. The only difference between this and Morgenthau (sadly) is that Morgenthau believes in the ideal of the philosopher-king who can exercise political wisdom through his [*sic*] intuition and save us from fatal excesses in the name of universality. But this is scant comfort indeed given that all manner of political murderers intuit that they are enacting God's will or some such equivalent source of universal morality.

The second problem with Morgenthau's mysticism is just as ethically disconcerting and again concerns its grammatical impossibility.[20] Morgenthau simply cannot escape the separation that forms the bedrock upon which his whole language game rests. Grammatically Morgenthau cannot make the transcendent 'this worldly' and as such the transcendent remains in a realm irredeemably severed from politics and therefore, irrelevant. Although we have seen that Morgenthau's solution to this problem is to appeal to concretisation with its attendant risk of totalitarianism, I want now to highlight the failure of this solution.

The transcendent and actual are separated by the differences in their ontology. On the one hand, the transcendent is divine, timeless, universal, philosophic, and perfect. On the other, the actual is particular, contingent, sensual, flawed and limited. These elements constitute the fabric of reality for Morgenthau. We saw this difference come to the fore in Morgenthau's picture of reason. Morgenthau's solution to the difficulty of political theorising was that international political theory should mirror the separateness of these two elements *via* a 'creative middle'. The apotheosis of true thought is an acceptance 'of this inner contradiction between vitality and reflection' (Morgenthau 1972: 57). This acceptance means that thought should represent the difference between the natures of the transcendent and actual.

In his picture of the subject, the ontological difference between transcendence and actuality is, again, grammatically productive. It produces a representation of humanity that is limited and sinful and is made conscious of this through the 'shock of wonderment'. But vitally, this awareness comes from man's link with the divine which provides him with both universal moral standards and moral capabilities so that he can realise himself to be limited in the face of perfection.

And a third time, in his picture of ethico-political space, the ontological separation is highlighted further by the need to justify and limit power as a reflection of the limited and imperfect nature of human action in politics. As such, Morgenthau's answer to the problem of ethics in international politics was to attempt to conjoin universal moral standards and politics through a notion of concretisation within the nation state that made the national interest an appropriate, universal standard of international morality. In all these pictures, the repetition of the difference between the transcendent and actual is the shadow of possibility cast by language on ethics in Morgenthau's language game. However, it is in Morgenthau's picture of ethico-political space where he most dramatically attempts to overcome the very separation that determined all the relevant aspects to his understanding of the problem of ethics in international politics.

How are we to judge the morality of action in international politics? Morgenthau is quite adamant that it is universal moral standards that must be used to evaluate the morality of all human action, including politics, or else we would be forced into a philosophy of moral relativism which he explicitly wanted to avoid. Furthermore, universal criteria provided the grounds by which he could judge political action as necessarily involving doing evil. Yet, when we look at his picture of reason, he tells us that the standard for evaluating political action should be political success. Indeed, this is why the ethic of responsibility is supposed to be an appropriate ethic for international morality because it safeguards the national interest and concomitantly it, and its citizens' survival. Grammatically, the two standards (political success and universal morality) for evaluating political action are mutually exclusive. But, he says, 'Both individual and state must judge political action by *universal moral principles*' (Morgenthau 1962: 109; italics added). However, he has 'always maintained that these universal moral principles cannot be applied to the actions of states in their abstract universal formulation but that they must be filtered through the concrete standards of time and place' (ibid.: 108). Herein lies the problem; a standard cannot, at one and the same time, be the same regardless of time and place and contingent. Either a standard is eternal and therefore, timeless or it is subject to change and time-bound; it cannot exist both in and outside time. I suggest that this means that Morgenthau's claim for the 'moral dignity' of the national interest fails. If we evaluate the national interest by universal standards (eternal), it is immoral and if we evaluate it by political success (contingent) it tells us nothing of morality only of the maintenance, extension or demonstration of power. Either way, the national interest is not moral within the rules of Morgenthau's own language game. What this reading suggests is that Morgenthau's notion of ethics which has its source in the transcendent cannot, even with his notion of concretisation and the exercise of the 'gift of intuition', be made 'this worldly'. Thus, when we read Morgenthau's political realism grammatically, ethics is hopelessly stranded in the realm of the divine because of the fundamentally incompatible natures of the transcendent and actual thus leaving the decisions of statesmen that Morgenthau was so desperately trying to counsel quite literally in the lap of the gods. Or worse, when put it into an alchemist's hands, a universalised, totalitarian nationalism is purported to be a divine universality embodied in the national interest. Only an intuition that comes from the theological experience of the 'shock of wonderment' can save us from making a fatal mistake. Such is the view from having climbed Morgenthau's mountains the way he asked us to. We have dug deep into our souls and beneath the surface of reality only to be re-confronted with the horror we sought to avoid for all time.

4 Ideal universality

Beitz, reason and the ghost of Houdini

In this chapter, I sketch the landscape of a form of universality in IR that is as equally familiar and seductive to scholars of the discipline as that of Realism, a liberal form of cosmopolitanism. I would venture to suggest that, for some of us, this landscape is so familiar that we almost no longer notice it. It's a bit like driving a route home that one has done hundreds of times so that one no longer notices the scenery along the way and the change of seasons. This kind of experience Wittgenstein pithily expressed as 'The aspects of things which are most important for us are hidden because of their simplicity and familiarity' (Wittgenstein 1958a: §129).

The chapter seeks to make conspicuous the overly familiar terrain of a liberal form of pictures of the subject and reason.[1] In a nutshell, and put too crudely no doubt, what is so familiar is a particular notion of reason and its wide acceptance as an important part of what it is to be a human being who can come to understand things and act accordingly. Everyday phrases and injunctions such as 'Be reasonable', 'Construct a reasoned argument', 'Tell me your reasons for x', 'Use your head', 'You're being over-emotional', 'Don't be so childish', 'Your belief in y is irrational', and so on, all betray this familiarity. The elevation of reason as a foundation for knowledge, as opposed to knowledge founded on divine revelation, say, is a marker of the Enlightenment as the intellectual precursor of liberalism. This is interesting for us even within the miniscule context of this chapter and the one that precedes it on Morgenthau. Whereas Morgenthau's grammar betrays a view of the world which has its provenance in Ancient Greek metaphysics and a strong form of intuitionism that has the divine as its object, in this chapter we have an approach that can be read historically as a reaction to it. One of the promises of the Enlightenment was to offer a 'corrective' to transcendent and metaphysical foundations of knowledge, namely, rationality as the grounds for critiquing existing political and social institutions, including Church and state. As such, the Enlightenment served as the basis for a form of secularist liberalism. It is the replacement of faith in the divine with a secular 'faith' in reason that most acutely distinguishes the universalities of Morgenthau and Charles Beitz as intellectual inheritors of these long traditions in western philosophy.[2]

As I hope this chapter demonstrates, Beitz puts his faith in reason as both a characteristic of the subject and as the means by which a diagnosis and resolution of the 'moral dilemma of international politics' can be obtained. Put bluntly, whereas for Morgenthau, it was our intuitions of God that could save us from the 'evil' that we do to each other, for Beitz, it is our reason that can remedy the injustices of the world. I seek to show that this faith in reason is also a form of metaphysical seduction: the seduction that reason is the spade with which we can dig beneath the surface of language to discover the solution to the moral dilemma of international politics and emerge satiated.

In International Relations, the cosmopolitanism of Charles Beitz is justifiably celebrated as having made a major contribution to 'international political theory', marking the conjunction of the fields of political theory and IR (Brown 2005; Caney 2005; Lu 2005; Miller 2005; Rengger 2005). The characterisation of his contribution in this way recalls a time when IR, as an academic discipline, was struggling to find ways of accommodating thinking about questions of justice and questions of ethics more generally. With the publication of *Political Theory and International Relations* in 1979, Beitz offered IR a way of theorising ethics that brought the insights of liberal, contractarian political theory to bear upon global politics (Beitz 1979, 1999). For our purposes, the importance of his work cannot be underestimated, not only because of his iconic status but because he offers particular pictures of reason and the subject as holding the key to locating a universalist solution to the moral dilemma of ethics 'and' international relations.

Like any author's work, Beitz's endeavour occurs within a particular context. Just as Morgenthau spoke of ethics as his reply to the ghosts of the Holocaust calling to him, Beitz was also being summoned, albeit by a different ethical concern. In Beitz's case, it was the injustice of the distribution of wealth in the world economic system. The question he sought to answer is whether what he calls an 'obligation of justice' exists so that it 'requires wealthy countries to increase substantially their contribution to less-developed countries, and to radically restructure the world economic system' (Beitz 1999: 127). This is a courageously ambitious task as it asks for nothing less than a set of moral justifications for the 1974 United Nations General Assembly's 'Declaration on the Establishment of a New International Economic Order' (Beitz 1999: 127).

Accordingly, Beitz's theoretical endeavour is to locate, articulate and justify principles or standards of international distributive justice that can regulate how 'goods'[3] are to be distributed in global politics so that the unjust distribution of wealth can be addressed. Essentially, the way Beitz believes this can be achieved is to 'argue that a suitable principle [of international distributive justice] can be justified by analogy with the justification given by John Rawls in *A Theory of Justice* for an intrastate distributive principle' (Beitz 1979: 8). Such a justification and argument are the role of theory, understood by him and the political theorist John Rawls, as procedural.

Therefore, Beitz has set himself the task of constructing a theory of international ethics which is an international application of Rawls' massively influential work *A Theory of Justice* (Rawls 1971).[4] It is vital to understand that Beitz's theoretical endeavour seeks to amend Rawls in important ways in order to provide the possibility of an international ethics. In *A Theory of Justice*, Rawls was satisfied to limit his concept of justice to domestic politics: 'the basic structure of society conceived for the time being as a closed system isolated from other societies' (ibid.: 8). Such a delimiter is clearly unhelpful for Beitz's international endeavour and so he seeks to show that Rawls is mistaken and that, when suitably corrected, Rawls' theory of justice can provide grounds for a specific form of universalism; what Beitz calls a 'cosmopolitan international morality' (Beitz 1979: vii).

In light of the above, this chapter reads Beitz's *Political Theory*, alongside his post-publication amendments to it, and sets out to demonstrate a number of things (Beitz 1979, 1980a, 1980b, 1983, 1991, 1999, 2005). It seeks to outline his grammar as a dichotomy that divides the ideal from the nonideal. This, of course, is essential to a grammatical reading as it provides the means by which to then show how grammar produces and regulates what Beitz takes to be the ethical problem that needs resolution and where he wants to lead us to go 'digging' for the answer. In effect, we shall see that the problem and, therefore, its resolution require a doubly universal conjunctive solution, a solution that can bridge both the ideal and nonideal, on the one hand, and the domestic and international, on the other.[5] As the grammatical reading unfolds, the chapter shows how Beitz's grammar then produces the very thing that Beitz's answer is constructed to avoid. The grammatical reading suggests that Beitz's endeavour ends in conjunctive failure so that (1) he cannot bridge the gap between the ideal and nonideal theoretically which, effectively, makes the 'nonideal' world disappear in an accidental Houdini moment; and (2) that he cannot bridge the gap between the domestic and international as he understands them and thereby, reinforces the Realist picture of international politics which he seeks to overturn. The chapter then concludes with a few grammatical remarks about how his grammar has produced a ladder that, once climbed, can be thrown away as it cannot offer the satisfaction of a metaphysical seduction being fulfilled (Wittgenstein 1922).

A grammar of the ideal and the nonideal

In Chapter 3, we saw that Morgenthau mobilised a grammar that included the transcendentally divine as the source of a universal moral code. The transcendental was grammatically juxtaposed with the actual, an ontological reality that Morgenthau conceived of as imperfect and a realm where the 'sinfulness' of man [*sic*] presented the primary obstacle to the possibility of ethics in global politics. Morgenthau's grammar is theologically driven and seeks, ultimately, to find an answer to how God can be *in* the world so that He has not abandoned us with no possibility of ethics among ourselves, and most importantly, among nation-states. This onto-theological grammar effectively stresses the conditions of impossibility (the 'tragic') as the 'moral dilemma' that requires a divine, universalist resolution embodied in the national interest.

In contrast to Morgenthau, with Beitz's grammar, we will see an emphasis on the conditions of possibility and a secular, liberal, diagnosis and resolution to the 'moral dilemma' of global politics. For Beitz, there is a difference in kind between ideal theory and the nonideal world which grammatically generates his construction of the moral dilemma of international politics as 'a problem of bringing about international distributive justice [which] is similar to that of escaping a Hobbesian state of nature' (Beitz 1979: 159). Despite wanting to escape a Realist state of nature (unlike Morgenthau), Beitz nevertheless shares some similarities with him in so far as Beitz also portrays the world/reality as imperfect, albeit for different reasons. For Beitz, the world is 'nonideal' which begs the question as to which standard of 'ideal' he is using in order to make this assessment of international political 'reality'. The separation of what Beitz calls the nonideal world and ideal theory is his grammar (Beitz 1979, 1999).[6] What, then, is the nature of ideal theory for both Rawls and Beitz?

First, for Rawls, an ideal theory of the principles of justice is concerned with investigating what 'a perfectly just society would be like' (Rawls 1971: 8). It is a strict compliance theory as opposed to a partial compliance theory in so far as 'everyone is presumed to act justly and to do his part in upholding just institutions' (ibid.: 8). Focusing on the nature and aims of a perfectly just society is taken to be 'the fundamental part of the theory of justice' (ibid.: 8). In other words, ideal theory, as an exploration into perfect conditions of justice in society, is necessary for providing the criteria not only of justice but also of *in*justice. In this sense, ideal theory is a necessary prerequisite of a partial compliance theory 'that studies the principles that govern how we are to deal with injustice' (ibid.: 8).

Applying Rawls' formulation of ideal theory, Beitz constructs his theory of cosmopolitan international morality in an almost identical manner. However, rather than limiting the focus of ideal theory to a perfectly just society, Beitz extends it to 'a description of the nature and aims of a just *world order*' (Beitz 1979: 170; italics added). As with Rawls, the aim is to provide 'a set of criteria for the formulation and criticism of strategies of political action in the nonideal world' (ibid.: 170). Again, the assumption is that it is only when criteria of justice have been established that judgements of the justice or injustice of political actions and institutions can take place. The important point to note, therefore, is that ideal theory serves as a ruler against which to measure justice in the nonideal world and indeed, it measures the world as falling short of the standards required.

Second, beyond just providing a 'ruler' for ideal justice, ideal theory is supposed to be applicable to 'real' world problems. How can this be so?

Both Rawls and Beitz postulate that ideal theory mediates our 'natural duty' to promote and support just institutions (Feinberg 1973: 268). The most fundamental natural duty for both Rawls and Beitz is the natural duty of justice (Beitz 1979: 170; Feinberg 1973, 1975; Rawls 1971: §19). The natural duty of justice for Rawls and, presumably, Beitz is 'derived from reason' (Rawls 1971: 115). Such a duty requires of individuals two things. First, support and compliance with already existing just institutions and, second, '[it] constrains us to further just arrangements not yet established' (Rawls, cited in Beitz 1979: 170). The mediating aspect of ideal theory for Beitz is then formulated thus: 'Ideal justice, in other words, comes into non-ideal politics by way of the natural duty to secure just institutions where none presently exist' (Beitz 1979: 171).

To sum up so far, ideal justice serves not only as the yardstick of justice against which to measure the justice or injustice of already existing institutions, but as 'a goal toward which efforts at political change should aim' (ibid.: 170). Thus, ideal theory provides the criteria and procedure by which justice should be applied and the natural duty of justice the individual impetus to act in accordance with its principles of justice. If, as Beitz wants, ideal theory is to be a *goal* (in the nonideal world), then he must assume that the natural duty of justice provides the motivation and grounds for fulfilling it. The two are inextricably linked. This is because if there were no natural duty of justice, then there would be no compelling reasons for individuals to apply principles of justice to the nonideal world. This would render the principles of justice derived from ideal theory irrelevant to morally substantive issues, such as the distribution of wealth globally. Needless to say, none of the above could be postulated were it not for Beitz's grammatical separation of the ideal (theory) and the nonideal (world) in the first place. Most importantly of all, as the rest of the chapter reveals, Beitz believes that reason is the key that can unlock the treasure chest containing this grammatically produced yardstick, goal and natural duty of justice.

The universal reasoning subject

Having only provided the briefest of sketches of Beitz's dichotomous grammar, we now turn to looking at how fundamental reason is in providing both the justification for a specific form of universality and its necessity in making persons the subjects of an international ethics (as opposed to states or communities). All being well, this should serve to further illustrate his grammar as described above and demonstrate that Beitz's grammatically produced picture of the subject is foundational for his universalism.

If one thinks about it, even briefly, it's pretty obvious that Beitz cannot valorise reason in the way he does unless he thinks human beings have the capacity to actually do it. It is important to state clearly here that, in Beitz's language game, the subject is the ultimate foundation for universality and in turn, reason (as the most important capacity of the subject) makes the ideal possible. For him, without reason there can be no ideal and therefore no universal ethic that the ideal can generate. From the point of view of a grammatical reading, however, this isn't quite the way to tell the story about his universalism. Rather, as Wittgenstein puts it, 'Grammar is the shadow of possibility cast by language on phenomena' (Wittgenstein 1974: §329). In other words, if we read how Beitz understands the phenomenon that is the subject we will be revealing the shadows of possibility that his grammar casts. In the case of Beitz's *picture* of the subject, in contrast to his version which is the subject *per se*, the shadows most importantly fall on the very possibility of there being such a thing as ideal theory and therefore, universal principles of international distributive justice. So, what is his picture of the subject?

Essentially, Beitz pictures the subject as universal. This subject is an ethical one that has moral worth and can make moral decisions using reason in ways that allow it to transcend any particular interests or socio-historical contexts that it may have. There's little point in developing any system of ethics that has the person (as opposed to nation-states or communities, for example) as its central focus unless you think persons have some moral worth in and of themselves. Beitz agrees saying 'it is the rights and interests of persons that are of fundamental importance from the moral point of view, and it is to these considerations that the justification of principles for international relations should appeal' (Beitz 1979: 55).[7] What makes this liberal picturing of persons so valuable in this language game is that they are moral ends in themselves whose interests should be treated equally. Persons have 'moral powers' that give them 'a capacity for an effective sense of justice and a capacity to form, revise, and pursue a conception of the good' (Beitz 1983: 595).[8]

Underlying this description of the moral powers of the subject is a Kantian notion of the person which regards, 'persons as both free and equal, as capable of acting both reasonably and rationally, and therefore as capable of taking part in social cooperation among persons so conceived' (Rawls 1980: 518). Equality, one of the sacred tenets of liberalism, is vital here. In an international context, Beitz attempts to ensure that his principles of international distributive justice can and will treat all persons equally. The way he does so is to devise a system called 'the global original position' wherein 'all persons should be respected as sources of ends' (Beitz 1983: 81). Each person in the global original position has an equal right to determine the first principles of international justice by which the world's distribution of goods should be ordered. The details of the global original position are discussed in the section below, but so far Beitz has painted a picture where persons are rational, free and equal and endowed with the related moral powers of an effective sense of justice and capacity for forming, revising and pursuing a conception of the good. This gives them moral worth as ends in themselves.

The moral powers of persons thus pictured are very powerful indeed as they are not only universal but facilitate, as human capacities, the very possibility of universality in the so-called nonideal world. Looking in more detail now, we shall see how Beitz attempts to capture this in his representation of the moral point of view which all persons have, including you and I. As the remainder of the chapter goes on to show, it's a hugely seductive picture that some find difficult to resist, perhaps because it appears to be so rational. If one agrees with Beitz's picturing of the subject, then the rest, his cosmopolitan international morality, seems to logically follow and make considerable sense, let alone be morally appealing. After all, how many of us would want to disagree with his basic ethical concern that the global distribution of wealth is uneven and that the effects of this are not 'OK' and need attending to? That he seems to provide an answer, just because it is an answer, is seductively comforting to an experience of despair with the injustices of the world. Beitz hears our heart-felt cry 'what can be done?' and actually replies to it.

There is a strong universalism attached to his representation of the moral point of view, a perspective that all subjects can and must take when seeking to discover what appropriate principles of justice are in international politics. In the vocabulary of this book, the moral point of view is Beitz offering us a spade that allows us to go digging for answers to our ethical problems. Of course, putting it this way postulates that Beitz thinks digging is a requirement and that we cannot proceed ordinarily by staying on the surface of language. In other words, Beitz wants to show us that we must have the capacity to theorise rationally (dig) to get what we want.

Beitz outlines the moral point of view in this way:

> Speaking very roughly, the moral point of view requires us to regard the world from the perspective of one person among many rather than from that of a particular self with particular interests, and to choose courses of action, policies, rules, and institutions on grounds that would be acceptable to any agent who was impartial among the competing interests involved.
>
> (Beitz 1979: 58)

What we have here is a picturing of reflective rationality as an essential part of what it is to be human. It is reason that makes it possible for us to be impartial, to transcend our own particular historical, social and material interests and therefore, to make rational choices.[9] We don't take *our* point of view but an abstracted, essentially human one. As human, 'one person among many', beyond the self and its own partialities (particularism), it is universal. This is a stark contrast to the previous chapter where self-interestedness and partiality simply cannot be escaped. For Beitz, the essential human capacity to take a moral point of view frees us from being forever bound to our selfish and material (power) interests.[10] The moral point of view does not eliminate the possibility of different, even conflicting, courses of actions, policies, rules, institutions and so on being available as choices but it does purport to eliminate the possibility of choosing the 'wrong' one(s). A 'wrong' choice is an irrational one. As he puts it, 'we typically assess the rationality of a decision by asking how effectively it advances the individual's system of ends or goals' (Beitz 1989: 70). A decision is irrational if it doesn't advance ends effectively, whether because of the decision itself or because a different decision wasn't followed. Vitally though, such choices must also involve other human beings, persons, so that they will agree to them. Beitz's reply to our cries of despair requires that agreement is possible as long as we are all being rational and impartial. Rationality, exercised by taking the moral point of view, postulates and necessitates that it is possible that we can and will *all* agree as to what would be the rational choice to make. In short, were we given the opportunity, we'd all figure it out the same way, using the same criteria and from the same perspective. Bluntly, that's about as literal an understanding of the universality of a reasoning subject as one can find.

In this section, we've spent a long time looking at Beitz's picture of the subject. It was to show that the subject serves as the ultimate foundation for universality in Beitz's liberal, contractarian language game.[11] Put differently, the subject is the wellspring of universality for Beitz. Without it, and in particular its capacities for reason as outlined above, Beitz would be unable to even begin to produce an international cosmopolitan morality as a form of universality and as an answer. So, what is grammatical about the sketch of his picture of the subject I've offered here?

Beitz's picture is his attempt to capture, represent, the essential features of a phenomenon (the subject). It is grammatical in so far as it reveals the shadows of possibility for humanity that his grammar produces. Beitz is wonderfully helpful in that his picture explicitly outlines several of the conditions of possibility for his form of universality as aspects of human capacities for reasoning. Reading this grammatically we can say that it his grammar that produces this particular picture of the subject. Beitz's grammar is one that separates ideal theory and the nonideal world. This grammar necessarily produces a puzzle about the very possibility of ideal theory. Where is it located? What does it consist of? And most importantly, how can it be possible? Beitz's picture of the subject is his answer to these grammatically generated questions. Were his grammar different, say, like Morgenthau's or Walzer's, he wouldn't need *this* picture with its in-built universality of a reasoning subject. That this is so can only really be more fully sketched by looking at what ideal theory is and how it brings all these essential features o f being human into play in the 'discovery' of principles of international distributive justice.[12] Now that Beitz's grammar has established that we need a spade and what it looks like, it now needs to provide a way of digging and its purpose. How to dig and what Beitz tells us we will find as the answer to whether there is an obligation of justice to redistribute wealth globally if we do, are what we turn to next.

Imagination: ideal theory and principles of international distributive justice

Knowing that we want to find principles of international distributive justice (but not yet what they might be) and suitably equipped with our spade of reasoning as moral subjects, how does Beitz suggest that we proceed? Earlier, we established that the moral point of view claims that were we to be given the opportunity to find principles of justice, we would all work it out rationally the same way, using the same criteria and sharing the same perspective. As a result we would, most crucially of all, agree on the same thing. Applying Rawls' *A Theory of Justice* to international politics, Beitz outlines in considerable detail what such an opportunity looks like and its content. It is the global original position, it is hypothetical (imagined) and unsurprisingly, it is a product of our reasoning capacities. It is, in sum, ideal theory as Beitz's picture of reason.

It is important to be clear that this hypothetical scenario is one that provides the opportunity for subjects, as members/representatives of humanity, to rationally choose principles of justice not 'negotiate' them as distinct individuals called George W. Bush, for instance.[13] What we are to imagine is establishing a hypothetical social contract.[14] 'We are to imagine rational persons meeting in an "original position" to choose among alternative principles of justice' (Beitz 1979: 130). As a product of our reasoning capacities, the global original position must be an imagined exercise of impartiality. It must, because it occurs from within a moral point of view, eliminate all morally irrelevant particularities – the things that would make us partial – as well as things which are 'morally arbitrary' (ibid.: 138). This is exactly what Beitz's 'veil of ignorance' is designed to do so that we get to the bare bones of 'features we normally associate with moral choice' (ibid.: 130).

So, what would we be ignorant of if we allowed ourselves to be seduced by Beitz's picture of reason and imagined this? According to Beitz, the things to strip away as both morally irrelevant and/or arbitrary (undeserved)[15] are: parties' identities and interests (e.g. British), their generation and place in international politics (e.g. strong or weak), their history (e.g. knowledge of wars fought), 'their level of development and culture' (e.g. economically 'advanced' and liberal) (ibid.: 130). So far, this list is congruent with Rawls' own list of what the veil of ignorance excludes. However, vitally, Beitz extends Rawls' theory to the international realm by adding the distribution of natural resources as morally arbitrary in order to facilitate his desire for an international, as opposed to domestic, form of justice.

Including natural resources under the shroud of the veil of ignorance is a key move in Beitz's theoretical endeavours. Let us recall that Beitz is in the business of wanting to globally redistribute goods and wealth justly. He discounts knowledge of parties knowing what natural resources they and others have (i.e. how they are distributed) in the international original position because that's the very issue at stake for him, not how, as fact, they are distributed but how the benefits that accrue from having them *should* be distributed justly from the moral point of view. Natural resources are morally arbitrary for Beitz because 'The fact that someone happens to be located advantageously with respect to natural resources does not provide a reason why he or she should be entitled to exclude others from the benefits that might be derived from them' (Beitz 1999: 138). It's just the luck of the draw as to how natural resources happen to be distributed and not a matter of justice or injustice.[16] To further assist in making any principles agreed in the original position global, Beitz extends the veil of ignorance 'to all matters of national citizenship' (ibid.: 151). Parties don't know what nationality they are and nor do they know that it is for that society that they are imaginatively choosing principles of justice.

Having effectively screened out all the elements that make the nonideal world nonideal, what would the parties rationally choose as principles of international distributive justice? Thankfully for Beitz, because of his pictures of the subject and reason, there isn't going to be any disagreement amongst the parties because they will be choosing rationally from the moral point of view:

> Assuming that Rawls's arguments for the two principles are successful, there is no reason to think that the content of the principles would change as a result of enlarging the scope of the original position so that the principles would apply to the world as a whole. In particular, if the difference principle ('social and economic inequalities are to be arranged so that they are . . . to the greatest benefit of the least advantaged') would be chosen in the domestic original position, it would be chosen in the global original position as well.
>
> (Ibid.: 151)[17]

Bingo! Our spade and efforts at digging have found the treasure chest. At last, we have an international principle of distributive justice that will redistribute (rearrange) inequalities so that the least advantaged benefit the most. Beitz has provided us with a fulsome account of the conditions of possibility for a universal principle of justice. It is universal in several senses. First, it is universal in the sense that all persons (humanity) are represented in the global original position as equals and treated fairly from the moral point of view. Second, as such, his universal principle of justice applies to all members of humanity as moral ends in themselves. And, third, it is universal in the sense that it applies beyond the domestic to the global.

Before we move on to reading what, precisely, in the nonideal world is to be redistributed, how and why it can be, it is worth taking a grammatical pause. Grammatically speaking, what has happened with Beitz's way of digging (the global original position) is this: he is simply repeating his grammar of ideal and nonideal back to us in this picture of reason. In effect, the global original position, with its facilitating veil of ignorance, has screened out and off all the elements that make the world nonideal. This has happened because, grammatically, it must. Ideal theory must be juxtaposed with the nonideal world: that's what it's for. Ideal theory produces the yardstick of justice by which to measure the nonideality of the world, if we recall. It is designed to search for and describe a perfectly just world order (ibid.: 170). Therefore, any elements that make the nonideal world nonideal must be removed so that it can be perfect and produce a perfect yardstick. It is also why the whole exercise needs to be hypothetical in the sense of an exercise of the imagination going on in our heads deploying all our human capacities for reasoning. The global original position cannot, by definition, happen in the nonideal world as a practice of international politics. Why? Obviously, it cannot because then it would be *in* the nonideal world, riddled with its partialities and interests, and not in the realm of ideal theory. Beitz's grammar requires that the ideal and nonideal are fundamentally separate. Therefore, they must both: (1) be clearly differentiated and differentiable from each other; and (2) never be conflated. Both Beitz's pictures of the subject and reason are filled with his brushstrokes that demonstrate how they are different from each other, albeit with an emphasis on the ideal thus far. These brushstrokes are the shadows of possibility of both these pictures coming together. In effect, Beitz has painted us a landscape of the ideal: what makes it possible (his picture of the universal reasoning subject) and what is made possible by this (his picture of reason as ideal theory and a principle of international distributive justice).

Having noted that we can see the shadows of the separation of the ideal from the nonideal in these two pictures, we can begin to see more clearly why Beitz's larger landscape is going to require a conjunctive solution as an answer to the moral dilemma of international politics, one that can form a universal bridge between ideal theory and the nonideal world. It is, quite simply, because his grammar has produced a conjunctive problematic and therefore, demands it. That this is the case is well demonstrated by Beitz's, not grammatically misplaced, vexations about the occasions when, and how, ideal theory can actually be applied to the nonideal world (ibid.: 169–76). We will turn to examining this grammatically produced Gordian knot in the following sections.

Making universality possible in the nonideal world

Thus far, we've seen how Beitz has built up a rather seductive and beautiful pair of pictures that stress the possible. And, when it comes to picturing the nonideal world, he is no less optimistic. According to him, and his defence of cosmopolitan liberalism, what is now required is an empirical foundation and argument about what the international environment is like for the possibility of his recommended universalism (Beitz 1979: 215). The picture of ethico-political space that he sketches serves two important functions in his language game. The first is a foundational possibility for ideal theory and the second, the possibility of conjoining the domestic and international in order to make ideal theory applicable to the nonideal world.

In Beitz's 1979 version of his cosmopolitanism, he believes he needs his picture of ethico-political space, as interdependent, as a vital condition for the very possibility of his universalism. He says: 'To assert the possibility of international political theory [ideal theory] we must first reexamine the traditional image of international relations as a state of nature and purge it of its sceptical elements' (ibid.: vii). In other words, he asserts that for there to be the possibility of ideal theory and the universalism that it generates, we must rely on features of the nonideal world. That suggests that for him ideal theory is, ultimately, grounded in conditions of possibility that exist in the nonideal. Bluntly, the ideal depends on the nonideal. In one sense, at least as Beitz presents it, it is a straightforward move. Grammatically speaking, it is much less so. The ideal and nonideal, as both he and I have spent so much time demonstrating, are not only differentiated and differentiable but ontologically cannot and must not be conflated. Their conditions of possibility are supposed to be fundamentally different which is why they are grammatical. If we recall, choices of principles of justice in Beitz's language game are supposed be the product of reflective rationality exercised within the global original position (i.e. grammatical products of his pictures of the subject and reason) and not grounded in considerations of characteristics of the nonideal world, such as interdependence (his picture of ethico-political space). This grammatical problem with his picture of ethico-political space will come back to haunt him in the form of Houdini's ghost in his later work. In the interim, let us just remark that Beitz has told us we need his picture of ethico-political space as the foundation for the very possibility of ideal theory and the international distributive justice that it generates.

The second function of his sketch of ethico-political space, as interdependent, is to bridge the separation of the international and the domestic so that he can escape the Hobbesian state of nature and, therefore, liberate the possibility of principles of justice being relevant to international politics. We can say that, for Beitz, this function is theoretically driven as a product of his pictures of the subject and reason. As this section seeks to demonstrate, this move is also grammatically problematic for Beitz. In the end, he cannot escape the state of nature and this is, in the final analysis, because his grammatical separation of ideal and nonideal won't let him.

The nonideal world is Beitz's picture of ethico-political space. Writing in 1979, Beitz described the features of the nonideal world of international political practice as interdependent. Nearly thirty years later, we would use the vocabulary of globalisation. Nevertheless, in his opinion, the changes over this period of time have only served to strengthen his empirical portrait of international affairs (Beitz 1999: 198–214). Bearing this in mind, why does Beitz feel the need to come digging in the nonideal world looking for a conjunctive solution to the distinction between international and domestic? It is because of Realism and Rawls.

With regards to Realism, Beitz reads this as a position of moral scepticism and so needs to refute it in order to make space for morality and a cosmopolitan one at that.[18] Essentially, he takes this to require showing that international distributive justice can be brought about in a way which is 'similar to that of escaping a Hobbesian state of nature' (Beitz 1979: 159). So, from his point of view, all he needs to do is show that the international realm is sufficiently similar to the domestic so that it is not a 'state of nature'. The way he goes about this is by turning to Rawls to refute the Realists.

Rawls' theory of justice is constructed to identify principles of justice within a (domestic) society which he defines as a 'cooperative venture for mutual advantage . . . typically marked by a conflict as well as by an identity of interests' (Rawls 1971: 4). Primarily, principles of justice need to be identified in order to make choices about the division of advantages produced by the benefits of collaboration and 'for underwriting an agreement on the proper distributive shares' (ibid.: 4). That society is a cooperative scheme is fundamental to Rawls' theory. This is because without cooperation and the burdens and benefits it produces, there would be 'no occasion for justice, since there would be no joint product with respect to which conflicting claims might be pressed, nor would there be any common institutions . . . to which principles could apply' (Beitz 1979: 131). Beitz believes that Rawls' notion of a cooperative scheme is too restrictive and seeks to amend it by excluding the requirement that parties in a social scheme need *actually* cooperate in social activities, or actually be advantaged by that scheme as opposed to its absence. For Beitz, then, global principles of justice apply to a cooperative scheme understood as 'institutions and practices (whether or not they are genuinely cooperative) in which social activity produces relative or absolute benefits or burdens that would not exist if the social activity did not take place' (ibid.: 131).

By amending Rawls in this way, Beitz creates the possibility of arguing that international politics satisfy the criteria of a cooperative scheme (*contra* Rawls) and consequently that general principles of political theory can apply to international theory, i.e. the possibility of a cosmopolitan normative international political theory. This move delivers to Beitz what he has been digging for in the nonideal world as a condition of possibility. He presents an aspect of his picture of the nonideal world of international politics as grounds for this. He says: 'If social cooperation is the foundation of distributive justice, then one might think that international economic interdependence lends support to a principle of global distributive justice similar to that which applies within domestic society' (ibid.: 144). According to Beitz, there are a number of factors that point to a sufficient amount of interdependence between states so that they constitute a cooperative scheme; these include transnational transactions such as trade, aid, communications, and foreign investment. The most important features of sufficient interdependence are the growth of international investment and trade. For Beitz, what is most important in terms of the applicability of principles of justice is that 'interdependence in trade and investment produces substantial aggregate economic benefits in the form of a higher global rate of economic growth as well as greater productive efficiency' (ibid.: 145). However, it is not only the benefits of interdependence that are significant in this regard but the burdens, or costs, also. Such burdens include a widening of the income gap between rich and poor states, political inequality (some states being more vulnerable to the effects of a breakdown in a trade relationship than others, e.g. oil-poor states) and 'domestic consequences' of which there are two types. First, the ability of domestic governments to control their own economies and, second, 'the domestic distributive and structural effects of participation in the world economy' (ibid.: 147). The important thing to note, is that for Beitz's argument to be successful, the details of *what* precisely the burdens and costs of interdependence are not directly relevant. All he needs to show, at minimum, is that the level of interdependence is *sufficient* so that it produces burdens and benefits whose existence fulfils one of his criteria of the applicability of principles of justice, namely, that 'social activity produces relative or absolute benefits or burdens that would not exist if the social activity did not take place' (ibid.: 131).

So, Beitz's digging around in the nonideal world has unearthed a cooperative scheme as an empirical state of affairs that provides the grounds for the possibility of ideal theory (i.e. international political theory). Again, he has stressed and sketched the conditions of possibility for his proposed universality. This time, he has done so with his picture of ethico-political space, with his sketch of what is possible in the world. All seems well.[19] We now have a 'real' (in the world) occasion and foundation for the need and possibility for principles of international distributive justice.

However, from the point of view of a grammatical reading, there are a number of problems with him adding this grammatically generated picture of ethico-political space to his pictures of reason and the subject. One problem is related to the ghost of Houdini discussed in the next section. The other has to do with whether Beitz has, grammatically, succeeded in escaping a Hobbesian state of nature and therefore has succeeded in offering interdependence as a conjunctive solution to the separation of domestic and international politics. Let us be clear, Beitz formulates the problem of the possibility of a cosmopolitan international morality as one which requires this 'escape' *as* a conjunction of international and domestic.

The horrible irony is that Beitz's formulation of the problem, the moral dilemma, grammatically reinforces that which he is trying to escape. 'A *picture* held us captive. And we could not get outside it, for it lay in our language and language seemed to repeat it to us inexorably' (Wittgenstein 1958a: §115). Beitz's picture of the nonideal world as he sketches it (above) with all its emphasis on conditions of possibility is not the whole of his picture of ethico-political space. His formulation of the problem of universality as being one of escape from a state of nature suggests that other aspects of his picture are holding him captive and that this is a product of the grammar of his language game.

As well as remarking how similar the domestic and international are, Beitz also takes them to be dissimilar in important ways that emphasise the international as a state of nature and anarchic. As well as there being no international sense of community so that it can act as 'motivational basis for compliance with laws and official decisions' (Beitz 1979: 155), he also says:

> There is no doubt that the main difference between international rela-
> tions and domestic society is the absence in the former case of effective
> decision-making and decision-enforcing institutions. There is no world
> constitution analogous to those explicit or implicit codes that define the
> structure of authority within states. And there is no world police force
> capable of enforcing compliance with world community policies.
>
> (Ibid.: 154)

Here, Beitz wants to maintain that anarchy is a distinguishing feature of the international contrasted with the domestic (ibid.). Though he admits that the international realm includes possibilities for reciprocal compliance (as per interdependence), the crucial point to note is that nonetheless 'one *cannot* plausibly argue that these are similar in extent to those characteristics of most domestic societies' (ibid.: 155; italics added). In order to illustrate why Beitz's picture of ethico-political space does indeed maintain the assumption of anarchy in a Realist form, and therefore fails to overturn it, we need to look more closely at the grammatical constitution of his understanding of the moral dilemma of international politics.

Beitz grammatically constitutes the practical problem of cosmopolitan universalism as one of realisation. In his language game, ideal theory cannot be undermined by empirical features of the nonideal world, most notably a lack of effective global institutions and a lack of a sense of world community. After all, the veil of ignorance screens out features like this in the imagined conditions under which persons would rationally choose and agree upon ideal principles of international justice. Beitz argues that ideal theory is immune to objections that point to the implausibility of a just global order in the present. As ideals the principles of international distributive justice that would be chosen in the global original position can only be invalidated, if and only if, the 'social facts that are supposed to render the ideal unattainable in the present' are immutable i.e. immune to the possibility of change (ibid.: 156). Nevertheless what a lack of effective global institutions and sense of community do tell us is that 'their relevance is not to the ideal of global distributive justice, but rather to the problem of realizing the ideal' (ibid.: 158). Grammatically, then, the strict separation of ideal theory from the nonideal world inevitably produces the problem of international ethics as one of realisation. The principles themselves, and any possible objections to them, are cordoned off as strictly ideal – untouched and untouchable by non-immutable, nonideal features of the world. All that's left for Beitz to worry about is putting such ideals into practice by realising them, i.e. finding a conjunctive solution to bridging the ideal and nonideal.

The problem, grammatically speaking, is that this sets up the problem of realisation in a way which endorses, rather than escapes, Realist assumptions about anarchy as a state of nature and the nonideal world and therefore, fails to bridge the gap between the domestic and international by overturning them quite as Beitz had hoped. Beitz's picture of ethico-political space can be summarised thus: ethico-political space is divided into international and domestic, states are not self-sufficient because conditions of interdependence exist, the international realm is characterised by ineffective global institutions that produce a problem of compliance and, the international realm lacks sufficient motivation for reciprocal compliance because there is no world community with an attendant 'sense of community' that could be a motivation. According to Beitz, the ethical problem of the realisation of international principles of justice is a question of how to secure compliance in the international (nonideal world) when there are limited assurances because of anarchy.

There is a grammatical conjunctive failure here for Beitz. A Realist could accept all these characteristics as a pithy statement of the characteristics of international politics as a state of nature (anarchic) and ironically, agree with his diagnosis of the moral dilemma of international politics. For Beitz, what distinguishes him from the Realists and their moral scepticism is his claim about the existence of interdependence. However, the existence of interdependence wouldn't be denied, even by a neo-realist like Waltz (Waltz 1979). Realists and neo-Realists alike may well disagree with Beitz as to the significance of interdependence, particularly over which possibilities it offers for cooperation, but wouldn't quarrel that it is a contemporaneous feature of international politics (Baldwin 1993). And, equally, we know from the preceding chapter that, in the case of Morgenthau, even were there to be little or no interdependence (as was the case when he was writing), this does not amount to a position of moral scepticism anyhow. Although there is a difference between the moral standards that might be applied to the international between, say, Morgenthau and Beitz, the underlying picture of ethico-political space which both their language games produce shows us that the realm to which they can or cannot be applied is significantly similar. In the case of Morgenthau, we saw that his notion of moral standards was grounded in the Ten Commandments. In the case, of Beitz, they are international principles of justice rationally and impartially chosen in a global original position. However, in both cases the issue is one of how to 'realise' (Beitz) or 'concretise' (Morgenthau) such standards in the realm of the international as opposed to the domestic. Either way, both thinkers tell us that the ontology of ethics and international politics are separate and if there is to be ethics *in* the world, then somehow this difference needs to be bridged. Unfortunately, Beitz's first move to pave the way for this by conjoining the domestic and international has grammatically failed. It has also, as this section has hinted, not sat well with his other two pictures of the subject and reason. In the next section, we will look to see how he tries to remedy some of this and how, alas, this takes him further away from the answer he so sincerely seeks.

The ghost of Houdini and the great disappearing act

In 1918, Harry Houdini famously performed a sensational magic act called 'The Vanishing Elephant' in which he made a 10,000-lb elephant disappear in the Hippodrome Theatre in New York City (Cannell 1973). How, exactly, Houdini did this has been lost but it was a major triumph to make something so large, apparently, disappear. In this section, I seek to demonstrate that Beitz pulls off a greater vanishing feat than Houdini's by making something even larger disappear: the nonideal world. It is, as the reading will show, a grammatical 'whoops!' that this happens because it certainly isn't what Beitz intends. Beitz's great disappearing act doesn't use smoke and mirrors to make the nonideal world vanish but rather the shadows of his grammatical separation of the ideal and nonideal along with the pictures it produces.

If we recall, Beitz's pictures of the universal reasoning subject and of reason provided a wonderfully rich and detailed landscape of the conditions of possibility for the ideal (ideal theory). So, not only did these pictures tell us what the ideal is, but also, importantly, what the ideal cannot be: the conditions of its impossibility. The ideal, these pictures made quite clear, do not, must not, and cannot have any morally arbitrary or irrelevant features of the nonideal world within them. After all, that's what an ideal theory is. It's ideal and therefore, untainted by grubby, factionalist, self-interested features of international politics. Were such features to be there, the ideal would be impossible. No wonder, then, that Beitz changed his mind about the role of his picture of ethico-political space as a condition of possibility for the ideal.

What did this change of heart entail for him and why, grammatically, does it end up making the nonideal world vanish? Essentially, his change of heart reasserts his grammar, reiterates and enhances his picture of the subject and maintains the separation of the ideal from the nonideal. However, this comes at a high price: the disappearance of the nonideal world as morally relevant.

According to Beitz, the interdependence argument misses the point precisely because

> the argument for construing the original position globally need not depend on any claim about the existence or intensity of international social cooperation [interdependence]. Of course, the construction would be pointless if there were no feasible scheme of institutions to

which principles of justice could apply. But a *feasibility* condition is different from an *existence* condition, which I had earlier thought was necessary.

(Beitz 1983: 595)

The point about ideal theory being relevant to international politics, for the revised Beitz, is that the principles of justice that it generates can serve as an ideal or goal. As such, what is vital is not that such principles can be applied now (an 'existence condition'), but that they might be in the future (a 'feasibility condition'). Thus, interdependence as an existence condition is irrelevant to the construction of a global original position that generates the principles that need only be feasible at some time in the future.

This move is deeply problematic, grammatically speaking, for two reasons, both of which occur because he has, effectively, removed the non-ideal world from consideration of principles of justice. First, because he has removed the foundation for the very possibility of ideal theory (Beitz 1979: vii) and, second, because he ends up reinforcing the separation of ideal theory with the nonideal world leading to a second conjunctive failure. The two problems are fundamentally related as they are both grammatically produced with the second problem being, one could say, the ladder we are left with which, perhaps, can be thrown away.

With regards to the first, Beitz's rationale for postulating the need for a digging expedition in the nonideal world was because without it there would be 'no occasion for justice . . . to which principles [of justice] could apply' (Beitz 1979: 131). What Beitz told us in 1979 is effectively saying that unless we incorporate a picture of ethico-political space, there is no point in having ideal theory. Why bother with principles of international distributive justice if the world doesn't need them and/or they can't be applied? After all, Beitz's whole ethical endeavour was because of the injustice, particularly the unjust distribution of wealth, he sees in the world. When he argued that the nonideal world was an interdependent cooperative scheme it was to establish that there are, now, benefits and burdens that need to be redistributed justly. Now, he is saying that it doesn't matter and 'need not depend on *any* claim about the existence or intensity of international social cooperation' and therefore, any benefits or burdens that may be produced (Beitz 1983: 595; italics added). What has happened here? To say that his interdependence argument 'misses the point' is a politics of forgetting why he thought the need for an international theory of justice was so urgent in existent conditions. Grammatically speaking, he seems to have suspended the application of his principles of international distributive justice to non-immutable 'things', such as international institutions like the World Trade Organisation, for some theoretically possible time in the future. After all, he's made it explicit that because they may not be applied now, it doesn't mean that the principles are wrong. This is a significant shift. Now, he seems more concerned with defending the integrity of his theory (the ideal) than addressing the injustice that exists in the world at present. In that sense, he has retreated even further away from the world and into ideal theory for comfort against the cry of 'what can be done about the injustices in the world?' The nonideal world is disappearing from his language game as he has got distracted by defending himself against criticisms that his theory is, well, 'too ideal' in its conceptualisation of interdependence (Brown 1992, 2002; Caney 2005; Miller 1999, 2000; Rawls 1999; Rengger 2005).

That this may be so can be further illustrated by what he offers instead of interdependence in more detail. I call this his 'accidental Houdini moment'. If, then, membership of the global original position no longer relies on the interdependence argument, what replaces it? Here Beitz invokes his picture of the subject claiming,

> If the original position is to represent individuals as equal moral persons for the purpose of choosing principles of institutional or background justice, then the criterion of membership is possession of the two essential powers of moral personality – a capacity for an effective sense of justice and a capacity to form, revise, and pursue a conception of the good.
>
> (Beitz 1983: 595)

Where has he taken us digging? Not back to the nonideal world and the injustices there that provide an occasion for justice. He has taken us back to his picture of the subject. Of course, subjects live in the world and in that sense he hasn't left the world entirely. But, which features of the picture of the subject is he emphasising? He is emphasising the universal reasoning capacities that the subject has so that they can take the 'moral point of view'. Grammatically, this is far more consistent with his language game as we saw that the subject, ultimately, is the foundation for the possibility of his universality (and not his picture of ethico-political space). It is the reasoning capacities of the subject that make the choice of international principles of justice possible because it is they that allow the possibility of the exercise of imagination so that they can be under a veil of ignorance in the global original position. And what is screened out by the veil of ignorance? The features of the nonideal world that make it nonideal (the world) are screened out. Beitz's argument is a not just a reassertion of his grammatical separation of the ideal and nonideal that makes clearer what the conditions of possibility are for the ideal. It is a prioritisation of the ideal over the nonideal. The nonideal 'misses the point' about the possibility of his universalism whereas the ideal does not. Abracadabra! The nonideal world is no longer relevant to his language game as a justification, occasion or foundation for principles of justice. Only the global original position (his picture of reason) and its members (his picture of the subject) are. In this sense, Beitz has pulled off a Houdini moment so that the nonideal world has disappeared because of the shadows of possibility that his grammatical separation of ideal and nonideal has cast. This is a conjunctive failure because the ideal and nonideal have not been bridged. If anything, there has been a retreat into the comforting seduction of the ideal where universal subjects and principles of justice are possible without all the messiness and intractability of the nonideal world.

No doubt there are other ways of reading Beitz than the way offered here, and indeed there are.[20] Nevertheless, as a grammatical reading, this chapter sought to 'assemble reminders for a particular purpose' (Wittgenstein 1958a: §127). It has not engaged with the truth or falsity of any of Beitz's pictures as this is not part of its aim.[21] What it has done, I hope, is to show how and why Beitz has produced his universalism in the way he has. I want to emphasise that his ethical endeavour is motivated by a sincere concern. Personally speaking, in part, I chose to discuss Beitz because I too am seduced by his cry of exasperation at the injustice of the distribution of wealth in the world and a sense of 'But, what can be done?' and I remember how I felt when I first read *Political Theory*. I felt hopeful that he could provide an answer because I desperately desired one for such an important issue. I don't think I'm entirely alone in this regard as his work is, justifiably in my opinion, much celebrated. However, what a grammatical reading has shown is that the answer he gives cannot satisfy this seduction.

In the end, the grammatical reading showed that a retreat into the ideal just takes us too far away from the motives of why we are concerned in the first place. Beitz's pictures of the universal reasoning subject and of reason are beautifully seductive. It's not even that one might wish that they were true that is my point here. Rather, it is the way in which these grammatically produced pictures show us how Beitz has put his faith in the endeavour of theorising as a way of 'escaping a Hobbesian state of nature' (Beitz 1979: 159). In other words, he offers us an ideal, theoretical articulation of universality as the solution to his Hobbesian moral dilemma of international politics. Beitz's language game, which is the theoretical practice of being a universal reasoning subject, in the end cannot deliver the answer that he so desperately seeks. To say this is to make a mystical grammatical remark about Beitz's picture of the subject. Wittgenstein's mysticism, which a grammatical reading deploys, is simply a remark about the limits of theory and, in the case of Beitz, the limits of reason understood as a capacity of being human. Beitz's beautifully reasoned defence of his ideal principles of international distributive justice were rational, logical and consistent with his language game. We saw that was so when we looked at his Houdini moment as being consistent with the demands of his grammar that led him to take retreat and comfort in the ideal. As Beitz himself put it: 'we must apply an understanding of people's motivational capacities and limitations at the appropriate level of abstraction' (Beitz 2000: 683). But, alas, the grammatical reading also showed that he accidentally made the world disappear as morally relevant. So, what is one to conclude? I, at least, conclude that theorising such as this cannot provide the comfort that we seek because it digs.

No matter how well equipped we may be with our spade of reason, a grammar of ideal and nonideal doesn't deliver us safely to our grammatically required destination; a domestic/international conjunctive space where a Hobbesian state of nature has been escaped and where there is the opportunity to apply principles of distributive justice to the world. Even when the grammar of language games, such as Beitz's is deployed 'consistently', the language games unravel. I suspect that this has 'something' to do with grammars of universality themselves.[22] We've seen how Beitz's grammar of ideal and nonideal ended up unable to offer a conjunctive solution as a form of universality. Why such failures happen, as the two grammatical readings of Morgenthau and Beitz have so far shown us, is a story for Chapter 6. In the interim, I close this chapter with an apparent *non sequitur*. The grammatical reading here isn't really a critique of Beitz or of his universalism. It is an assembly of reminders of where we might feel seduced into digging for foundations of universality and what happens when we do. In Beitz's case, just as for Morgenthau, the place to dig was, in the final analysis, the picture of the subject.

critiques in academic circles and became a standard, if not the sta...
on courses on the morality of war alongside his more recent...
(Walzer 1977, 2004a).[2] Walzer's *Just and Unjust Wars* has b...
a 'modern classic' (Boyle 1997; Hendrickson 1997; Ko...
1997; Smith 1997; Walzer 1997a). Needless to say, it is...
desirable, to review all of Walzer's work and the m...
ture that it has generated. Instead, the point of...
grammatical reading of a very familiar, com...
salism. This is what Walzer offers us for the...
scapes of universality and ethics in Interna...
Accordingly, I seek only to assem...
showing that Walzer postulates two...
thin, and that this binary universal...
its foundations in, his picture...
produced' in order to highlig...
grammatical distinction b...
reading Walzer this way...
subject, as phenomen...
two shadows: a un...
members (the th...
going', but the...
of both uni...
to all' tha...
ling th...
dig...
ac...

is possible and both agree ...
mental characteristics of the subject.[1]

Of course, there are disagreements between Beitz, Morgenthau and Walzer too, but not over the question of choosing either the one or the many. Instead, there is a difference between the kind of universalism that Walzer wishes to defend and the reasons why. Beitz has postulated a form of ideal universalism, Morgenthau a divine universality, and Walzer, I will argue, a binary universalism. The irony is that, while Walzer is so often portrayed as a particularist (i.e. favouring the many and denying the possibility of the one), I think he may well be the most thoroughgoing universalist of the three theorists we have read grammatically simply because he attaches universality to each, rather than just one, of the two elements of his grammar.

Michael Walzer's work has been hugely influential and, justifiably, highly respected in IR. The 1977 publication of *Just and Unjust Wars*, in particular, has generated a far-reaching response in the form of review essays and

...ndard, text
...contributions
...en described as
...ntz 1997; Nardin
...not possible, or even
...assive secondary litera-
...this chapter is to offer a
...munitarian, form of univer-
...purposes of exploring the land-
...tional Relations.
...ble reminders for the purpose of
...kinds of universality, the thick and the
...ty is grammatically produced by, and has
...of the subject. I say it is 'grammatically
...t that his picturing of the subject relies on his
...etween members and strangers. In the end,
...allows us to see the shadows of possibility that the
...on, casts in terms of universality. Obviously it casts
...versality for strangers (the thin) and a universality for
...ick). That's why his universalism is binary and 'thorough-
...re's more to it than this. It is the subject that is the foundation
...ersalities and is the referent object: the element that is 'common
...t makes universality possible. Thus, even when passionately extol-
...e moral desirability of pluralism and difference, Walzer cannot resist
...ing below the differences to find something that is the 'same' in order to
...t as a foundation for his universality. It is the move of someone metaphysically seduced. Why? Because it is an enactment of the view that if we can
locate the relevant 'thing' to which morality refers in global politics, then we
can *justly* sort out the rest. If you like, it is a result of Walzer bumping his
head against the limits of language. When Walzer, and those like him, say
'we are all different', they think the word 'different' must refer to a 'thing'
that we all share: something that is the same. Once we dig a bit deeper we
can find out what that 'thing' is, so Walzer's grammar tells us, and we will
have located a foundation for universality and the possibility of building a
universal ethic for global politics. Rather neatly, for Walzer that 'thing' is
'we'. And, as we shall see, the 'we' is an essential and primary part of his
grammar.

So what is Walzer trying to grapple with in terms of global politics? What
is the moral dilemma of global politics for him?[3] In what he considers to be
the practice of international politics, it is a question of when a state's rights
to sovereignty and territorial integrity should be preserved and the circumstances under which it should not. In other words, when and under which
circumstances states should intervene in the business of other states. Even
his, perhaps, best-known work to IR, on just and unjust wars, can be
subsumed under this concern (Walzer 1977, 2004a). War, whether just or

unjust, is necessarily a form of state intervention and a violation of principles of sovereignty and territorial integrity. In this chapter I seek to tell the story of Walzer's moral engagements with global politics grammatically, hence, we could express his moral dilemma a little differently. Walzer's dilemma is when, and under which circumstances, to evoke and follow either a thin or a thick universality. It is a grammatically produced dilemma, in the details of Walzer's configuration of his language game, because were it not for his grammar, he wouldn't be posing the question in quite the same way, nor look for an answer quite where he does, and nor, of course, would he outline the resolution the same way. As a grammatical reading seeks to show, all this adds up to Walzer's grammar repeating itself back to him because he is held captive by a picture – most of all, his picture of the subject.

It goes without saying that Walzer doesn't consider himself as captivated by a picture, any more than Morgenthau or Beitz do. He believes that he is accurately representing the world of global politics: 'This is how things actually are' (Walzer 2004b: 126). The moral dilemma of global politics is as 'real' for Walzer as it is for Morgenthau and Beitz. Each believes that they are accurately representing the obstacles that global politics creates. Of most relevance to us here, global politics is a landscape of moral dilemmas (mountains) that requires some attempt at conquest (if universality and, therefore, ethics are to be possible. If we climb these mountains, so the grammatical logic of these language games tells us, perhaps we will see the world as it 'really is' from the summit. What all of this looks like for Walzer is the content of the sections below.

In the meantime, it is perhaps worth remarking that I'm not suggesting for one moment that Walzer is deliberately metaphysically seduced and intentionally wants to 'dig' to find something essential, common to all. It's a grammatical accident that he does so, like the other accidents that occurred in the preceding two chapters.[4] Walzer himself says, and with passion, 'I have never been drawn to essentialist definitions of anything' (Walzer 2004b: 118). I completely believe he is sincere but that's the funny thing about being captivated by certain pictures and the grammar that produces them; they can take us to places where we don't want or intend to go. That's what a grammatical reading is, among other things, designed to show; that what theorists want may not be where they think it is, nor dependent upon what they think it must depend on (Diamond 1995: 24). In the end, I seek to show that Walzer is unable to hold onto a thin universalism. If you like, he can't resist fattening up the thin. Nor can he resist thinning the thick. This is deeply problematic within his bifurcated universalist international ethic because, without the thin, he cannot set limits on the universality of the thick. More accurately, in the absence of a delimiter to thick universality there can be no exceptions to the presumption that all states are legitimate and that there should never be any intervention. Without an ability to postulate the thin, *as* thin, thick universality will always trump it and, for

Walzer, that would be wholly morally unacceptable. It would amount to a universalised moral argument that, in the face of the Holocaust or other actions that 'shock the conscience of humankind', would permit us to shrug our shoulders, turn the other way and say 'that's got nothing to do with us' (Walzer 1995: 55). Equally, thinning the thick takes him into forms of essentialism he wants to avoid as a 'wrong intuition'. Just as was the case in the previous two chapters, Walzer doesn't want to end up here, but, alas, his captivation with his grammar pulls him along.[5]

A grammar of belonging and estrangement: members and strangers

The importance of the notion of community is pervasive in Michael Walzer's thought and would be difficult to overestimate (Walzer 1977, 1980, 1981, 1983, 1984, 1985, 1987a, 1987b, 1987c, 1989a, 1989b, 1989–90, 1990, 1994a, 1994b, 1994c, 1995, 1996, 1997b, 2004a, 2004b). As Rosenblum puts it, the 'radical *political* claim' of Walzer's work, is that 'membership in a *community* of shared moral meanings is "conceivably" the greatest good' (Rosenblum 1984: 582). One of the keys to Walzer's version of international ethics is the relationship he postulates between community, politics and ethics in the concept of political community as moral community. His seminal *Spheres of Justice*, published in 1983, offers us an extended elaboration of what he believes are the relationships between political community, statehood and justice (Walzer 1983). If, as seems undeniable, community is vital to Walzer's political and moral commitments, then we can look to see how grammar plays a role in his account of the constitution of community. This chapter seeks to show that the distinction he makes between members and strangers is the grammar of his language game and therefore, produces his delineation of ethics into two forms of universality: one for members and one for strangers. Only by distinguishing between members and strangers is Walzer able to locate community, for it is '*we who are already members* [who] do the choosing' (ibid.: 32; italics added). And, of course, grammatically, it works the other way too. Walzer needs the distinction in order to locate who the strangers are. For him, it's straightforward. If someone is not a member of our political community then they are a stranger. Walzer uses the term stranger synonymously with foreigner, member of a different community and/or state and to refer to immigrants (ibid.). Members, for him, are simply those who share a common life. Equally, that means that as members of our own communities we are strangers to people who belong to communities other than our own. Thus, not only does Walzer's grammatical distinction between members and strangers map onto a division of 'them' and 'us' but it maps onto 'us' *tout court* also. 'We', whoever 'we' are, are also bifurcated. We are, equally and at the same time, members when we look inwards towards ourselves and strangers to others who look upon us from the outside.

While we could quarrel with this, perhaps, over-simplistic view of how, if at all, to distinguish between members and strangers, it's really not the point of reading grammatically. Rather, what this chapter is trying to understand, is how and why Walzer's universality looks the way it does and the pictures he is seduced by in order to make it look so.[6] As we shall later see, Walzer's communitarian language game provides an inescapable tension for him that is most acutely revealed as a tension between the elements of his binary universality that, after all, is binary precisely because of his grammatical separation of members and strangers.

Just before we move on to looking at the details of his grammar, it is important to remember that grammar is arbitrary. That means it has no ultimate justifications beyond or outside itself. There comes a point where there are no more reasons one can give for why a grammar may be the case. We can say that grammar is an ungrounded grounding. As Wittgenstein puts it: 'If I have exhausted the justifications I have reached bedrock, and my spade is turned. Then I am inclined to say: "This is simply what I do"' (Wittgenstein 1958a: §217). There comes a point where there's no more digging to be done in other words. Walzer's grammatical distinction between members and strangers is just that: the point at which his spade is turned. Mind you, we will see that his bedrock grammar nevertheless provides him with the foundations to do plenty of digging elsewhere, and even a bit of gardening, before we turn his spade for him.

Nancy Rosenblum argues that the significance of Walzer's member/stranger distinction is the result of Walzer's view that 'belonging to a community of character is an independent good' (Rosenblum 1984: 586). Although it cannot be denied that community is a good for Walzer, what can be questioned is the role the member/stranger distinction plays in his language game. Rosenblum is suggesting, so to speak, that community comes first and membership second. Indeed, this is why she says, like many others, that Walzer's position is begging for a theory of community. I disagree somewhat and the reasons for this are grammatical. Given that grammar produces, the question is a different one: 'How does Walzer's understanding of community even get off the ground?' In other words, what is accepted or taken as a 'given' *before* Walzer can go on to show the political and moral importance of community (what commentators refer to as his communitarianism)? What is accepted, the given, in Walzer's communitarianism are the concepts of members and relationally, strangers.

The grammatical significance of the member/stranger distinction is pervasive in Walzer's work and can be traced as far back as his 1970 collection of essays in *Obligations* (Walzer 1970). In this work, membership is fundamental, for according to him, 'Obligation . . . begins with membership' (ibid.: 7). And, indeed, the essays go on to discuss and elucidate what he believes to be the political and moral obligations that are attendant on membership, whether it be of a corporation, an oppressed group or a state, for example. In all cases the starting point, what I call his grammatical bedrock, is the distinction between members and strangers that allows

Walzer to locate political communities by their membership. As will become clearer throughout the rest of the chapter, it is not only obligations that begin with membership, but the whole of Walzer's bifurcated universalist thinking about 'moral argument at home and abroad' (Walzer 1994c).

That Walzer's distinction between members and strangers is antecedent to his notion of community and therefore, is his grammar, is probably best illustrated by his account of the constitution of political community in *Spheres of Justice*. Vitally, Walzer's claim is that the distribution of membership constitutes political community.[7] For him communities are constituted by decisions concerning 'their present and future populations' (Walzer 1983: 31). As such, choices need to be made as to who should be admitted as members and who is to be excluded, which criteria to adopt, and so on. As Walzer is well aware, this begs the question as to who it is that makes the choices concerning the constitution of political community. Walzer is clear about his answer and it is worth quoting in full:

> We who are already members do the choosing, in accordance with our own understanding of what membership means in our community and of what sort of a community we want to have. Membership as a social good is constituted by our understanding; its value is fixed by our work and conversation; and then we are in charge (who else could be in charge?) of its distribution. But we don't distribute it amongst ourselves; it is already ours. We give it out to strangers. Hence the choice is also governed by our relationships with strangers – not only by our understanding of those relationships but also by the actual contacts, connections, alliances we have established and the effects we have had beyond our borders.
>
> (Walzer 1983: 32)

What this means is that 'we who are already members' constitute the community in two senses: first, in the sense that 'we' are that community, and second, 'we' constitute the community in the sense that it is 'us' who make the choices about the type of community we want. Rather than this begging the question of community, this begs the question as to who 'we' are. Posing the question this way reveals a grammatical circularity in Walzer's account.

First, to say, as he does, that 'we who are already members do the choosing' as to who shall count as members, is not of itself an account of membership. This is because it presupposes the very thing it is supposed to account for. In other words, Walzer's account of membership (by which he can then go on to provide an account of the constitution of political community) relies on a pre-existing membership. As he puts it, membership 'is already ours'. As such, it is presupposed that 'we' already know who 'we' are (i.e. members and not strangers).[8]

Second, Walzer tells us that the criteria of membership such as who should become members, under which circumstances, and so on, are grounded in the shared understandings of the community. Thus, the choices that are made regarding the constitution of political community express the values of a particular community. If, however, what is at stake is the question of how political community is produced in the first place, then an answer that rests upon community understandings is of no use. This is because for there to be the kinds of understandings that Walzer takes as significant, there must already be a pre-existent membership in order to constitute the community that have the shared understandings. In short, Walzer's answer begs the question because *shared* understandings presuppose the 'we' (i.e. members) who do the sharing.

Funnily enough, Walzer himself gestures towards his own unquestioned acceptance of the distinction between members and strangers when he says,

> It is certainly possible that a deeper criticism would lead one to deny the member/stranger distinction. But I shall try, nevertheless, to defend that distinction and then to describe the internal and the external principles that govern the distribution of membership.
>
> (Ibid.: 34)

As we shall see below, Walzer himself does not question the distinction and nor does he offer grounds for its maintenance as his defence of it. Rather, grammatically speaking, his defence lies in what the distinction produces: his pictures of the subject, reason and ethico-political space. In short, its application, which he believes shows us the political and moral benefits of maintaining it. Walzer shows us 'how to go on', and it is precisely the ability to do this that the unquestioned status of grammar provides. Walzer's spade may be turned, but he has it in his hands and defends his communitarianism by showing us where to go digging and most of all, why, morally speaking, we should. It is in this sense then, that the member/stranger distinction is a grammatical feature of Walzer's understanding of political community and the binary nature of the ethical universality that it produces.

Belonging, common humanity and the divided self

Who and what are 'we', according to Walzer? What is his picture of the subject that serves as the foundation for both forms of his universalism? Whatever we might be, Walzer's grammar ensures that we are never strangers unto ourselves (though we are to others) and that we can and do know who we are. In his communitarian language game, this operates in three, overlapping related, senses: first, we can know ourselves as members of particular political communities; second, we can know ourselves as members of common humanity; and third, we can just know ourselves, as individuals, by introspecting. And indeed, knowing of ourselves in these ways provides the possibility to recognise this in strangers and therefore, can provide foundations for a universalism that can be both local and global in scope. Rather neatly, as we will see after this section, picturing the subject this way allows Walzer to tackle the double whammy of international ethics head on with a doubly universalist resolution. That is to say, he provides two conjunctive solutions to the apparent difficulties posed by the purported difference between domestic and international politics: the first whammy. And he also provides two conjunctive solutions to the question of choosing between universality and particularism: the second whammy. The two solutions in each case have a 'thick' and a 'thin' version, both are universal and, as universal, both are conjunctive.

This all sounds a little vague at this point, so let's now look at his picture of the subject more closely. Basically, the subject is 'a wonderfully complex entity, which is matched to, which reflects and is reflected in, the complexity of the social world' (Walzer 1994c: 85). The element of complexity is introduced through the particularism and plurality of social meanings created by subjects living within a political community. Social meanings (whose understanding is shared) are the complex fabric of the social world in which humanity is reflected and reflects. Thus, a fundamental part of being human for Walzer is the ability to create meaning. As he says, 'We are (all of us) culture-producing creatures; we make and inhabit meaningful worlds' and in that sense, all human beings are equal to one another (ibid.: 27).

Because we are *all* meaning and culture-producing beings, Walzer reckons we can all have a 'decent respect for the opinions of mankind' [*sic*] and therefore, the possibility of some kind of universalisable justice (Walzer 1983: 320). As he states, 'Our common humanity will never make us members of a single universal tribe. The crucial commonality of the human race is particularism: we participate, all of us, in thick cultures that are our own' (Walzer 1994c: 83). The point Walzer is making is that we don't need to be members of the same tribe so that 'members of all different societies can acknowledge each other's different ways' (ibid.: 8). Instead, he is saying that membership itself, the experience of it as particular, means that all human beings *qua* humans have the ability to recognise particularity and difference in people other than themselves (strangers). What is universal about this aspect of his picture of the subject is the particularism of humanity. It provides a 'trans-cultural critical principle' (Mulhall and Swift 1992: 145). As we will later see, this will become increasingly important as moral decisions are made as to whether to intervene to 'save strangers' from events such as massacres and genocides (Wheeler 2000).

How did Walzer hit upon a universalisable trans-cultural principle so quickly, grammatically speaking? Walzer has dug beneath the surface of language and his spade has hit something. That something is the postulation of a characteristic of the subject as a referent object; something that is common to all instances of humanity upon which universality can be founded. In this case, it is difference that serves as what is common to all. Expressing it this way serves as a sharp reminder of how the word (its

meaning) and that to which it refers have been both postulated and separated by Walzer. The meaning of the word 'difference', the way Walzer uses
it, is to emphasise differences in the *content* of thick cultures. This is why he
is a pluralist and a communitarian. However, this aspect of his picture of the
subject is also claiming that what difference refers to is a common, shared,
experience of membership as simply thick, *regardless* of content. The simple
experience of thick*ness* as referent object, opposed to the word's meaning,
has no thick content itself. To emphasise the shared experience of difference is to view humanity a bit like a container that we, as culture-producing
creatures, will fill in whatever ways are particular to our shared ways of life
and understandings. In other words, the container of meaning, i.e. the
referent object (humanity), is itself thin. Walzer himself doesn't say this
explicitly but by reading grammatically we can see that it's what his
language game is *doing*. Without this implicit move, Walzer wouldn't have
the grounds for universalising (1) an international ethic that seeks to protect
the pluralism of ways of life in different political communities; (2) members
being able to recognise the moral value of pluralism for everyone including
strangers; and (3) also being able to recognise when a political community
belonging to strangers is failing 'to allow people equally to create the
cultural constructions by which they live' (Mulhall and Swift 1992: 145). To
postulate a referent object is a picturing move: a move that allows Walzer to
generate a trans-cultural, thin, principle from an aspect of humanity that is
deeply encultured and thick.

What Walzer's picture of the subject is consciously trying to resist is what
he calls a 'wrong intuition' whereby all individuals begin with a set of core
moral principles and values that are precedent to the meanings created by
their society (Walzer 1994c). This is precisely the sort of intuition that
Morgenthau and Beitz have. In contrast, Walzer wants to insist that particular, local shared understandings are decisive in moral reasoning. In fact,
they are so decisive that he wants to argue that his thin universalism has
thick (i.e. particularist) roots. However, Walzer seems unable to fully resist
this wrong intuition himself because of his grammar and desire to limit the
universality of particularism and what it morally allows. As we will see in
the next section, Walzer wants to be able to accommodate a moral obligation towards strangers and for that he needs to have another digging expedition below the surface of shared meanings and find more elements upon
which a trans-cultural critical principle might rest, but this time to find one
that doesn't wholly rely on membership.

Although it is the case that common humanity is particularist for Walzer,
this is not the only characteristic he attaches to it in his body of work. All
human beings, for Walzer, have a right to life and liberty by virtue of their
common humanity. As he puts it himself, 'Individual rights (to life and
liberty) . . . are somehow entailed by our sense of what it means to be a
human being' (Walzer 1977: 54). The significance of an individual's, as
opposed to a state's, rights to life and liberty cannot be understated in

Walzer's work. In *Just and Unjust Wars*, they form the basis of his just war theory providing a delimitation of justifications both for going to war (*jus ad bellum*) and actions in war (*jus in bello*). Indeed, he says that, 'the judgments we make (the lies we tell) are best accounted for if we regard life and liberty as something like absolute values' (ibid.: xvi). So unlike other rights which follow from shared understandings the rights to life and liberty 'follow from our common humanity' (Walzer 1983: xv). As such, they are transcultural, transhistorical and essential to what it means to be human: they are 'natural' rights that one has simply *qua* human.

If Walzer has failed to resist his own 'wrong intuitions' as I've described them, one should expect that these rights are not conferred upon an individual through their membership to any particular state or political community. We just have them because we are human, not because we are members of political communities who have shared understandings around them. And, sure enough, Walzer later tells us 'Individual rights [to life and liberty] may well derive, as I am inclined to think, from our ideas of personality and moral agency, *without reference* to political processes and social circumstances' (Walzer 1985: 234; italics added).

There's a grammatically generated tension that we can highlight in Walzer's understanding of the rights to life and liberty that won't and can't go away simply because it is grammatical. It's the same difficulty that occurred when we looked at how Walzer universalised particularism and difference as a feature of common humanity. There I suggested that Walzer made the thick thin by separating the word 'difference' from its referent object. Here, what seems to have happened is the same move but with an opposite effect: the thin needs to become thick. The rights to life and liberty refer to referent objects/features as absolute values that are not thick, i.e. are not particularist, enculturated understandings of them. Therefore, these rights are universally thin, for Walzer, and can be used to make judgements about the actions of strangers who may violate them. However, this is a real tension for Walzer, because most of the time (but not always, hence the ambiguity and tension in his work) he wants to insist that everything must be thick first and thin afterwards. As he says 'maximalism in fact precedes minimalism' (Walzer 1994c: 13). With regards to the rights to life and liberty it seems that these are thin (minimalist) first and get fattened up later when they become maximal. There's little point in trying to resolve this tension for Walzer because it can't go away because it's generated by his grammar. Bluntly, his grammar makes it a problem for him because he separates members from strangers and therefore, has urges to bridge the gap between them. As we will later see, these urges are driven by mountain climbing tendencies to resolve the double whammy of international ethics. So far, we've looked at ways in which members are like strangers *via* features of their common humanity that are shared: difference and the rights to life and liberty. And thus far, his picture of the subject, as 'we', includes all of humanity and is whole-heartedly universal.

But what happens when Walzer moves from 'we' to 'I'? If the tension I've described thus far is indeed grammatically produced, we should be able to locate it here too. To find out, we need to look at the third sense of his picture of the subject as a divided self. It is important to look here for further aspects of his picture of the subject because, as Walzer himself says, 'it supports the versions of pluralism I have defended in domestic and international society' (Walzer 1994c: 86): his ethics.

Walzer thinks the self is divided in three ways and his description constitutes a fabulously fulsome elaboration of what he means by describing the subject as 'a wonderfully complex entity, which is matched to, which reflects and is reflected in, the complexity of the social world' (ibid.: 85). First, the subject is divided in that it has many interests and roles e.g. 'citizen, parent, worker [etc.]'. Second, it is divided by its identities, 'family, nation, religion, gender, political commitment and so on' (ibid.: 85). It is the third element that is most crucial wherein the subject 'also divides itself among its ideals, principles, and values; it speaks with more than one moral voice – and that is why it is capable of self-criticism and prone to doubt, anguish and uncertainty' (ibid.: 85). Put these all together and what Walzer wants to present us with is a picture of 'I' or 'me' as 'a complex, maximalist whole' (ibid.: 96); thick, in other words.

Of course, what he's trying to avoid is the 'wrong intuition' of the subject as thin: abstract, pre-social, and sovereign over itself. The kind of subject that liberal political theorists, like Beitz, postulate so that the subject can take an unsituated 'view from nowhere' (Nagel 1986). What Walzer wants to achieve is a position where 'thick, divided selves are the characteristic products of, and in turn require, a thick, differentiated, and pluralist society' (Walzer 1994c: 101). This is absolutely essential because, as we shall later see, Walzer's understanding of ethico-political space is his picture of the subject writ large, both domestically and internationally. The subject will therefore function as his conjunctive solution to bridging the gap between the domestic and international and as such, can serve as the foundation for the very possibility of a universalist international ethics. In fact, he goes so far as to say:

> The reality is this: specific sets of thick selves find themselves more or less at home in specific complex societies. There are always mismatches, but we can try to draw the (*internal and external*) boundaries of the society in such a way as to reduce the pain they cause.
>
> (Ibid.: 101; italics added)

So what is he picturing as the subject who is capable of being a self-critic? First, we need to ask why he poses the question in the first place. Walzer thinks the issue of asking who the self-criticising 'I' is, arises from the immediacy of the experience of 'doubt and division' when one is not sure 'which part is our best part, which roles, which identities or values are fundamental'

(Walzer 1994c: 92). This experience is the experience of internal pluralism that presents us, sometimes, with difficult choices and where it isn't clear which of our many aspects should have the final say. We feel divided or even schizophrenic as there seem to be so many 'me's' the way Walzer describes it. Which one rules? Who is it, really, that decides among many choices of moral values that we have internalised from our societies, for example? Well, for Walzer, whoever it is has agency. It has to be 'imagined' as 'capable of manoeuvring among my constituent parts' (ibid.: 100). Although this 'I' is not (regally?) sovereign it is, he tells us, 'like a newly elected president . . . [a] commander-in-chief' (ibid.: 99). It's like 'a democratic state' where 'I' am presidentially at the centre and all my pluralistic aspects are like my cabinet and advisors (ibid.: 98). For Walzer, the question then becomes how there is any consistency to who 'I' am. How do I avoid becoming schizophrenic and not lose my self and become 'utterly fragmented' (ibid.: 98)? Walzer answers again by drawing an analogy with a democratic state. The divided self has agency and so it is never entirely lost, just as 'In similar fashion, a democratic public changes its character without losing its collective identity or sense of agency, as it listens and responds to social criticism' (ibid.: 100). Thankfully, a grammatical reading isn't going to engage with the truth or falsity of this picture, only look to see what it produces in the form of universality and an international ethic based on it.

Given this picture of the subject, it will come as no surprise that later Walzer will offer us a picture of ethico-political space that is modelled on a democratic state, the United States of America specifically, when he gives his account of global pluralism. An ethico-political space such as this would provide the best match to what we are as human beings and 'reduce the pain'. In effect, Walzer is going to globalise his picture of the divided self and he will universalise it because, we as human beings, are *all* like this. That's the 'reality' of it, or so he tells us. 'Divided selves are best accommodated by complex equality in domestic society and by different versions of self-determination in domestic and international society' (ibid.: 103). Walzer has made a very clever move here. He has offered us his conjunctive solution to the separation of international and domestic politics. It is his picture of the subject, in all its fabulous entirety as outlined throughout this section of the chapter.

Before we move on to exploring this universalising move into ethico-political space, we should take a grammatical pause for breath. Is there a grammatical tension in this 'I', just as there was in his understanding of 'we'? Is he able to keep his 'I' thick and avoid the 'wrong intuition' of making it thin? Yes and no, respectively. Walzer's centre of the circle, the 'I' who has agency, is perdurable. That is to say, this 'core self' is permanent and stable and is the one that does the manoeuvring among its constituent parts. Now, while Walzer insists that this core self's configuration changes over time and in that sense is a historical and social product, he is nevertheless making a distinction between this 'I' and its 'internal critics'. The internal critics are also historical and social products for Walzer. Taken together, the core self and the internal critics are a grammatical product of membership. We are not strangers to ourselves in any sense. All our purported aspects belong to us as 'I'. What seems to be happening here is yet another form of essentialism in his picturing of the subject, albeit accidental since Walzer doesn't intend it.

The reason is this. The 'I' whose 'configuration changes over the course of its endurance' is somehow socio-historically pre-existent so that it is there *to be* shaped over time (Walzer 1994c: 101). It seems that for Walzer what makes us individuals, i.e. different from other selves, is the way in which the core self is shaped and influenced by its internal critics. This appears to be the implication behind him saying 'Every self is its own self, responsive and resistant in its *own* ways' (ibid.: 101). There seems to be a point where the core self seems to have control over the extent of its responsiveness and resistance to contingent forces (what Walzer seems to attribute to personal rather than social construction). At base, the *existence* of the core self is not dependent upon time and place, though its *shape* may be. It is nowhere. If we recall, Walzer likened the perdurability of 'I' to the continuing character of a democratic state in response to social criticism. Grammatically, we have already noted that Walzer takes it as bedrock that a distinction can be made between members and strangers. In other words, he takes membership of any community for granted though sees its configuration as socio-historically contingent. Membership is the perdurable part of any political community. 'We' always know who 'we' are grammatically speaking. Likewise, the core self is an individualised form of membership to itself and taken as bedrock in Walzer's picture of the subject so we can introspect and be transparent to ourselves: 'I' can know who 'I' am. Just as the political community may agree to change its criteria of membership over time, so too may the core self choose to change its relationship with its internal critics. But the point remains that the agential nature of the core self, as membership (of itself), is a grammatical given. It is simply assumed as bedrock. As such, all Walzer seems to have done in relation to a 'wrong intuition' is add an element of plurality; there are more internal critics in his picture than the liberal one, and therefore, there is more than one line of criticism. Placing 'I' in the centre of a pseudo-democratic circle, rather than at the top of super-agential hierarchy as a 'wrong intuition' does, isn't much of a displacement at all. Walzer's 'I' can respond and autonomously resist its internal critics which sounds precisely like the kind of hierarchical, sovereign, 'superagent' that Walzer wants to avoid (ibid.: 89). And 'I' can only do so because it is not reducible to, nor is the same as, its internal critics. Walzer's thick 'I' now looks rather skinny because his grammar has made it so.

We've looked at the grammatical production of Walzer's picture of the subject in considerable depth and detail. It has been a necessity because, as we will now go on to explore, it pretty much explains why Walzer makes all the other moves he does to defend a binary form of universalism and why each form of universality remains in permanent tension with the other. Let's turn to those now.

Binary universality: reason, the thin and the thick

Given Walzer's picture of the subject, he is going to present to us with a way of digging beneath the surface of language for answers to the question of international ethics that suits us, as human beings. This is his picture of reason. It isn't, self-consciously at least, going to be like Beitz's way of digging which involved abstraction and imagination as the best-suited expression of a universal reasoning subject. Beitz's cosmopolitan way of proceeding to understand the world we live in, our place in it, and therefore, the kind of international ethics that is possible would be based on a wrong intuition for Walzer.

Reading Walzer's work, in my opinion, is a refreshing experience and to be recommended. He has an immediate, clear writing style. He comfortably uses the pronouns, 'we', 'ourselves', 'us', and so on, that draw the reader in as though he really is talking to us.[9] Walzer's writing style is no accident. It is a carefully crafted expression of his picture of reason; of how we can come to understand the world we live in and, most importantly for us, how ethics is possible in global politics. Walzer wants to be intelligible to his readers. It's more than just wanting to be 'reader-friendly' though that is rare enough in academia. It reveals a much deeper and ambitious desire to expound 'our' shared understandings, whether of justice, the morality of war, or ethics more generally. As he says 'if my readers find my arguments incomprehensible and bizarre [it will be] . . . because of my failure to grasp and expound our common morality' (Walzer 1977: 20). Thus, Walzer is proposing a picture of reason whose role it is to reflect, to mirror accurately, our shared understandings of morality.[10] Put differently, his picture of reason is supposed to be an accurate portrait of 'our' picture of 'our' shared understandings around, for example, moral reasons. It is quite literally a *picture* of reason.

For Walzer, the content of shared understandings are social meanings. Reason, therefore, is 'radically particularistic', just as we are (Walzer 1983: xiv). And, understanding is itself 'the inevitable product of historical and cultural particularism' (ibid.: 6). In relation to ethics, it means that morality is socially dependent and as such, standards of rightness and wrongness, justice and injustice, and so on, depend on and are relative to shared social practices and understandings. Reason is thick. So, *how* do we dig to find answers for Walzer? We dig as 'ourselves'; as subjects who are situated. And we dig, as his picture of reason tells us, not to find abstracted, ideal answers to international ethics, but 'our' answers; we dig to discover 'ourselves' – to gaze upon our own collective reflection. No wonder his picture of the subject is so foundational in his communitarian language game then. It's the locus of the answers we seek.

Given the intimate, mirroring relationship between reason and the subject, Walzer's grammatically produced tension resurfaces in his picture of reason. He wants reason to be 'thick', to be particularist and pluralist. Can he keep it thick and avoid thinning it accidentally? Let's look into Walzer's mirror more closely.

In Walzer's picture of reason, 'the mirror [is] a critical instrument' (Walzer 1994c: 42). The critical potential of mirroring rests on being able to mirror society accurately in order to 'show us as *we really are*' (Walzer 1994c: 42. Original italics). Grammatically this presents Walzer with considerable tension and difficulty. Walzer clearly does not believe that reality exists independently of any social understandings we might have about it. So, the kind of mirroring that he is suggesting is not the construction of an accurate representation of trans-social, trans-cultural, trans-historical timeless elements of reality. He is not, therefore, drawn to naturalism.[11] Although it is the case that what he wants to represent is not a reality, but rather social realities, this leaves open the question of representation itself. What does it mean for Walzer to show us as '*we really are*'? For Walzer, as we already know, it involves a description of shared understandings, social meanings, and so on. The difficulty with Walzer's mirroring notion is that it seems to imply that there is only one correct representation of 'our' shared understandings that constitute 'our' society – the one that reveals how we '*really*' are. Given everything that Walzer has said about the importance of social meaning, in particular, its pluralism, then what gives Walzer a privileged position from which to mirror/represent society accurately, so that his is the only correct one? This difficulty arises, I think, for grammatical reasons. Walzer, it seems, does not see representation or more accurately, forms of representation as relative to social meanings. Mirroring assumes a separation of the object that is reflected (social realities in this case) and the subject who views the reflection (Walzer theorising and social critiquing). It is the wrong intuition that has come to haunt Walzer again.

Despite himself, or more accurately as a grammatical accident, Walzer has fallen prey to at least one aspect of Descartes' legacy, that 'my task as a representer is to represent accurately; correct action will follow (only) from correct representation' (Edwards 1982: 166). Walzer believes that correct action, i.e. morally just and justifiable, will follow from an accurate (true), as opposed to inaccurate (false), representation of 'our' shared understandings. We will explore this in detail in the following section when we shall see how his representation of international and domestic society leads him to offer the form of universalist ethics that he does. In the interim, suffice to note that all his works are attempts at providing accurate representations of our shared understandings, of 'us' (whether 'we' or 'I') so that 'we' can better understand the just course of action to take, as 'we' understand it in 'our' own terms. Ultimately, for Walzer, just action will be to follow the ways of a bifurcated universalism: the ways that his picture of the subject tells us are available to 'us' and that reason can locate.

James Edwards pithily calls the Cartesian legacy, as described above, 'an insidious kind of self-forgetfulness' (ibid.: 166). What he means by this is that the notion of rationality-as-representation privileges the accuracy of the representation; but does it mirror the state of affairs? This has the effect (desirable for Descartes, though certainly not for Walzer) of removing the observer from playing an essential role in what is being represented because there is a separation of the represent*er* and what is being represent*ed*.[12] Clearly, this is not what Walzer wants to happen as the possibility of impartiality and objectivity is an anathema to him because of his picture of the subject. We must always be thickly situated. Nonetheless, accepting a picture of reason as representational leads to Walzer having placed himself in a spot that has a view from nowhere. Consequently his picture of reason is no longer thick but thin. He's dug himself straight into the waiting arms of his wrong intuition once more via a form of self-forgetfulness.

Even were we to try to wiggle Walzer out of this, perhaps by asking what kinds of privileged position we have available to us as human beings, we wouldn't succeed. Walzer's picture of the subject already raised this question when he explored the divided self and asked how we choose the best part of ourselves to act upon and follow. There, he suggested, we take the position akin to a newly-elected president. The section above demonstrated that that too led him into a thin, wrong intuition as a grammatical accident. So, what does his grammar of members and strangers have to do with the aspect of his supposed thick picture of reason presented thus far?

Walzer's purportedly thick picture of reason tells us that we can know ourselves. What we find when we dig as 'ourselves' is a mirror within which we can recognise our own reflection as 'our' selves with all 'our' pluralistic shared understandings, meanings, notions of right and wrong, and so on. Our own reflection as 'us' is not that of strangers. That is only possible because of his unquestioned grammatical acceptance of what membership produces. It produces a clearly defined 'us' as a community of shared understandings, and so on. His grammar assumes, as it must, that there can be a clear demarcation between 'we' who share understandings (members) and those who do not (strangers). There are standards and/or criteria established by a pre-existent membership as to who belongs to the authentic inside of the community and those who are excluded and of course, it is the authentic inside that Walzer is trying to mirror (as thick). Grammatically, then, membership is far more than a good to be distributed as Walzer would have us believe. It is necessary for morality and our *reasoning* about it – for moral life, criticism, argument and intelligibility. Walzer's digging has unearthed no ordinary discovery. It's a reasoned excavation of a thick *universality*. No matter who the 'we' may be, *all* human beings belong to a 'we' because, as human beings, we cannot be strangers to everyone nor to ourselves in his grammar. It's how things '*really are*' apparently. Grammatically, we can now say that, for Walzer, thick universality has its foundations in his picture of the subject and that reason shows us, as a reflection, that this is so.

Recalling that his grammar produces a subject that is both at once a member to those it lives a shared life with and a stranger to those with whom it doesn't, what kind of reasoning can be extended to the stranger then? How are we to criticise or even understand moralities that are as strangers to us? Walzer grapples with this because his grammar compels him to.

Walzer is puzzled. Given all his claims about the universality of thickness he nonetheless finds himself 'recalling a picture' of marchers in Prague, 1989, carrying banners saying 'Truth' and 'Justice' (Walzer 1994c: 1). What puzzles him is that 'I knew immediately what the signs meant – and so did everyone else who saw the same picture. Not only that: I also recognised and acknowledged the values that the marchers were defending – and so did (almost) everyone else' (ibid.: 1). Blimey! If universality is nothing *but* thick, knowledge, recognition and acknowledgement such as this should be impossible. Other than those who share membership with the Prague marchers, strangers like Walzer, let alone 'everyone' or 'almost everyone', shouldn't be able to do what he has just described.

Walzer satiates his grammatically induced puzzlement by postulating a thin universalism or moral minimalism. He accounts for everyone being able to understand the banners' pleas for justice and truth for two, mutually dependent, reasons. The first, as he presents it to us, depends upon the second. First, then, what is required is the 'liberation of minimalism from embeddedness' (ibid.: 3). Since Walzer wants to argue that moral mini-malism (thinness) has its roots in a thick morality, any moral resonance of thickly understood terms such as 'justice' and 'truth' beyond 'our' local understandings will have to be dislocated from their particularist roots. Second, for the uprooting of the particular to be successful, it must be re-located to the universal. Walzer is doing more than just digging with his spade now. We could say that he is gardening, transplanting moral shoots of justice and truth from their home soil to a universal patch elsewhere. This can *only* happen, he tells us, if there is a wider 'common understanding' of an aspect of a term (ibid.: 3).

To get to the heart of what Walzer is envisaging, we need to be clear what it is that thin 'common understandings' rest upon. Let's look at Walzer's example of justice. He says,

> Whatever the origins of the idea of justice, whatever the starting point of the argument in this or that society, people thinking and talking about justice will range over a mostly familiar terrain and will come upon similar interests – like political tyranny or the oppression of the poor.
>
> (Ibid.: 5)

Here, Walzer is acknowledging the thick origins of justice. But, there's an additional claim which is that there is 'something' special about justice, however it may be locally understood, that connects it to a terrain that will be familiar to everyone, or almost everyone, like an opposition to tyranny. It's the additional claim that makes re-location, or transplantation, possible. More importantly, it's Walzer's bid for the existence and possibility of a thin form of universality.

Predictably, this is problematic. The problem is this: Walzer's description of justice cannot avoid slipping into an essentialist claim about the uprooted nature of justice itself. Just the sort of thing Walzer wants to avoid as his injunctions elsewhere make clear. Despite himself, he's claiming that it is the structure (terrain) of justice that can trans-socially and trans-linguistically connect it to tyranny and oppression of the poor. This is the equivalent of claiming that the nature of justice is so that all societies, regardless of their own specific elaborations of justice, have *within* their notions of justice an essential characteristic, e.g. an opposition to tyranny. It's an essentialist claim because Walzer is implicitly arguing that there is a feature, its terrain, that is common to all instances of justice and more significantly, is recognised and acknowledged as such. Without it, there could be nothing 'common' about thin 'common understandings' in his communitarian language game.

This move to make universality thin doesn't work, because justice now looks as if it's put on a considerable amount of weight and is thick. Justice isn't just 'justice' any more in its purportedly thin version. It's now, 'justice implies oppression to tyranny in every society and can be recognised as such by everyone in the world' and 'justice implies the oppression of the poor in every society and can be acknowledged and understood as such by everyone in the world'. Apart from having fattened up the thin considerably, Walzer has just shifted the problem. How does everyone in the world understand 'tyranny' and 'oppression of the poor'? Walzer might answer by gardening for more common understanding of these terms' terrains instead. But this would quickly lead us into infinite regress, e.g. tyranny implies a form of totalitarianism. What does everyone, globally, understand by 'totalitarianism', and so on *ad infinitum*?

To sum up so far, Walzer's picture of reason reveals, by mirroring, two forms of universality: the thick and the thin. Thickness is universal because 'we' are, *all*, thick. That's what we see when we dig to hold up a mirror to society as a picture of reason; we see ourselves, our shared understandings of justice and injustice, etc., and our situatedness. This is true of everyone if Walzer's picture of reason is to hold us captive. Everyone who has been socialised into being able to reason in thick ways can hold up a mirror and see themselves as members not strangers. Given that Walzer tells us that every human being belongs somewhere and therefore, has membership somewhere (his picture of the subject), thickness is universal. Equally, thinness is universal because, when we hold up a mirror, we can also see that 'our' values may contain within them 'common understandings' which can be re-located anywhere and need not be confined to home soil. These common understandings may have their origins in local membership, according to Walzer, but we can share them with strangers.

Walzer's picture of reason shows us that his binary universality is grammatically produced by his separation of members and strangers. He is a thoroughgoing universalist because he has: (1) universalised the characteristics of membership as thick universalism; and (2) universalised an experience of estranged familiarity. Understanding the Prague marchers' banners, for Walzer, is evidence that sometimes even strangers' pleas for justice can make sense to everyone globally. Hence, he has produced a notion of thin universality attached to strangers. So, we have two universalities: one for members and one for strangers. But, it's important to remember this, for Walzer, we share membership with those whom we live among in a shared way of life, but because of that we are also strangers to others who do not share our membership. As human beings then, we have access to both forms of universality. And, of course, that's unsurprising in Walzer's language game because his picture of the subject told us it had to be like this. His picture of reason simply confirmed this for him as he asked us to dig in search of a mirror within which we would see our own dual reflection, as both members and strangers.

Now that we've established what Walzer's universalism is and why, we can see that he has resolved the whammy of whether there can be ethics in global politics by settling firmly on the side of universality. He's climbed the mountain of asking whether there is one universal ethic or many particular ethics that can be applied to global politics and the view from the top is a conjunctive solution that simply universalises both. Believing that he has accurately represented the ways things actually are, both particularism and thinness exist. That means that when it comes to developing a universal ethics for international society, both must appear and be accommodated. The question now becomes how to resolve the second whammy of international politics and that is, how can the differences between domestic and international politics be resolved so that a dual universality can find a space, a locus, for its accommodation in practice? To discover that, we need to look at his picture of ethico-political space.

Fat chance: communities, states and international society

If Walzer is right, he's going to need to find space for two types of justice that, together, will provide a (binary) universal ethic as a conjunctive solution that can incorporate the moral requirements of both domestic and international politics. First, Walzer seeks to find a justice that accommodates the universal moral value of thickness that is best served by the ethico-political space of political community locally and a form of global pluralism internationally. And, second, he seeks a thin ethico-political space to be used only in a 'supreme emergency'.[13] Such emergencies only arise in the event of a state no longer accommodating the moral value of thickness. The thin, then, is necessary as a universal limiting condition on any unjust excesses that the thick might produce. Without the thin being able to do this, Walzer would find himself endorsing a universal ethic that he absolutely wants to avoid; one that would allow genocides, for example, to occur with impunity in the lands of strangers. His sense of justice is one where it is an absolute moral imperative that such impunity must be avoided. There's a very good reason for this. The ghosts of the Holocaust haunt Walzer, like Morgenthau. His position is 'driven . . . by [his] own memory and reflection on the struggle against Nazism' (Walzer 2004a: 33). This is what drives the moral dilemma of international politics for him. When, if ever, should we involve ourselves in the lives of strangers outside our own political community? When do we stick to the thick or abandon it and evoke the thin? Technically, that is a question about locating the moral extension, the limits, of a state's rights to political sovereignty and territorial integrity. It's a grammatically produced dilemma because (1) the question of when to make a moral choice about thickness or thinness only arises if they are both postulated as existent in the first place; and (2) we need to find out when a situation demands the application of the thick or the thin because correct actions will follow from a true, accurate, representation of the situation (state of affairs).

Unfortunately for Walzer, when we read him grammatically, we see that he is unable to avoid his own nightmare. The primary reason for this is because he is unable to resist fattening up the thin. It's a grammatical accident because of the irresolvable tension that his grammar creates, a tension that we've already explored in the context of his pictures of the subject and reason. Regrettably, when we look at how this tension reappears in his picture of ethico-political space, Walzer's grammatical chance of binary universality producing the kind of global justice he seeks is a fat one.[14] Accordingly, we will first look at the spatial accommodation of humanity's thickness and then move on to the occasions when thin universality needs to be evoked as a limiting condition. We'll conclude by showing how Walzer ends up in conjunctive failure, just as Morgenthau and Beitz did.

Walzer is a communitarian because he holds that 'The community is itself a good – conceivably the most important good' (Walzer 1983: 29). The key to universal justice in international politics, according to him, is the relationship between the state and community. Walzer conceives of global politics as an 'international society' whose members are states (Walzer 1977). It is states, therefore, that are best placed to defend the community as 'the most important good' and to protect individuals' rights to life and liberty as well as their common humanity as culture-producing creatures.

What is the relationship between state and political community so that states have a 'moral standing' in international politics (Walzer 1980)? A state consists of a political community and its government (Walzer 1985: 220, 35). The political community has rights to territorial integrity and political sovereignty that are derived from the individual's rights to life and liberty and these rights belong to the state also. The state has these rights through its members' consent of 'a special sort' (Walzer 1977: 54). Through consent, members form a metaphorical 'contract' with the state that it should protect the common life which they have shaped through 'shared experiences and cooperative activity' over a long period of time (ibid.: 54). For Walzer, the state's primary role is therefore to protect the common life, the historical community, that members have created. In other words, the state is an ethico-political space that best accommodates his picture of us as subjects because it is thick. That's why it has moral value. The moral value couldn't be any higher. As he puts it, 'The survival and freedom of political communities – whose members share a way of life, developed by their ancestors, to be passed on to their children – are the highest values of *international society*' (ibid.: 254; italics added).

For Walzer, what seems to allow the transfer of moral value from community to state is the idea of state legitimacy as 'fit'. He says, 'A state is legitimate or not depending upon the "fit" of government and community, that is, the degree to which the government actually represents the political life of its people' (Walzer 1985: 222). What he seems to mean by this is that there exists a fit between government and community if 'a people [is] governed in accordance with its own traditions' (ibid.: 220).[15] In other words, what needs to be pictured accurately, so that right moral action (justice) can follow, is domestic ethico-political space *as* legitimate. As we shall see, once we have the correct picture of ethico-political space, we can know which universality to evoke: the thick or the thin.

When there is a fit between community and government it is, empirically, the occasion for a thick universal international morality that should uphold two state rights: the rights to territorial integrity and the right to political sovereignty. Accordingly, Walzer proposes that our guiding principle in international ethics should be a form of what he calls 'presumptive legitimacy'. In other words, we should in the main presume that a state is legitimate 'unless the absence of "fit" between the government and community is radically apparent. Intervention in any other case usurps the rights of subjects and citizens' (ibid.: 222). This is Walzer's pluralism that seeks to respect and protect difference writ on a global scale, an international society where different ways of life, understandings, and so on can be protected by the international practice of state sovereignty.

Presumptive legitimacy is the first point at which Walzer's grammar resurfaces in tension with itself in his picture of ethico-political space. Given the two elements of his grammar, members and strangers, it shouldn't come as a surprise that he postulates that there are two kinds of moral standing of states. A state, as ethico-political space, can have bifurcated legitimacy. It can be 'presumptively legitimate in international society and actually illegitimate at home' (ibid.: 222). Basically, there can exist judgements of legitimacy from a member's point of view and from a stranger's point of view.[16] Walzer's picture of reason told us that this could happen. For the most part, any judgements we make are bound to be thick: they are 'our' judgements and situated in 'our' ways of life in 'our' own political communities. It's because of this that Walzer wants us to presume that other states are legitimate most of the time. We just aren't in a position to really tell what it's like to be a member of a different state and therefore, whether the government really is protecting their communal way of life. In other words, we can't be objective about it and so, we must refrain from universalising 'our' way of life as the only legitimate way of life in a political community. It's thick universality as an internationalised politics of difference.

But here's an odd, grammatically produced, thing. Apparently, there can be 'objectively illegitimate' states so that their members' 'opinions are not relevant, for whatever they think, we can argue that such a government does not and cannot represent the political community' (Walzer 1980: 216, 15). Who is the 'we' in that sentence? Strangely, it's 'we' as philosophers. He tells us there's a 'simple distinction' to be made and held between the 'philosophical question [which is] . . . transnational or universal [and] the political question' (ibid.: 216, footnote 11). The philosophical issue seems to be answerable objectively, regardless of what its own members think, a state can be illegitimate. The political question, of what members want to do about the position they find themselves in when their state is objectively illegitimate, is 'answered by some national process of decision making' (ibid.: 216, footnote 11). The distinction between the philosophic/universal and the political in this instance allows Walzer to conceive of presumptive legitimacy as 'the politics of *as if*' (ibid.: 216). Except under exceptional circumstances, discussed below, 'we' must *act* 'as if' a state is legitimate. But, here's the oddity again, 'anyone can make such judgements' that a state is objectively illegitimate (ibid.: 214). That's a distinction between who can judge and who can act. Only members are permitted to act since that is what a respect for the pluralist character of self-determination entails, but everyone else, including philosophers and strangers it seems, can judge.

The importance of Walzer's distinction between who can act and who can judge cannot be understated grammatically. 'Anyone' can judge. That means both members and strangers can. But, and here's the key, only members can act faced with a government that may be objectively illegitimate *unless*, in effect, they are rendered unable to act for themselves by its actions: that they are strangers that need to be rescued (Walzer 1995). Let's unpack this.

'Anyone' can judge. But *how*, in this instance, thickly or thinly? On the one hand, Walzer's notion of presumption emphasises how we cannot escape the thickness of our reasoning. It's why we are prohibited from acting on our judgements and must presume to uphold a state's rights to political sovereignty and territorial integrity. This is his 'politics of *as if*'. Thickness, and the ethics and politics it has now generated in international society, are a grammatical feature of membership. On the other hand, though, Walzer is telling us that we can make judgements that do not require membership in the particular community we are judging; we can stand outside not only theirs but ours and be objective. If this isn't an outright contradiction, it's certainly a tension in his picture of ethico-political space. The reason for the tension is predictably grammatical. 'Anyone', which means 'everyone', is bifurcated according to his picture of the subject and its grammar. We are all, at the same time, both members and strangers. So, we have the capacity to make judgements thinly as strangers and to make judgements about strangers. But how do we know when to act on our universally thick judgements, *as if*, and leave political communities to their non-democratic ways of life even though they are objectively illegitimate? And when do we act on what our judgements tell us universally thinly? They're the same question: when must strangers, in the name of justice, act? Walzer has an answer, as he must. If he's going to postulate this grammatically produced bifurcation of not only universal judgement but action, for members and strangers, he has to distinguish between them and then make a choice. This choice, according to the rules of his language game, will be determined empirically with a correct representation of the state of affairs that are morally relevant.

Walzer argues that it's only in 'supreme emergencies' that strangers can act on behalf of members whose membership of political community they do not share. Then we must choose a thin 'emergency ethics' that captures 'some minimal fixed values ... [and] minimum solidarity of persons' (Walzer 2004a: 40). In such cases, we are 'free to do whatever is militarily necessary to avoid the disaster, so long as what we do doesn't produce an even worse disaster' (ibid.: 40). The looming disaster cannot be 'anything less than the ongoingness of the community [being] at stake, or ... communal death' (ibid.: 46). The community, after all, is the greatest good in his ethics because, empirically, 'It is a feature of our lived reality, a source of our identity and self-understanding' (ibid.: 49).

Walzer describes when those moments of disaster are upon us as his three 'rules of disregard' (Walzer 1977: 1980). What is to be disregarded is the presumption, the *as if* element, that a state's political sovereignty and territorial integrity must not be violated. They are his answer to the moral dilemma of international politics which is the 'paradox' that 'moral communities make great immoralities morally possible' (Walzer 2004a: 50). The way to resolve the paradox is to set a limit on what immoralities the universality of the thick make morally possible. Thinness sets the limit. In the case of humanitarian intervention, the three rules relate to empirical conditions within a state where there is either (1) a struggle for national liberation or secession; or (2) a civil war; or (3) the massacre, enslavement or expulsion 'of very large numbers of people' (Walzer 1980: 218). In each of these cases, the fit between government and community has broken down and is 'radically apparent', even to strangers (ibid.: 214). In the case of (1), the community is fragmented and wants to break away into separated parts to create new, more coherent, political communities that better reflect what is shared between its members. In the case of 2) the community is again fragmented and its factions fighting each other. In both cases, what was the community is no longer there in any meaningful sense. It is being reconfigured and therefore, there are no more obligations towards the old configuration of the community as a state with its attendant rights of political sovereignty and territorial integrity.

Given Walzer's memories of the Holocaust, it's the third element, the case of genocide, massacre and mass expulsion, that he is most impassioned about. They are also the kinds of case where, since he first postulated presumptive legitimacy in 1977, he has 'found it easier and easier to over-ride the presumption' (Walzer 2004a: xiii).[17] Genocide, massacre, and mass expulsion are the kinds of action that '"shock the conscience" of human-kind' (Walzer 1995: 55). No matter how thickly situated we may be, every-one's conscience will be shocked, the lack of fit radically apparent to all, and therefore, military action (and the immoralities it brings in its train) permis-sible to stop it from continuing.[18] It's an obvious appeal to the universality of thinness, the sort of experience where any notion of justice, however locally understood, can recognise the political tyranny of genocide and its existential threat to a community along with the life and liberty of its indi-vidual members. The rules of disregard are the moral limit of thickness, the point at which thickness' possible immoralities are held in check by the universality of the thin. Thin universality, in supreme emergencies, then must *always* trump thick universality. If it doesn't, we have only thick universality wherein we stand by, do nothing and let any acts like the Holocaust continue unchallenged because we must presume such a state is acting legitimately. This is exactly what Walzer's universal international ethic, more than anything else, is designed to avoid.

But, grammatically, can he avoid it? Can the thin really do this for him? For such a limit to be placed on thickness, the thin would have to remain steadfastly thin. It must not descend into thickness or else there is nowhere that we could locate minimal fixed values and solidarity among strangers. It's precisely at the time when genocides are occurring that Walzer thinks thickness is the problem and not the solution, so any moral respect or regard for it must be cleanly eliminated from consideration.

Unfortunately, a grammatical reading shows us that Walzer cannot fully succeed and that we are confronted with conjunctive failure. He can't stop the thin from putting on weight and becoming thick. Appealing to minimal values and minimal solidarity among strangers evokes his understanding of thinness that we examined in the previous section. Minimal values, that is to say thin values, rest on 'common understandings'. These common under-standings form the basis of a minimal solidarity so that we can figuratively march alongside the protesters in Prague. Equally, and for the same reasons, humankind can find its conscience shocked in the face of gross injustices, like genocide. Our particularistic membership makes no difference here; it is our common humanity and what it provides for us as the possibility of universally common understandings that do. The limits on the excesses of thick immoralities therefore, rest on common humanity, a non-particularistic aspect of the subject. It's the ethico-political space of humanity and effectively, Walzer's picture of the subject that can and should save strangers.

There are three pertinent, thin, aspects of common humanity in Walzer's picture of the subject. First, the possibility of possessing common understandings. Second, the rights to life and liberty. And, third, the divided self who can make moral choices. In each case, Walzer tried to set limits to the thick. In the case of common understandings, while the origins of understanding may be thick, there comes a point when they be removed from their particularist roots and made sense of anywhere and by anyone. In the case of the rights to life and liberty, the same applied. Walzer believes that they are 'something like absolute values' and again, not dependent on membership for their moral force but common humanity (Walzer 1977: xvi). And the divided self, 'I', in the final analysis is perdurable through particularistic time and circumstance and, therefore, not dependent upon thickness for its moral choices, only its own agency. Taken all together, these add up to aspects of common humanity that are essentialist, possessed simply by virtue of our humanity and not our membership to any community and they are not relative.

However, in each case, Walzer cannot help but fatten them up and make them thicker because of his grammar. The very possibility of common understandings, under which the rights to life and liberty can be subsumed, rested on the possibility of each particularistic understanding of justice, for example, having a feature that is common to all of them. That feature is 'a mostly familiar terrain . . . [with] similar interests' (Walzer 1994c: 5). However, such a feature is not thin. It is thick and prone to infinite regress. In the case of Walzer's third rule of disregard, it's more accurately described as the proposition,

> justice implies that everyone, everywhere, because of their common humanity, will have a moral objection to genocide, act upon it by supporting the use of military force to stop it and be able to recognise that it is occurring in a way that doesn't depend on their own thick understandings of events and their moral significance.

That's an awful lot to uproot from its thick origins. What are the common understandings of 'genocide', 'military force', 'stopping' a genocide, 'common humanity' and 'everyone', for example? To answer that would then require more sketches of terrains, which in turn would require another, and so on *ad infinitum*.

And how does the 'I' succeed in being, ultimately, the creator of its self and therefore, have agency that is not wholly dependent upon its thick internal critics? By being democratic, Walzer tells us. By listening and responding to its 'advisors', each of which is a social product. But, given that what is doing the shaping of the 'I' here is, by necessity, thick, it's impossible for 'I' not to put on weight. It's what it lives on.

The fattening up of the thin is (as is the thinning of the thick) an unavoidable product of Walzer's grammar. Membership and estrangement are his grammatical bedrock. Walzer may consider them to be a distinction and neatly separable but we have seen throughout this chapter that they define each other. There are no strangers unless there are members and there can be no members if strangers cannot be distinguished from them; they are each other's constitutive outside and, grammatically speaking, co-dependent. What this means, as we have seen, is that part of what membership means in Walzer's language game *are* the features of estrangement and vice versa. As such, they can't help but creep back in and produce conjunctive failure either as a fattening of the thin, or a thinning of the thick. This is morally disastrous for Walzer's binary universality.

In sum, what kind of view of universal international ethics do we have once we've done all the digging and gardening Walzer has asked of us? We don't have the view that Walzer wants, needs and desires – a landscape where thin universality can stop the moral excesses that an unfettered thick universality would allow. Yet again, just as was the case with Morgenthau and Beitz, a grammatical reading reveals that Walzer cannot find what he seeks, how he seeks it and where he seeks it. Instead, we find Walzer confronted with his own worse nightmare as a grammatical feature of conjunctive failure. Walzer wanted to avoid an ethic of international political practice that would find the following response morally justifiable in the face of a genocide; 'We shouldn't do anything to help because we may have misunderstood what is going on and anyhow, people should be left free to sort out their own problems their own way.' Walzer wants that sentence to be true but *only* when empirical conditions determine that a state is legitimate, or presumptively so. That's his commitment to thick universality. However, he doesn't want that sentence to be true when states are illegitimate and massacring their own citizens. At that point, thin universality must trump the thick. But, of course, that presumes that we can clearly distinguish between the two sorts of universality. Without that, thinness cannot act as a limiting condition on the immoral excesses of the thick as Walzer wants. Unfortunately, as each of the three grammatical readings have shown, grammars can produce dangerous effects whether we want them or not.

6 In defence of universality
(Im)possible universalism

We have grammatically read universality thrice. What has this achieved? My wish is that it has achieved as little as possible. I hope that it has added nothing special at all to universality and ethics in International Relations. Most of all, I hope that what grammatical readings produce is an outcome that is completely and utterly ordinary: one where we 'bring words back from their metaphysical to their everyday use' (Wittgenstein 1958a: §116).

The grammatical readings in this book have sought to show how Morgenthau, Beitz and Walzer have been metaphysically seduced: that's what makes them diggers. This isn't a critique of them *per se*, neither of the sincerity of their commitment to ethicality nor of their association of ethics with universality and the subject. The book is not really about them at all but rather about how language games (practices) of ethics and universality in IR seduce us into thinking that words refer to problems and things that 'have the character of *depth*' (ibid.: §111). Tackling 'ethics', 'universality', 'the subject', 'international political reality', and so on can seem like a profound search for the answer to Life, the Universe and Everything (Adams 1982). I will happily admit that I have been so seduced in the past (maybe I still am?) and that I have, consequently, theoretically vexed over them for far too long. It doesn't mean, for one moment, that these words don't have very significant meanings for us. They clearly do and it all matters ethico-politically; possibly much more than we might have initially thought. Accordingly, what I shall do in this concluding chapter is talk about why these words are not deep and do not point to something profound (metaphysical), and why their lack of depth is what makes understanding their use an ethico-political endeavour that may matter much more than our theories would have us *think*. It will amount to a defence of universalism.

'You can't always get what you want':[1] depth, digging and the drawing of lines

Reading grammatically is a response to 'the problems arising through a misinterpretation of our forms of language [so that they] have the character of depth. They are deep disquietudes; their roots are as deep in us as the forms of our language and their significance is as great as the importance of our language' (Wittgenstein 1958a: §111).

What have we done, so far, by grammatically reading a Realist language game (Morgenthau), a cosmopolitan one (Beitz) and a communitarian one (Walzer)? Importantly, we have tried to stay within their language games in order to get a sense of the contours of their form and the sense of depth that they consequently produce. As far as one is able, that has involved learning how to be a speaker of their language games.[2] It isn't insurmountably hard to do such a thing and there's nothing particularly special about it. We do it all the time. Most people are conversant in a large number of language games, even from a young age. Using the same language, English in this case, my child has mastered several different sorts of contextually driven language games: football, playing on X-box Live, being with his grandparents, being a pupil at school, friendships with his peers, and so on. Each has variations in the use of words that alter their meaning according to the practices of the language game (context) that is being played, e.g 'bad'.[3] As someone who studies IR, and I imagine a few of you reading this book may also, a part of that studying is learning different language games. We do this by reading the work of other people like Morgenthau, Beitz and Walzer, for example. In their work they show us the meaning of their words by how they use them, the range of use – what the words can and cannot mean, can and cannot imply, and so on. In this way, we can become trained in their language games and sometimes, even teach them to our students if we are teachers. Of course, we also argue as to what authors may have meant and they may even argue with us over what they really meant to say.[4] But, even those argumentative conversations depend on us speaking roughly the same language game and having learnt them to some degree (better or worse). It also means that the same words can appear in different language games but mean different things because how those words are used differ. 'Universality' is one of those words and is a word just like any other. There's nothing special about it in and of itself. What makes 'universality' special, appear deep, is how it is used in the language game: the form of the language game that is regulated by its grammar.

Given the title of this book, it's the use of the word 'universality' that these grammatical readings have sought to render conspicuous. What I've tried to show is what happens when we completely immerse ourselves in language games on their own terms and according to their own grammars. I have not only tried to show what universality means for the three thinkers, but why it does, and what that then implies for the range of the term's use for them. It adds up to an assemblage of reminders for a particular purpose. My primary purpose has been to show the range of what is made possible and, by implication, impossible by the differences in the range of the use of the word 'universality' in the three language games read. In each grammatical reading I sought to locate a grammar, show how each grammar produces three pictures (the subject, reason and ethico-political space), produces a particular understanding of what the moral dilemma of international politics is, show how these grammatical products are the putting into practice of the range of possibilities that universality and ethics are said to imply and, finally, to show how all of that adds up to a purported conjunctive solution to the double whammy of international ethics. In effect, a grammatical reading is seeking to locate the limits of each language game and, in so doing, trace out the contours of its form.

Why be so interested in the limits of language (games)? Because it's where we bump our heads and find ourselves theoretically troubled and vexed. It's where, it seems in the case of the three readings here, the urge to go beyond them becomes irresistible and produces the character of depth and deep disquietude. It is the point at which the urge to dig below the surface of language can get the better of us and where we will find ourselves metaphysically seduced, captivated by the notion that we have hit upon the fundamental *nature* of the problem or the phenomenon and that the roots of it are just as 'deep in us'. And, given that the language games we've looked at here belong to theoretical approaches to global politics, going beyond the limits of language really is a head-bumping exercise that not only can lead to brain-ache but, vitally, show us the limits of what can be accomplished by theorising as a digging exercise. Grammatically reading the limits of language, therefore, can also render conspicuous what we *think* about the world and how our ideas have effects that regulate not only how but, who can live in the world.[5] In other words, tracing how grammar produces the limits of language can show us how and why ethics and universality matter ethico-politically. It's because *representations* of us (as pictures of the subject), how to think (as pictures of reason) and reality itself (as pictures of ethico-political space) are grammatically produced.

How does that happen and what happens when it does? That grammar can produce such far-reaching effects only happens if we are seduced by the notion that language functions to represent reality and all that is contained in it, including us. That we are in the business of representing reality when we use language relies on there being an object that is being named by a word: a word–object relation. If we honestly believe that that is what happens, we will very quickly find ourselves below the surface of language, somewhere deep, locating named but mysteriously functioning phenomena/ objects and trying to figure out the relationship between them like 'universality' and 'ethics'.[6] That's precisely what Morgenthau, Beitz and Walzer have done. They each assume that they are representing/picturing the world when they theorise and that therefore, what they have located is not only accurate (true) but 'real'. I'm not going to philosophically quibble with the use of the word 'real' here and find myself digging so that I am tempted to represent what real *really* means. I'll just end up with a headache from having bumped my head. Instead, let's highlight some things that have happened in the language games of universality that we have read grammatically.

Wittgenstein's notion of language *games* is a heuristic device in several ways. It's there to serve as a reminder that for a game to be a game it does not need to share some essential, named, feature that is common to all. For example, canasta doesn't have a feature in common with rugby, but both are games. Both are rule governed, though, so it is important to remember that the rules are different. Equally I may share no features at all with my cousin three times removed but we still belong to the same family. The most that we may find, as we look at the three grammatical readings, are family resemblances. Accordingly, as I draw conclusions about Morgenthau, Beitz and Walzer's language games, I am not looking for an essential feature that they all share so that, were I to dig it up and unearth it, we may then be able to deduce something fundamental about the nature of universality: the *real* answer. I will just limit myself to making grammatical remarks and staying on the surface of language.

The first grammatical remark to make, then, is that we haven't discovered a single kind of universality that is common to all. What we've got is a family of universality: divine universality (Morgenthau), ideal universality (Beitz) and binary universality (Walzer). They aren't entirely and neatly unrelated to each other though. All of them are grammatically produced but their grammar differs. All of them believe that the foundation of a universal international ethic lies 'deep in us' because each postulates their picture of the subject as its foundation yet their pictures of the subject differ. Each thinks they are representing international political reality in their pictures of ethico-political space but what that looks like also differs in its details. And each offers a way of digging so that we can unearth what they have in their pictures of reason. Nevertheless, how to dig, what our spade looks like and what we may find when we do, differ in each case. Consequently, their universalist formulation and resolution of the moral dilemma of international ethics are different. The differences between them are not absolute or neat. There are no hard lines around each language game. There's plenty of overlap in some areas such as anarchy as a feature of international politics and the conundrum of one ethic over many (the double whammy), none in others, vague similarities in some, strong similarities in others, and so on. But the point is, it is the context/practices of meaning use that make the differences between them and therefore, as we have seen, the differences in what universality means for each.

Bearing in mind the above, the second grammatical remark I want to make is about grammatical remarks. They are nothing more or less than a reminder for a particular purpose. They aren't going to be an ontological claim about the *real* reality of universality, ethics, the subject, reason or ethico-political space, for example. There's nothing metaphysical about them. Grammatical remarks are, as a feature of language, also context-driven rather than driven by the nature of the objects to which the words, purportedly, refer for their meaning. In this case, the context is set by the purpose of the reminders I wish to make which are to do with universality, ethics, IR and reading grammatically. I could, as could anyone else, have chosen a different purpose that would, accordingly, make the kind of reminders (grammatical remarks) they would like to make different. There's nothing objective about a grammatical reading and neither is it wholly subjective (personal to me and the goings-on in my mind). Language is public and shared. We couldn't understand each other if it wasn't or this book would be nothing but a set of meaningless marks on the paper to anyone reading it and wholly inaccessible to anyone other than me.[7] The grammatical remarks made are the ethos of reading grammatically. And, as such, I take them to be ethico-political. They are an engagement with the grammars of universality, politics and ethics in order to trace their effects on the things that are the purpose of the reading.

The third, and final, grammatical remark of this sub-section is about conjunctive failure, pithily summed up as 'You can't always get what you want' (The Rolling Stones, 1968). Having fully immersed ourselves in three language games of universality in IR, we saw that each couldn't hold on to the answer that they sought most dearly and that would fully satiate their desire for one. Morgenthau desperately, and understandably, wanted to avoid constructing an international ethic that would ever repeat the logic of the Holocaust. In his case, the moral dilemma of international politics was a question of how to avoid the morality of the nation being universalised as either a utopian and/or totalitarian endeavour in practice. Alas, he ended up doing the same thing through his attempt to reconcile his own grammar of the transcendent and actual by concretising the divinely universal within the nation-state as the national interest. With great passion, Walzer too wants to avoid any international ethic that would allow another Holocaust to take place with others just passively standing by and letting it happen. In his case, his grammar produced the moral dilemma of international politics as an issue of when the community should be left to its own self-determination and protected by the state's rights to sovereignty and territorial integrity and when it should not. His answer was to offer us a thin universality that could counteract the immoral excesses of the universality of thickness embodied in communal life. And again, unfortunately, the grammar of his language game took him straight into the cruel embrace of universal non-intervention as his grammar made him unable to resist fattening up the thin. Finally, Beitz who so wanted to engage with the injustice of distribution *in* the world ended up making it disappear and become morally irrelevant in his language game. The thing he thought could save us, ideal universality, ended up taking him into his own nightmare where ideal theory has no relevance at all to the nonideal world. Neither language game produced the answer that they wanted and indeed, more than that, took them exactly where they didn't want to be: into the horrors of conjunctive failure.

How does that happen? It happens because all three are diggers (metaphysically seduced) and so their grammars produce this effect. Grammar and seduction go together in each of their cases. Each reading located a grammar that turned out to be a binary distinction: transcendent vs actual (Morgenthau), ideal vs nonideal (Beitz), and members vs strangers (Walzer). I must admit that I didn't expect this when I first began to read grammatically. It's just the way it turned out because, to locate a grammar, I asked myself the same question in a series of ways (in no particular order): What, in relation to universality and ethics, is the assumption that cannot be questioned in this language game?; What is the grammatical bedrock that allows us to 'go on'?; What is it that, were one to question it, would conceivably make the language game unable to get off the ground?; Why does x think that y is a problem?; and what is being assumed that makes the problem a problem in the first place?[8] At first, I located one thing, for example, the transcendent in Morgenthau. But then I asked similar questions about transcendence and came to the view that, grammatically speaking, Morgenthau's meaning of the word 'transcendent' couldn't really get off the ground without having assumptions about its opposite as what it is not – the 'actual'. Grammatically, the relationship between transcendence and actuality is a word–word relation and obviously, a grammatical reading holds that it is from here (and not reference to named objects) that meaning is generated. So, it turned out that the grammar I located for the purposes of assembling reminders about universality in IR were binary distinctions.

That rather self-indulgent little segue into how I came to locate grammars is there to serve as a reminder of something too. It is a reminder of the difference between digging and reading grammatically: of what one may hold to be the 'great . . . importance of our language' to return to the quotation at the beginning of this section. Diggers assume, as they must, that their words name some 'thing' – an object of some sort because they assume that for language to have meaning, it must represent certain states of affairs in reality: real 'things' in the world and their arrangement. What happens consequently, returning to the grammars contained in the three readings, is that seemingly deep problematics begin to appear in their language games. They have the character of depth because the diggers think they refer to deep 'things'. Each word must refer to an object: transcendent, actual, ideal, nonideal, member, and stranger. They become an ontological feature of reality for each respective language game. As soon as that happens, we seem to be confronted with deep questions about the nature of reality and the things in it. In the case of these three readings, they are confronted with a primary grammatical disjunction (e.g. transcendent and actual) that generates problematics around (1) what each one *is*, fundamentally; and (2) what the relationship might be between them. Such problematics, with their adopted ontological status as a fundamental feature of reality, take on the character of real-world problems and are suitably all the more vexatious for having done so.

Accordingly, if one is so seduced, one is drawn into feeling compelled to answer, to dig to find out, *actually*, what the nature of each element is and the relation between that and its opposite. But, grammatically speaking, this must assume that the two elements of the binary distinction are distinct so that the relationship between them requires figuring out. It's somewhat like the use of the word 'and' that separated ethics and IR that we explored in Chapter 2. As soon as you separate out the transcendent from the actual, the ideal from the nonideal and membership from estrangement as though they named some 'thing', you're going to get the urge to conjoin them so that you have produced a coherent theory. It's this metaphysical urge that leads them to not always get what they want and find themselves confronted with the horror of having failed to bridge the gap between them.

Why? Grammatically speaking, it's because their language games need both elements, not for metaphysical reasons that generate meaning, but for reasons just to do with meaning *tout court*. I have tried to show in each grammatical reading why each grammar is grammati*cal*: a bedrock that allows the rest of the proceedings (everything else each thinker wants to say) to go ahead. In each case, the thinkers could not establish the meaning of each term without reference to its opposite. It's what generates the meaning. So, for example, Walzer cannot make sense of all the rich and varied things that he attaches to membership without reference to strangers. His language game must keep them distinct. They must remain separate so that they can be distinguished. That's one, but not the only, reason why conjunctive failure is an inevitable grammatical outcome. For the theory (which is each thinker's language game) to work, they must never fully be put together. Were they to be fully conjoined, all that the distinction generates would disappear because it would become conflated or blurred. Blurriness would be intolerable only because diggers assume that the words must refer to different objects. They draw distinctions as hard differentiating lines that go deep into reality because what is delineated must be represented as either/or.

The second reason why conjunctive failure happens is again grammatical and to do with word–word relations. The thing is that, grammatically, the meaning of members and strangers, for example, isn't neatly separable, as diggers would have us seduced into believing. They are dependent on each other for their meaning. Consequently, the opposite of any word is included by its exclusion.[9] Put another way, membership means not only thick ways of life and understanding but also 'not stranger'. Stranger appears inside the meaning of member by its exclusion as 'not'. As inside the meaning, stranger is always there. Estrangement can never be wholly expunged, kept out, as that which is absolutely 'not' membership. And, of course, the reverse is the case too. This creates a haunting of each word by its opposite which no exorcism can cast out. The effect of this haunting, grammatically, is another reason why the grammatical distinctions cannot hold between the transcendent/actual, ideal/nonideal and members/strangers. Each thinker's conjunctive solution was an attempt to put each element together with a bridge but nonetheless keep both sides of the river distinguishable from the other. However, what reading grammatically shows is that: (1) the need for a bridge is a grammatical product; and (2) each side of the river is not clearly independent from the other and therefore, clearly distinguishable. That sounds esoteric but isn't. Let's give an example using Walzer again.

When we read Walzer grammatically, we saw that he couldn't help but fatten up the thin and conversely, thin the thick. I tried to show that this was because of his grammar of members and strangers. Walzer couldn't help but fatten up the thin because the thick is inside the thin as part of what 'thin' means. As such, he can't hold the line between thick and thin universality just at the point when he needs and desires it the most. He desperately needs to keep the line (distinction) he has drawn because without it the thin cannot be evoked as a clear alternative, something different to, the moral excesses that the thick can sometimes produce, like genocides. However, because thickness haunts thinness from the inside, the line can't be held and his conjunctive (bridging) solution fails. He can't always get what he wants.

Drawing distinctions is drawing lines. Making distinctions is a feature of language and unavoidable because that's how words get their meaning – in different relations to each other including, sometimes, opposition.[10] Were this not so, the whole of language would be just one, extremely, long word! However, the implication of my grammatical remarks is that it is only if we are metaphysically seduced that we draw distinctions as *hard* lines that go deep into reality and deep into us as subjects so that we can neatly separate the world into its component elements and features. Such a seduction, and the digging expeditions it can send us on, only arise if we are unable to let go of the idea that each word must refer to an object, name some 'thing' in the world. That's not to say that some words don't name objects. They do. An ordinary English language grammar book calls them nouns. The problem that Wittgenstein alerts us to, with his use of the metaphor of games, is quite basic really. It's that we should refrain from generalising, which is very much harder said than done. That some words name objects doesn't mean that all words do and derive their meaning that way or even primarily so. In IR, philosophy, and so on, we have words that seem to be bursting with special meaning such as 'universality' and 'ethics'. So much seems to pour out of them that it can feel quite overwhelming. In my opinion, that sense of depth, profundity and grappling with Life, the Universe and Everything only happens if we, even inadvertently, find ourselves pulled towards the idea that some 'thing' lies beneath them. The ethical sting in the tail is that if we don't relinquish this seduction we will not find what we think we are looking for where we think we will find it, nor how we think we will find it. The three grammatical readings showed that where we end up instead is exactly where we don't want to be and embroiled in what we have tried so hard to ethically avoid.

'But if you try sometimes, you just might find you get what you need':[11] (im)possible universalism

Given everything I've just said in the section above, why would I want to defend universalism? What do those grammatical remarks have to do with politics and ethics?

I want to defend universality, no matter what its form, simply because it serves as a reminder for particular purposes which I, personally, hold to be ethico-politically desirable. The section above and the grammatical readings were all about failure, about not finding the answers that we seek by digging. They were, in effect, about ethico-political endeavours that are attempts at representation and the horror it can bring in its wake. I want to defend universalism because it must always fail. I absolutely will not defend it because it can succeed now or possibly in the future. For me, the ethics of universality lies in it never being fully possible: its grammatical (im)possibility. This is the moral value of what Morgenthau, Beitz and Walzer, for example, have given us.

Before I go any further, let me explicitly say that I am not offering a new, different, kind of universalism: a 'fourth way' to add to the three we have already read. Neither am I offering (im)possible universalism as a conjunctive, bridging, solution of some sort. My greatest hope is that I'm offering no 'thing', and adding nothing, whatsoever. I hope that the universality that I am defending will 'in no way interfere with the actual use of language; it can in the end only describe it. For it cannot give it any foundation either. It leaves everything as it is' (Wittgenstein 1958a: §124).

The grammars that produce the meanings of 'universal' are fascinating, not least for all the things that they can produce like the language games of international ethics that Morgenthau, Beitz and Walzer have offered us in IR.[12] But also, universality is a fantastic word because, with no need to get metaphysical at all, in everyday usage its meaning always evokes implications of all cases and/or everyone. It's an all or nothing kind of word. It makes no sense to say, in ordinary language, 'that's about 38 per cent universal' or 'that's a lot universal', for example. Were one to say such things, we could reply, 'you seem to have misunderstood the word universal'. Leaving metaphysics aside, then, I would like to defend universality and our uses (practices) of it whether in language games of IR theory, language games of universal human rights, or everyday language, for example, because it always evokes senses of all and/or everyone. That it makes such an all-embracing universal claim leaves open, always, the possibility of questioning whether it does include everyone and/or all cases of something. All it takes to throw universality into a crisis of meaning where it is no longer universal is to find one example of exclusion: one person who is left out; one case that isn't covered, and so on. After all, the meaning of universality seems to have gone awry if someone claims, 'Well, never mind that my understanding of universal humanity doesn't include humans who are suspected terrorists in the "war on terror", it's still universal.'

The first reason why I want to defend universality, then, is a very superficial one. The use of the word is always an invitation that asks whether there are any exceptions – asks if we have drawn lines, where and how *hard* – and

I want to defend the ethics of such an invitation. Personally, I want to accept the invitation as an ethico-political opportunity to challenge the practices of hardness that universality can render conspicuous. Were we to 'try sometimes', we may find that staying on the surface of language is an ethico-political practice of challenging the drawing, legitimisation, policing and authority of lines as though they were hard (The Rolling Stones, 1968). As this chapter now works towards its ending, I will keep revisiting the significance of such an opportunity with the grammatical remarks that follow.

The second reason why I want to defend universality is also superficial and, again, is related to line drawing. Accepting now that we are no longer seduced by the notion that universality names 'the real thing', like a bottle of Coca-Cola, we can let go of our deep disquietude and move on. What I see, from having read the three universalisms earlier, is this: a grammar of (im)possibility that produces universality.[13] I openly admit that calling such a grammar (im)possible is nothing deeper than heuristic: a short-hand for assembling reminders for the purpose of challenging hardness in this case.

The three grammatical readings each located a binary grammar: transcendence/actuality, ideal/nonideal and members/strangers. Given my remarks above about how meaning is produced and what must be assumed in order for it to be possible for a language game to get off the ground, we could, only for convenience's sake, summarise these elements of meaning production as another grammatical binary: as (im)possibility.

Taking Beitz as an example, we can say that the conditions of possibility of the ideal imply its own conditions of impossibility and, at the same time, the conditions of possibility of the nonideal. Equally, and at the same time again, the conditions of the nonideal imply its own conditions of impossibility and, at the same time, the conditions of possibility of the ideal. They are co-dependent and co-constitutive. One cannot be without the other. They include each other by exclusion. So, when Beitz outlines the ideal, he is outlining its conditions of possibility. He does this explicitly. It's his global original position. He's telling us what conditions need to obtain, the veil of ignorance, a moral point of view etc., for the ideal to be possible. He's drawing a line around the ideal, around what is possible. As he does draw this line, he is, simultaneously, offering the line as a marker of conditions of impossibility. He's telling us what must not cross the line and those things are the nonideal which are, basically, all the things that the veil of ignorance screens out like interests attached to nationality, gender, and so on. Not only is he telling us what cannot cross the line as nonideal, he's also offering the line as a shared boundary with the nonideal and its conditions of possibility. In this case, that the nonideal's conditions of possibility are all related to interests, situatedness, and so on. And it works the other way round too. For the sake of shorthand, because we need it, I'm calling this (im)possibility to render conspicuous how the drawing of lines (between the possible and impossible) produce meaning.

In each grammatical reading, we saw that this was what happened and, we saw that it led to failure. And the necessary failure of universality is what I want to defend. Having cleared the ground, so to speak, and staying firmly on the surface of language, I now want to say more about where I see the space and time for an ethics of universality which I am defending. To augur my answer rather bluntly, I see the space and time for it in failure and as ever present. It isn't anywhere special. There's no digging, no mountain climbing, no great search needed. It's right here and now. I want to say we have left everything as it is. It's why I believe that engaging with universality grammatically (i.e. superficially on the surface of language) may matter ethico-politically much more than we think. So, two questions: What do the ever-present spaces of the failure of universality look like and why are they so ethico-politically important?

With regards to the first question, they look leaky! Because I see impossibility and possibility including each other by exclusion, each is leaky and bleeds into the other. The line between them is necessarily porous. They can't ever fully keep each other out as each other's absolute other because they internally, as well as externally, belong together in their co-constitution. That's why no exorcism can banish the ghost of the other that haunts it and why universality always fails as the section above, and the grammatical readings, sought to demonstrate. If, as I am suggesting, forms of universality are (im)possible, they are always leaky.[14] Practices of universality, even when they try to draw the lines as hard lines, contain within themselves their own failure all the time. That means the invitation I talked of earlier is always there. And in practice, the invitation is often accepted. The language games around universality always provide the space and opportunity to say, because leakiness makes it so, 'I am not included in your universal' and to unmake it. (Im)possible universalism then, isn't a 'fourth way', another form of universality to add to the others. It's just a grammatical remark about universality and its meaning in use (practice).

That the line between impossibility and possibility is porous, and is not anchored to (founded upon) objects that either side of the line name, means that it's not hard, grammatically speaking.[15] Turning to the second question then, why is this so ethico-politically important and to be defended as a grammatical feature of universality? It matters because it brings us firmly and inescapably back into the world of ethico-political practice as opposed to abstracted, theoretical, metaphysical digging expeditions. Grammatical questions now become ethico-political practical ones about line drawing: How are lines drawn? Where are they drawn? Who draws them? Who polices them and how? What are the effects of these lines on people's lives and subjectivity? What must be assumed to draw them? And most important of all, how do some answers to these questions add up to a set of practices which draw lines as *hard* lines, as though they located and mirrored some inevitable ontological reality?

Viewing grammar this way implies that politics is the practice of drawing lines everywhere. Politics has unavoidable ethical implications because it draws lines (makes distinctions) between what kinds of lives and subjects are politically permitted as possible or impossible: politically legitimate or illegitimate, legal or illegal, human or inhuman, masculine or feminine, normal or abnormal, desirable or undesirable, true or false, and so on.[16] When, as all too often happens, such lines are drawn as hard lines, the very possibility for politics is expunged. When a line is taken to demarcate the difference between ontological phenomena (by naming them), the line becomes, seemingly, unquestionable. After all, if such lines really did represent reality, we are faced with a *fait accompli*: a reality that cannot be changed – 'This is how things are' (Wittgenstein 1958a: §114). It becomes illegitimate, supposedly, to ask why the lines have been drawn where they have and how they have excluded certain forms of life. Political contestation of the lines themselves is expunged as illegitimate by the very practice of drawing a hard line between legitimacy and illegitimacy (politics) itself. However if, as I have argued, lines are (im)possible they cannot be hard in this sense and so the possibility and occasion for politics can never be fully expunged. Ethico-political engagement is always possible because of grammatical leakiness. This is why the significance of grammar has 'roots [that] are as deep in us as the forms of our language and their significance is as great as the importance of our language' and is much more than we *think* (theorise) it is (ibid.: §111). The 'more' is the world we live in with other people. A grammatical reading of universality has tried to show that the surface of language is ethico-political because it traces the contours of practices that make possible and impossible, rather than name, lives being lived and the people who live them.

Defending universality, then, is a defence of staying on the surface of language. It challenges the hardness of line drawing. It is a defence of one of the most obviously available practices of politically contesting the drawing of lines because universality draws them so blatantly and grandly. (Im)possible universalism, the porosity of the line between possibility and impossibility, reminds us that attempts at holding the line must always fail. And, ever-present conditions of failure are what make ethico-political contestation and engagement possible. Such a possibility, whether enacted or not, is the ever-present invitation that universality offers us in practice. Universality, it seems to me, is defensible because it is an easy, uncomplicated, reminder that we can always accept the invitation to ethico-politically engage.

Mysticism, the universal subject and hunting for Snarks

In this third and final sub-section, I want to say something apparently bonkers in the context of International Relations as a discipline belonging to the social 'sciences'. I want to say that the three grammatical readings have revealed the mystical.[17] Everything hinges on how I am using 'the mystical', of course. Accordingly, I will re-visit Wittgenstein's purported mysticism, first discussed in Chapter 1, its relation to grammatical readings of universality, pictures of reason and, most important of all for this section, pictures of the subject. Evoking the mystical, as the final hoorah of a book that has explored the undesirable ethico-political effects of metaphysical seduction, seems a bizarre 'wrong move'. After all, what could be more metaphysical than the mystical? It *is* a wrong move if understood wrongly. Understood rightly, it is a grammatical joke. Evoking the mystical is to open a space for a free burst of laughter at the sheer strength, tenacity and absurdity of our desire to go beyond the limits of language. The mystical, we might say, is a way of reminding us that we need a reminder. Using the word 'mystical', itself, is an example of the ways in which we are so attached to going beyond the limits of language that we need to stretch, twist and break words in order to show that trying to go beyond a word's limits is, indeed, what we are doing. It's the seriousness with which we are driven to perform such intellectual, theoretical and linguistic acrobatics that I, at least, find so funny. Good jokes may indeed make us laugh at ourselves, but I hope they also leave a nagging discomfort with where we find ourselves as a result of some of the beliefs and assumptions to which we cling. Lewis Carroll's poem, *The Hunting of the Snark: An Agony in Eight Fits*, is a helpful heuristic device to explore this further (Carroll 1891).

The Hunting of the Snark is the tale of a crew of eight men who sail the sea in search of a Snark. A character called Bellman captains them. Bellman has a map. It is a sheet of paper that is 'a perfect and absolute blank'. In the end, the crew don't capture a Snark. It turns out that the Snark was a Boojum. That's the tricky thing about Snarks. Until you encounter them, you can't tell if they are the sort of Snark which are, in fact, a Boojum. And if you do find yourself face to face with a Boojum 'you will softly and suddenly vanish away, and never be met with again' (Carroll 1891). What I want to talk about in this section are the virtues of blank maps and Snarks being Boojums: the mystical.

Maps, unless they are Bellman's, literally consist of lines that represent the world accurately. So accurate are they that they provide the means to locate one's destination, where one is, and perhaps most of all, chart the most direct course towards the destination one seeks. What I've tried to show, via the three grammatical readings of universality, is that each theorist is attached to theory as map drawing and each displayed a dependency upon their map, and its deeply drawn lines, to chart a course towards what it is that they sought. The readings showed that they didn't find what they wanted (let's call it a Snark) but ended up encountering a Boojum instead. The Boojum was conjunctive failure, (im)possibility, and it's the Boojum that I am defending as a defence of universality.

Wittgenstein's *Tractatus Logico-Philosophicus* is the apotheosis of mapping propositions as completely as possible. It is a picture of reason. In the *Tractatus* he explored only six propositions, the first of which was simply 'The world is everything that is the case' (Wittgenstein 1922: 1.0).

Wittgenstein's complex numbering system of his remarks is renowned and often times adopted. The number 5.4711, for example, refers to the primary proposition '5', the fourth component of that proposition, the seventh component of the fourth, and the first component of the first component of the seventh component.[18] It amounts to an incredibly detailed map, we might say. The interesting thing about the *Tractatus*, and the picture of reason that his numbering system conveys, is what Wittgenstein concludes after all this detailed, laborious, effort. He ends the *Tractatus* with one proposition, 7.0, with nothing that follows it. The proposition is 'Whereof one cannot speak thereof one must remain silent', so he does. Proposition 7.0, and what precedes it, is Wittgenstein's mysticism. My point is not to engage in the thriving academic field of Wittgenstein commentary here, but to render conspicuous what I take to be the relationship between this kind of mysticism, reading grammatically, and pictures of the subject.

Returning to the mystical then, what can we take from proposition 7.0? I think the first thing is the failure of theoretical endeavours, of this mapping kind, to satisfy our need for an answer to questions of universality, ethics and International Relations. Bearing in mind that grammatically reading a realist, communitarian and cosmopolitan language game revealed that they were a mapping (digging) endeavour, just as the early Wittgenstein's was, we can re-visit the implications of Wittgenstein saying,

> My propositions are elucidatory in this way: he who understands me finally recognises them as senseless, when he has climbed out through them, on them, over them. (He must so to speak throw away the ladder, after he has climbed up on it.)
> He must surmount these propositions; then he sees the world rightly.
> (Wittgenstein 1922: 6.54)

There's much that could be said about this but, mixing metaphors, I want to emphasise that the lines on the map are akin to the rungs of the ladder. Just as the ladder should be thrown away to see the world rightly, so too should the map *when* all is said and done. The argument I want to make, and have been making in defence of universality, is not that the theorising of Morgenthau's, Walzer's or Beitz's sort shouldn't necessarily be done. This is why I will maintain the readings are not a critique of the language games involved *per se*. Rather, my argument is that the ethico-political value of such endeavours does not lie in the success of the endeavour's outcome: the answer. Nor, from the point of view of a grammatical reading, does it lie in the act of mapping, nor in the lines that have been drawn through the act of mapping. Instead the ethico-political value of language games of universality is that they remind us that we need to throw away something, and that when we do, then we may see the world rightly. Put simply, I want to emphasise the point that theorising in ways that assume a representation of the world – how things really are – show us that we have *missed* the point. This is their ethico-political value and what makes a defence of universality, no matter what its form, defensible but only once the ladder has been thrown away.

Reading grammatically *is* the act of climbing through, on, over, up on the rules of language games (the rungs) to show their limits. It is, ironically, the act of not being captured or seduced by the grammar and rules of language games, nor the answers that they produce, *by* climbing each rung. The implication is that the ladder can't be thrown away after climbing it unless you do, actually, climb it first. It's vital to climb it because, without doing so, we can't discover for ourselves that we haven't got what we wanted. That's what grammatical readings do. In that sense, they leave everything as it is. The only difference is, hopefully, that rather than holding on to the ladder (the language game and all that it produces), we throw it away after noting what it has shown us: the mystical.

So, to recap, proposition 7.0 of the *Tractatus* reminds us that we need to throw away something: our belief that theorising can represent (map) universality, ethics or anything else. We need to lose our desire to understand the world as though language/ethico-political practice has ontological depth. We have missed the ethico-political point if we hold onto our ladder. Another way of putting it is to say 'Not *how* the world is, is the mystical, but *that* it is' (Wittgenstein 1922: 6.44). The mystical, in this context, is Bellman's blank piece of paper. In the end, the point about theorising in these ways is that we are no worse off with a blank: silence. Nevertheless, it's important to remember that an appreciation of the beauty of a blank piece of paper is, perhaps, only possible because we have come to see how a piece covered in violently deep lines and scribbles cannot deliver us to our destination safely. Silence is only golden when it appears in the context of unwelcome and relentless noise.

Evoking the mystical is simply another way of emphasising what I take to be the ethico-political value of reading grammatically and why I seek to defend universality *when* it has been read thus and not before. Reading grammatically requires climbing through, on, over and up the rules of language games. In other words, it requires full engagement with ethico-political practices: seeking to understand them from within their own parameters and assumptions no matter how distasteful or delicious we might find them. Only then, I suggest, can we see what is so seductive about them and therefore so powerful and pervasive. In the end, to say that what is seductive is that they have drawn lines hard is a metaphor. It simply means that when ethico-political practices make distinctions between human and inhuman, violent and peaceful, legitimate and illegitimate, legal and illegal and so on, the task is: (1) to understand that this is indeed what is happening which is why locating a grammar is vital to rendering this conspicuous; (2) to look to see which grammatically generated rules are being deployed to maintain the seduction of the language games so that it retains its hold on us or whomever is captured by it (violently imprisoned sometimes); (3) to recognise that no matter how hard these grammars are policed they can never fully succeed. The porosity of grammar, failure, makes the occasion for ethico-political engagement ever-present; and (4) to throw away the ladder. In other words, throwing away the ladder is to resist and refuse to be seduced by language games that draw these distinctions deeply and violently (hard). Reading grammatically simply suggests that one way of doing this is to remain on the surface of language in order to keep the superficial, that is to say, the porosity of (im)possibility in view, doing ethics and politics. As Cora Diamond noted about the mystical, to proceed this way 'will change what we want to do in ethics' (Diamond 1995: 24). I defend universality because, when read grammatically, I take it to show this.[19] I've resorted to calling it mystical only to highlight the superficiality of language. It only seems mystical if we are seduced by the urge to understand superficiality as a profound notion and/or phenomenon! That's the grammatical joke, but I hope I have conveyed that accompanying my laughter there is great discomfort with the acts and effects of line drawing on people's lives.[20] Of course, my conveyance of the implications of this on people's lives is strictly limited here. That's because I have only grammatically read theorists' language games of universality and ethics and assembled reminders for a particular purpose. That purpose was to simply argue that theorising as map drawing, digging or building rungs of a ladder, is to *miss* the point. Universality seemed like a helpful example because it is one of those words that seems to burst with special, profound, meaning. Bearing in mind that my point is an insignificant one – that we have missed the point – a book that really did address universality, ethics and global politics wouldn't and couldn't be *this* one.

So much for the mystical in relation to Bellman's blank sheet of paper – but what of Boojums and Snarks? I began this chapter by claiming that reading grammatically is a response to

> the problems arising through a misinterpretation of our forms of language [so that they] have the character of depth. They are deep disquietudes; their roots are as deep in us as the forms of our language and their significance is as great as the importance of our language.
>
> (Wittgenstein 1958a: §111)

I will now end the chapter by claiming that our failure to find a Snark is something to be defended because we find ourselves encountering a Boojum instead. It is the final aspect of a grammatical defence of universality.

We've already discussed, at length, the (im)possibility of the desire for an answer being fulfilled by endeavouring to represent the world/reality. I now want to make a few grammatical remarks about this in relation to subjectivity by, again, evoking the mystical. In each of the grammatical readings a picture of the subject (let's call it a Snark) was taken to be the foundation for universality. In the final analysis, the readings revealed that, for each theorist, the grounds and therefore, possibility for universality lay deep within *us* – that universality's 'roots are as deep in us as the forms of language' (ibid.: §111).

Morgenthau's grammar was the transcendent in opposition to the actual. His picture of the subject was that of a form of human nature that was also in opposition with itself whereby man [*sic*] could know the difference between good and evil but could not help but sin. The knowledge of good came from that part of human nature that is divine (the shock of wonderment). The ability to act on it, other than imperfectly came from the actual; selfishness and the lust for power as the non-divine elements of humanity. So, in Morgenthau's case, it seems clear enough that his picture of the subject is a grammatical product. The subject is bifurcated, deeply, along the grammatical line between the transcendent and the actual. Consequently, Morgenthau offers us his solution to international ethics as a transcendent universalist conjunction whereby the transcendent can be reconciled with the actual through the national interest. A concession is given to selfishness and the lust for power in his understanding of an ethic of responsibility but equally, a concession is given to the transcendent through its actualisation in the nation-state. The grounds for a universalist ethic therefore, lay in it being accommodating of *this* picture of the subject. The implicit assumption is that for universality to work and be possible, it must reflect the subject.

In the case of Beitz, his grammar was that of the nonideal distinguished from the ideal. His picture of the subject was of one endowed with the capacity for a moral point of view through reason (the ideal). However, the subject also possesses nonideal aspects which are self-interested and therefore, partial. These nonideal aspects needed to be stripped away when choosing global principles of justice, hence his global veil of ignorance. Beitz's conjunctive solution of ideal universality reflects this picture of the subject perfectly. We have a purported solution that accommodates the moral point of view, prioritises it as the grounds for his cosmopolitanism while at the same time seeking to acknowledge that partiality and interests will make such a solution morally necessary.

And, for Walzer, he attached his communitarianism to a grammatical distinction between members and strangers associating the former with the thick and the latter with the thin. His grammar produced a subject that was both a member and a stranger to those with whom it does not share membership. Indeed, his grammatical distinction is so acute at times that he even labels his picture of the subject a 'divided self'. Again, just as Morgenthau and Beitz did, his binary universalist conjunctive solution mirrors the grammatical separation as something deep within *us*.

What's intriguing here is not only that their universalities have their foundations in their pictures of the subject and reflects them, but that the subject functions *as* the answer to a universalist international ethics.

Grammatically speaking, their pictures of the subject are, in the end, *the* answer to ethics in global politics because that's what is being universalised. Were we to push each theorist and ask, 'In the final analysis, what makes your form of universality possible and what's its point?' I believe each has to answer, 'We, as human beings, do and we are the point.' The logic of this doesn't seem terribly misplaced at first glance. If nothing else, ethics is about how we should treat each other in the world. A focus on the subject as an ethical one with attendant postulations of moral value, responsibility and capacity makes sense. This is what the three pictures of the subject we explored attempted to capture for us.

Grammatically, the interesting thing is how the logic of this seduces us into a particular sort of search: a search to capture what is, ethically, most important about being human. Were we able to capture it, we would, so the language games we've read tell us, have hit upon the foundations of our universal answer to ethics in global politics. We can simply say, foci on the subject of *this* kind send us on a hunting of the Snark (subject). Lewis Carroll's poem tells us that if we encounter a Snark that is Boojum we 'will softly and suddenly vanish away, and never be met with again'.[21] There is virtue in encountering a Boojum I suggest.

The belief that we can capture the subject (Snark) by representing it arises from the misinterpretation our forms of language as deep (Wittgenstein 1958a: §111). I've already argued that when we do that we encounter the failure of the endeavour and a reminder that we need reminding of what it is that we've done. The subject cannot be fully captured by language because, whatever it might be, language does not serve to name or locate what is essential/deep about us. Attempts at capturing subjectivity simply remind us that our mistaken attachment to the notion that we *are*, universally, that which has been represented is an opportunity to make such pictures of the subject 'softly and suddenly vanish away, and never be met with again'. Rather than seeing the lines that form pictures of the subject as hard, deep lines, we would see them for what they are: as soft. So soft, in fact, that their significance to us as markers of what ontologically divides us from one another and/or from what is possible and legitimate may vanish never to be encountered as such a 'thing' again. It's an opportunity to kick away the ladder once and for all and do something else that 'may in no way interfere with the actual use of language; it can in the end only describe it. For it cannot give it any foundation either. It leaves everything as it is' (ibid.: §124).

Just as the world is superficial/mystical, so too is subjectivity. To paraphrase Wittgenstein, it's not how we are that is the mystical but *that* we are. There are so many ways of being in the world, so many ethico-political language games of subjectivity, so many overlapping practices of subjectivity that each person enacts and is subject to, that to map them all and the details of their terrain is an impossible endeavour, let alone finding the elements which are common to all. And, as I've tried to argue throughout this book, we don't even need to try. We can stay on the surface of language and engage with the ethico-political practices of picturing the subject and their effects. We can trace instead how attempts at universally capturing, representing, 'us' impact on the possibility and impossibility of specific people living in specific ways. We can just content ourselves with assembling reminders for a particular purpose. There's no more than that that can be done unless we want to bump our heads against the limits of language and by so doing have removed ourselves from the world and each other by theorising. Given that, I have next to nothing to say about subjectivity, *in itself*, except that there is nothing to be said. To remain silent about that should return us to the rough ground of multiple, ethico-political practices of attempts to say something as the drawing of hard lines.

Closing remarks

This book has been a book about diggers, ways of digging, what has been dug up and how this kind of endeavour cannot satiate our deepest desires for an answer. It is not a pessimistic piece of work but one filled with hope, the hope that our desire to live in the world with others remains with us and that we seek to take every opportunity to remind each other, and ourselves, of what it is that we do (politics as the drawing of lines) that closes our hearts to the possibility of letting some one just live and be. It doesn't mean that 'anything goes' and that all ways of living and being in the world are ethically and politically desirable (Feyerabend 1975). On the contrary, the (im)possibility of universality shows us, by the assembly of reminders for a particular purpose, the danger and harm that come from drawing lines as though they had the character of depth. Were we to kick away the ladder and abandon the requirement of depth, I suggest that the return to the rough ground will keep us where we want to be and where we are anyhow: in the world living with others. Needless to say, a plea to return to the rough ground is not the same as doing it. That's why this book isn't really one that engages with universality, ethics and global politics. It's more accurately a story about how easy it is to be seduced into avoiding such engagement but reminding us that, even then, the opportunity is never fully lost.

Bellman's map of the Ocean, the blank sheet of paper, is a beautiful reminder that as soon as we begin to draw hard lines and believe that we have, indeed, mapped the world, the subject and our course, we may have lost our way and with it our ability to find quite what we are looking for. It is the mystical.

Notes

Introduction

1 See Chapter 6.
2 Later referred to as pictures of the subject.
3 Later referred to as pictures of reason.
4 Later referred to as pictures of ethico-political space.
5 For the moment let's satisfy ourselves by saying that this refers to the way we usually speak to people in, for example, the corner shop when popping in to buy a pint of milk; assuming we are not talking about ideas theoretically or philosophically.
6 *Collins Dictionary of the English Language*, ed. Thomas Hill Long (London and Glasgow: Collins, 1979).
7 Grammatical readings need not be confined to just ethics, universality and IR. For example, Jenny Edkins and Véronique Pin-Fat, 'Jean Bethke Elshtain: Traversing the Terrain Between', in *The Future of International Relations: Masters in the Making?*, ed. Iver Neumann and Ole Waever, *The New International Relations* (London: Routledge, 1997a); Jenny Edkins and Véronique Pin-Fat, 'The Subject of the Political', in *Sovereignty and Subjectivity*, ed. Jenny Edkins, Nalini Persram, and Véronique Pin-Fat (Boulder, CO: Lynne Rienner Publishers, 1997b); Jenny Edkins and Véronique Pin-Fat, 'Through the Wire: Relations of Power and Relations of Violence', *Millennium: Journal of International Studies* 34, no. 1 (2005); Véronique Pin-Fat, 'Why Aren't We Laughing?: Grammatical Investigations in World Politics', *Politics* 17, no. 2 (1997b); Véronique Pin-Fat, '(Im)Possible Universalism: Reading Human Rights in World Politics', *Review of International Studies* 26, no. 4 (2000); Véronique Pin-Fat and Maria Stern, 'The Scripting of Private Jessica Lynch: Biopolitics, Gender and the "Feminization" of the US Military', *Alternatives: Global, Local, Political* 30 (2005); Robin Redhead, 'Imag(in)Ing Women's Agency', *International Feminist Journal of Politics* 9, no. 2 (2007).
8 Published as political and social philosophy, in the same year, was Janna Thompson, *Justice and World Order: A Philosophical Inquiry* (London and New York: Routledge, 1992).
9 See, for example, Molly Cochran, *Normative Theory in International Relations: A Pragmatic Approach* (Cambridge: Cambridge University Press, 1999); Nigel Dower, *World Ethics: The New Agenda*, Edinburgh Studies in World Ethics (Edinburgh: Edinburgh University Press, 1998); and Kimberly Hutchings, *International Political Theory: Rethinking Ethics in a Global Era* (London: SAGE, 1999).
10 I am not claiming that all Realists and all communitarians are universalists. Not only would such a claim be beyond that which is substantiated in this work, it

also stands the risk of being a gross generalisation. All I can say is that beyond the grammatical readings in this book there may be other examples, but one would need to do the reading to demonstrate that this was, indeed, the case.

11 There is absolutely no implication that (im)possible universality is a 'third' way, some other kind of universalism, or indeed a resolution to what it may be. As Wittgenstein puts it, 'One of the greatest hindrances to philosophy is the expectation of new, unheard of, discoveries', in Anthony Kenny, ed. *The Wittgenstein Reader* (Oxford: Blackwell, 1994), p. 270. (Im)possible universality simply denotes the grammar of universality. To say that universality is (im)possible is a grammatical remark. See Chapter 6.

1 Reading grammatically: reading, representation and the limits of language

1 A much earlier, and cruder, version of this appears in Véronique Pin-Fat, 'Ethics and the Limits of Language in International Relations Theory: A Grammatical Investigation' (PhD dissertation, University of Wales Aberystwyth, 1997a); Pin-Fat, 'Why Aren't We Laughing?: Grammatical Investigations in World Politics', *Politics* 17, no. 2 (1997b): 79–86. The difference between what I had earlier called a grammatical investigation and what is now a grammatical reading is that the former had not entirely 'thrown away the ladder'.

2 See Edkins and Pin-Fat for the implications of refusal in relation to sovereign power and biopolitics; Jenny Edkins and Véronique Pin-Fat, 'Life, Power, Resistance', in *Sovereign Lives: Power in Global Politics*, ed. Jenny Edkins, Véronique Pin-Fat, and Michael J. Shapiro (New York: Routledge, 2004) and Edkins and Pin-Fat, 'Through the Wire: Relations of Power and Relations of Violence', *Millennium: Journal of International Studies* 34, no. 1 (2005).

3 The latter is analogous to Wittgenstein's example of 'forming and testing a hypothesis'.

4 A fulsome exploration of this in relation to universality is discussed as the theme of Chapter 6.

5 The difference between a language game and form of life is that the latter provides a wider context of activities in which the activities of a language game make sense. This is *not* to say that forms of life provide the foundation or explanation of language games, which would simply be a metaphysical position, although Wittgenstein is often interpreted in this way. The discussions on forms of life among Wittgenstein scholars are extremely complex and cannot be entered into here. Suffice it to say that to understand the way in which Wittgenstein employs the metaphor of forms of life is often as a juxtaposition against epistemological claims. He says, 'So are you saying that human agreement decides what is true and what is false?' – It is what human beings *say* that is true and false; and they agree in the *language* they use. That is not agreement in opinions but in form of life'; Ludwig Wittgenstein, *Philosophical Investigations*, ed. G.E.M. Anscombe and R. Rhees, trans. G.E.M. Anscombe, 3rd edn (Oxford: Basil Blackwell, 1958a): §241.

6 Ibid.: §124.

7 This quotation is particularly significant because he mentions two pictures: one classically metaphysical 'that men have souls' and the other classically empirical 'that this substance contains two carbon rings'. The notion of investigating the application of pictures therefore, applies equally to all propositions whether 'empirical' or otherwise.

8 Just as the communitarian interpretation of rule following is conservative.

9 This is an aspect of Morgenthau's picture of the subject. See Chapter 3.

10 This refers to an aspect of Beitz's picture of reason. See Chapter 4.

11 This refers to Walzer's picture of political space. See Chapter 5.

12 This is another way of saying that the meaning of a word is its use.
13 See Chapter 3.
14 Why this is only heuristic will become clearer when Wittgenstein's mysticism is discussed below. In the end, this distinction should be 'thrown away', at least in so far as one reads it to mean a distinction that locates differences that reflect 'how things must be'.
15 This is not to imply that there is only one way of playing the game of diplomacy, for example. Rather, there are many 'games', practices, that are involved here. Fierke's use of Wittgenstein stresses his relevance to 'politics' rather than the 'political'. This is a consequence of her interpretation of Wittgenstein that sees him as offering an alternative philosophical *method* relevant to IR and consequently, it marks where our approaches differ.
16 The reading of rule following advanced here therefore differs significantly from those who interpret Wittgenstein to hold a position that is doctrinal, for example, Saul A. Kripke, 'Wittgenstein on Rules and Private Language', in *Perspectives on the Philosophy of Wittgenstein*, ed. Irving Block (Oxford: Basil Blackwell, 1981); Norman Malcolm, 'Wittgenstein's Philosophical Investigations', in *The Philosophy of Mind*, ed. V.C. Chappell (Englewood Cliffs, NJ: Prentice Hall, 1962) or elucidatory, for example, G.P. Baker and P.M.S. Hacker, *Wittgenstein: Understanding and Meaning: An Analytical Commentary on the Philosophical Investigations*, vol. 1 (Oxford: Basil Blackwell, 1980); Hans-Johann Glock, *A Wittgenstein Dictionary* (Oxford: Blackwell, 1996); Paul Johnston, *Wittgenstein and Moral Philosophy* (London: Routledge, 1991); and Anthony Kenny, *The Legacy of Wittgenstein* (Oxford: Basil Blackwell, 1984). In International Relations, see, for example, the use of Wittgenstein in G. Duffy, B. Frederking, and S. Tucker, 'Language Games: Dialogical Analysis of Inf Negotiations', *International Studies Quarterly* 37, no. 3 (1998); K.M. Fierke, *Changing Games, Changing Strategies* (Manchester: Manchester University Press, 1998); K.M. Fierke, 'Links across the Abyss: Language and Logic in International Relations', *International Studies Quarterly* 46 (2002); K.M. Fierke and K.E. Jorgensen, eds, *Constructing International Relations: The Next Generation* (Armonk, NY: M.E. Sharpe, 2001); F.V. Kratochwil, *Rules, Norms and Decisions: On the Conditions of Practical and Legal Reasoning in International Relations and Domestic Affairs* (Cambridge: Cambridge University Press, 1989); Nicholas Greenwood Onuf, *World of Our Making: Rules and Rule in Social Theory and International Relations* (Columbia, SC: University of South Carolina Press, 1989). The problem with thinking that rules are settled by social practice is that (1) this is deeply conservative; and (2) raises the problem of relativism so often directed at 'Wittgensteinians'.
17 The relationship between universality and mysticism is explored further in Chapter 6.
18 Which is *not* to say that *all* theorists do; only the ones discussed in this book.
19 The distinction between time and place here is wholly artificial and is evoked only as a matter of written style in order to emphasise my point.
20 I refer the reader back to the first sentence of this book and Chapter 6. Reintroducing the 'rough ground' would involve writing a different book that looked at a variety of different practices of ethics in world politics that the theorists do not and cannot consider as ethical practices in world politics because of their fantasy of 'what is required'. The possible practices one could look at are so many that no book could cover them all. For single, but different, examples of going to the rough ground, see Edkins and Pin-Fat, 'Life, Power, Resistance', in *Sovereign Lives: Power in Global Politics*, edited by Jenny Edkins, Véronique Pin-Fat and Michael J. Shapiro (New York: Routledge, 2004); Edkins and Pin-Fat, 'Through the Wire: Relations of Power and Relations of Violence'; Pin-Fat,

'(Im)Possible Universalism: Reading Human Rights in World Politics', *Review of International Studies* 26, no. 4 (2000): 663–74; and Pin-Fat and Stern, 'The Scripting of Private Jessica Lynch: Biopolitics, Gender and the "Feminization" of the US Military', *Alternatives: Global, Local, Political* 30, (2005): 25–53.

2 Universality as conjunctive solution: ethics 'and' International Relations

1 The literature is now vast. A brief sample of books dealing with ethics and world politics might include Mark R. Amstutz, *International Ethics: Concepts, Theories, and Cases in Global Politics* (Oxford: Rowman & Littlefield Publishers, 1999); Charles Beitz *et al.*, eds, *International Ethics: A Philosophy and Public Affairs Reader* (Princeton, NJ: Princeton University Press, 1985); Charles R. Beitz, *Political Theory and International Relations* (Princeton, NJ: Princeton University Press, 1979); Chris Brown, *International Relations Theory: New Normative Approaches* (London: Harvester Wheatsheaf, 1992); Chris Brown, *Sovereignty, Rights and Justice: International Political Theory Today* (Cambridge: Polity, 2002); Hedley Bull, 'Order vs. Justice in International Society', *Political Studies* 19, no. 3 (1971); David Campbell, *Politics without Principle: Sovereignty, Ethics, and the Narratives of the Gulf War* (Boulder, CO: Lynne Rienner, 1993); David Campbell, *National Deconstruction: Violence, Identity and Justice in Bosnia* (Minneapolis: University of Minnesota Press, 1997); David Campbell and Michael J. Shapiro, eds, *Moral Spaces: Rethinking Ethics and World Politics* (Minneapolis: Minnesota Press, 1999); Molly Cochran, *Normative Theory in International Relations: A Pragmatic Approach* (Cambridge: Cambridge University Press, 1999); Jean Bethke Elshtain, *New Wine and Old Bottles: International Politics and Ethical Discourse* (Notre Dame, IN: University of Notre Dame Press, 1998); Mervyn Frost, *Towards a Normative Theory of International Relations* (Cambridge: Cambridge University Press, 1986); Mervyn Frost, *Ethics in International Relations: A Constitutive Theory* (Cambridge: Cambridge University Press, 1996); J.E. Hare and C.B. Joynt, *Ethics and International Affairs* (London: Macmillan, 1982); Virginia Held, Sidney Morgenbesser, and Thomas Nagel, eds, *Philosophy, Morality, and International Affairs* (London: Oxford University Press, 1974); Stanley Hoffmann, *Duties Beyond Borders: On the Limits and Possibilities of Ethical International Politics* (Syracuse, NY: Syracuse University Press, 1981); Stanley Hoffmann, *The Political Ethics of International Relations* (New York: Carnegie Council on Ethics and International Affairs, 1988); Kimberly Hutchings, *International Political Theory: Rethinking Ethics in a Global Era* (London. Sage, 1999); Michael Ignatieff, *The Lesser Evil: Political Ethics in an Age of Terror* (Edinburgh: Edinburgh University Press, 2004); K. Kipnis and D.T. Meyers, eds, *Political Realism and International Morality: Ethics in the Nuclear Age* (London: Westview Press, 1987); Andrew Linklater, *Men and Citizens in the Theory of International Relations* (London: Macmillan, 1990); Andrew Linklater, *The Transformation of Political Community: Ethical Foundations of the Post-Westphalian Era* (Oxford: Polity, 1998); Alastair J.H. Murray, *Reconstructing Realism: Between Power Politics and Cosmopolitan Ethics* (Keele: Keele University Press, 1997); Robert J. Myers, ed., *International Ethics in the Nuclear Age* (Lanham, MD: University Press of America, 1987); Terry Nardin, *Law, Morality and the Relations of States* (Princeton, NJ: Princeton University Press, 1983); Terry Nardin and David R. Mapel, eds, *Traditions of International Ethics* (Cambridge: Cambridge University Press, 1993); Richard Norman, *Ethics, Killing and War* (Cambridge: Cambridge University Press, 1995); Felix E. Oppenheim, *The Place of Morality in Foreign Policy* (Lexington, MA: Lexington Books, 1991); Ralph Pettman, ed., *Moral Claims in World Affairs* (London: Croom Helm, 1979); Fiona Robinson, *Globalising Care: Ethics, Feminist Theory, and*

International Relations (Oxford: Westview, 1998); Richard Shapcott, *Justice, Community and Dialogue in International Relations* (Cambridge: Cambridge University Press, 2001); Janna Thompson, *Justice and World Order: A Philosophical Inquiry* (London: Routledge, 1992); Kenneth W. Thompson, ed., *Ethics and International Relations* (Oxford: Transaction Books, 1985a); Andrew Valls, ed., *Ethics in International Affairs: Theories and Cases* (Oxford: Rowman & Littlefield, 2000); R. John Vincent, *Human Rights and International Relations* (Cambridge: Cambridge University Press, 1986); R.B.J. Walker, *Inside/Outside: International Relations as Political Theory* (Cambridge: Cambridge University Press, 1993); Michael Walzer, *Just and Unjust Wars: A Moral Argument with Historical Illustrations* (London: Allen Lane, 1977); Michael Walzer, *Thick and Thin: Moral Argument at Home and Abroad* (Notre Dame, IN: University of Notre Dame Press, 1994c); Michael Walzer, *Arguing About War* (New Haven, CT: Yale University Press, 2004a).

2 Nickolas Ashford and Valerie Simpson, *Ain't No Mountain High Enough*, performed by Marvin Gaye and Tammi Terrell (Motown, 1966).

3 By cognitive status what is meant is whether an ethical proposition can be either true or false and, therefore, count as a claim to knowledge rather than preference, for example.

4 A well-known example of a non-cognitive theory of ethics is A.J. Ayer's 'boo–hooray theory'. On his view, moral utterances do not state anything except the reactions of the speaker; a 'hooray' or 'boo'. A.J. Ayer, *Language, Truth and Logic* (London: Gollancz, 1936).

5 See, for example, Steven Forde, 'Varieties of Realism – Thucydides and Machiavelli', *Journal of Politics* 54, no. 2 (1992); Steven Forde, 'Classical Realism', in *Traditions of International Ethics*, ed. Terry Nardin and David R. Mapel (Cambridge: Cambridge University Press, 1993); Martin Wight, *International Theory: The Three Traditions*, ed. Gabriele Wight and Brian Porter (Leicester: Leicester University Press, 1994). However, it is by no means clear that Machiavelli is an amoralist; see Walker, *Inside/Outside: International Relations as Political Theory*, Chapter 2.

6 I follow Hollis in using positivism in the wider sense to cover positive science and logical positivism. As Hollis points out:

> At the narrow end, I have found Positivism used, especially in international relations, to mean a behaviourism so fierce that it rejects all psychological data and qualitative methods. This is clear enough, but, since it is a specialised usage, I suggest regarding it as a tendentious one, due to a disputable belief that, because only behaviour is observable, science should set its limits accordingly.
>
> (Martin Hollis, *The Philosophy of Social Science: An Introduction* Cambridge: Cambridge University Press, 1994: 42)

7 IR was so retarded in its consideration of these issues that it prompted Frost to, brilliantly, label IR 'the backward discipline'; see Frost, *Towards a Normative Theory of International Relations*.

8 In IR, the 'first debate' was the debate between Idealists and Realists and the 'second debate' between behaviouralists and classicists; Hedley Bull, 'International Theory: The Case for a Classical Approach', *World Politics* 18, no. 3 (1966).

9 There are certain disadvantages to calling this the 'third debate'. Primary among them is that this seems to imply that the problems of separating fact from value were not present in the 'first' and 'second' debates.

10 For an alternative, feminist, recounting of this story, see Christine Sylvester,

Feminist International Relations: An Unfinished Journey (Cambridge: Cambridge University Press, 2002).

3 Divine universality: Morgenthau, alchemy and the national interest

1 This chapter was first published as Véronique Pin-Fat, 'The Metaphysics of the National Interest and the "Mysticism" of the Nation State: Reading Hans J. Morgenthau', *Review of International Studies* 31, no. 2 (2005).
2 Jim George's book is one of the most sustained attacks on the purported positivism of Realism; Jim George, *Discourses of Global Politics: A Critical (Re)Introduction to International Relations* (Boulder, CO: Lynne Rienner Publishers, 1994). Others who claim that Morgenthau is a positivist would include Martin Griffiths, *Realism, Idealism and International Politics: A Reinterpretation* (London: Routledge, 1992); Justin Rosenberg, 'What's the Matter with Realism?', *Review of International Studies* 16, no. 4 (1990); Steve Smith, 'The Forty Years Detour: The Resurgence of Normative Theory in International Relations', *Millennium: Journal of International Studies* 21, no. 3 (1992); J. Ann Tickner, 'Hans Morgenthau's Principles of Political Realism: A Feminist Reformulation', *Millennium: Journal of International Studies* 17, no. 3 (1988). For a different form of argumentation which claims that Realism is necessarily unconcerned with ethics, see, for example, Jack Donnelly, 'Twentieth-Century Realism', in *Traditions of International Ethics*, ed. Terry Nardin and David R. Mapel (Cambridge: Cambridge University Press, 1993); Jean Bethke Elshtain, *Women and War*, with a new epilogue edn (Chicago: University of Chicago Press, 1995).
3 In IR, Kenneth Waltz is the most famous positivist and Realist. However, it goes without saying that he is no village idiot and offers a form of positivism that uses a deductivo-nomological model. See Kenneth N. Waltz, *Theory of International Politics* (New York: McGraw-Hill Publishing Co., 1979).
4 The pages to which I refer are his (in)famous 'Six Principles of Political Realism', in Hans J. Morgenthau, *Politics among Nations: The Struggle for Power and Peace*, 3rd edn (New York: Alfred Knopf, 1964), 3–15. For more sensitive readings of Morgenthau, see, for example, William Bain, 'Deconfusing Morgenthau: Moral Inquiry and Classical Realism Reconsidered', *Review of International Studies* 26, no. 3 (2000); Murielle Cozette, 'Reclaiming the Critical Dimension of Realism: Hans J. Morgenthau on the Ethics of Scholarship', *Review of International Studies* 34 (2008); A.J.H. Murray, 'The Moral Politics of Hans Morgenthau', *Review of Politics* 58, no. winter (1996); Ulrik Enemark Peterson, 'Breathing Nietzsche's Air: New Reflections on Morgenthau's Concepts of Power and Nature', *Alternatives* 24, no. 1 (1999); Hans Karl Pichler, 'The Godfathers of "Truth": Max Weber and Carl Schmitt in Morgenthau's Theory of Power Politics', *Review of International Studies* 24, no. 2 (1988); Benjamin Wong, 'Hans Morgenthau's Anti-Machiavellian Machiavellianism', *Millennium: Journal of International Studies* 29, no. 2 (2000).
5 Russell also focuses on the details of Morgenthau's metaphysics which underlie his separation of thought and action in G. Russell, *Hans J. Morgenthau and the Ethics of American Statecraft* (London: Louisiana State University Press, 1990).
6 Due to the limitations of space I shall not address the gender-bias in Morgenthau's notion of 'man' and 'human nature', though it is acknowledged that this is an important aspect of his language game. For a detailed argument that addresses this point, see Tickner, 'Hans Morgenthau's Principles of Political Realism: A Feminist Reformulation'.
7 The implications of Morgenthau's view of the relationship between sense-objects and knowledge deny the possibility that he is an empiricist or a positivist. See the section on reason for a sustained elaboration of this theme.

8 An anonymous reviewer pointed this out to me, for which I am grateful.
9 Morgenthau's definition of man's 'consciousness of the divine' is as the unfulfilled longing for union with God in perfection.
10 Here I am in agreement with Griffith's statement that Morgenthau's understanding of human nature 'invokes a metaphysical and religious conception of "fallen man"'. See Griffiths, *Realism, Idealism and International Politics: A Reinterpretation*, 38. This mitigates against a reading of Morgenthau as a positivist.
11 This argument is only compelling if one accepts that the single criterion of selfishness is self-reference. On this formulation, selfishness is unavoidable in so far as every action requires an actor.
12 See also Hans J. Morgenthau, 'The Intellectual and Moral Dilemma of History', *Christianity and Crisis* (8 February 1960); Hans J. Morgenthau, 'The Sanctity of Moral Law', *Christian Ethics Today: Journal of Christian Ethics* 3:4, no. 12 On-Line (1997).
13 However, what Plato and Aristotle believed to be universal differs. In the case of Plato, it was the Forms (*eide*) and, in the case of Aristotle, substance (*ousia*).
14 Aristotle, quoted in Russell, *Hans J. Morgenthau and the Ethics of American Statecraft*, 79.
15 For a discussion of Weber's notion of a world disenchanted, see Alkis Kontos, 'The World Disenchanted', in *The Barbarism of Reason: Max Weber and the Twilight of Enlightenment*, ed. Asher Horowitz and Terry Maley (Toronto: University of Toronto Press, 1994).
16 The links of Morgenthau's work with Weber are now well documented. See Michael Joseph Smith, *Realist Thought from Weber to Kissinger* (Baton Rouge: Louisiana State University Press, 1986); S.P. Turner and R.A. Factor, *Max Weber and the Dispute over Reason and Value: A Study in Philosophy, Ethics and Politics* (London: Routledge & Kegan Paul, 1984). Although Morgenthau only explicitly references Weber once in his work (*Politics Among Nations*), in later life he acknowledged his intellectual debts to his thought. He later said,

> Weber's political thought possessed all the intellectual and moral qualities I had looked for in vain in the contemporary literature inside and outside the universities . . . While as a citizen he was a passionate observer of the political scene and a frustrated participant in it, as a scholar he looked at politics without passion and pursued no political purpose beyond the intellectual one of understanding.

See Hans J. Morgenthau, 'Fragment of an Intellectual Autobiography', in *Truth and Tragedy: A Tribute to Hans Morgenthau*, ed. Kenneth W. Thompson and Robert J. Myers (Washington, DC: The New Republic Book Company, Inc., 1977), 7.
17 On the importance of 'speaking truth to power' for Morgenthau, see Cozette, 'Reclaiming the Critical Dimension of Realism: Hans J. Morgenthau on the Ethics of Scholarship'; Hans J. Morgenthau, *Truth and Power: Essays of a Decade, 1960–1970* (London: Pall Mall Press, 1970); Robert J. Myers, 'Hans J. Morgnethau on Speaking Truth to Power: A Profile', *Society* 29, no. 2 (1992); Kenneth W. Thompson and Robert J. Myers, eds, *Truth and Tragedy: A Tribute to Hans Morgenthau* (Washington, DC: The New Republic Book Company, Inc., 1977).
18 Morgenthau accepted this, repeating Weber's position almost verbatim in Hans J. Morgenthau, *Scientific Man vs. Power Politics* (Chicago: University of Chicago Press, 1946), 195.
19 Guenther Roth and W. Schluchter, *Max Weber's Vision of History* (Berkeley: University of California Press, 1979), 85.

20 This is not the only difficulty, of course. The whole notion of transcendent, time-less, eternal universals, the existence of God, and so on, is deeply contentious. I do not address well-rehearsed criticisms here.

4 Ideal universality: Beitz, reason and the ghost of Houdini

1 The picture of ethico-political space will also be examined but the chapter seeks to show how and why it is dependent upon pictures of the subject and reason.
2 I am using the word 'faith', not theologically, but in an everyday sense in order to evoke the idea of complete trust or confidence in something. In this case, it is reason.
3 Precisely what is to be distributed internationally will be discussed below.
4 Chris Brown locates *A Theory of Justice* as a key moment in the 'revival of normative ethics' Brown, *International Relations Theory: New Normative Approaches* (London: Harvester Wheatsheaf, 1992), 177. Rawls' work has also been characterised as 'a return to the ground-level study of desirability' Chandran Kukathas and Philip Pettit, *Rawls: A Theory of Justice and Its Critics* (Oxford: Polity Press, 1990), 6. And as 'a welcome return to an older tradition of substantive, rather than semantic and political philosophy' Norman Daniels, ed. *Reading Rawls: Critical Studies on Rawls' 'A Theory of Justice'* (New York: Basic Books, 1989), xi.
5 Effectively, this is Beitz's version of what I have called elsewhere the double whammy.
6 The terms 'nonideal world' and 'ideal theory' are Beitz's own; Beitz, *Political Theory and International Relations* (Princeton, NJ: Princeton University Press, 1979).
7 See also ibid.: 152.
8 See also John Rawls, 'Kantian Constructivism in Moral Theory', *Journal of Philosophy* 77 (1980), 521.
9 Beitz knows full well that this is not an easy position to argue. As an 'assemblage of reminders for a particular purpose' this book cannot provide sufficient detail on the nuances of his argument. Beitz disagrees with the more constructivist elements of Rawls' Kantianism. See Charles R. Beitz, 'Cosmopolitan Ideals and National Sentiment', *Journal of Philosophy* 80 (1983); Rawls, 'Kantian Constructivism in Moral Theory'.
10 Accordingly, much of *Political Theory* is a critique of Realism and also specific aspects of Morgenthau's work.
11 It is important to note that I am using the term 'liberal' differently to the way in which Beitz would.
12 It also requires the other chapters on Morgenthau and Walzer to see how their grammars, both different to Beitz's, lead them to picture different subjects to his.
13 In other words, the subject that occupies the global original position occupies it by virtue of the essential features of being human and in that sense, is represen-tative of humanity and not a specific individual.
14 Hence Beitz, as Rawls, is a liberal contractarian.
15 Beitz, *Political Theory and International Relations*, 139.
16 Beitz establishes this by drawing an analogy between natural resources and Rawls' treatment of natural talents. Charles R. Beitz, *Political Theory and International Relations*, 2nd edn (Princeton, NJ: Princeton University Press, 1999), 136–43.
17 Rawls' two principles, as cited by Beitz, are:

> 1. Each person is to have an equal right to the most extensive total system of equal basic liberties compatible with a similar system of liberty for all. 2.

> Social and economic inequalities are to be arranged so that they are both:
> (a) to the greatest benefit of the least advantaged, consistent with the just
> savings principle [the difference principle], and (b) attached to offices and
> positions open to all under conditions of fair equality of opportunity.
>
> (Ibid.: 129–30)

18 However, in the 2nd edition of *Political Theory* he accepts that there is more to
   Realism than this; ibid.: 185–91. It is also clear that a grammatical reading of
   Morgenthau does not agree with Beitz's characterisation of Morgenthau as a
   moral sceptic. See Chapter 3 of this book.
19 At least according to the arguments Beitz presents in the first edition of *Political
   Theory*.
20 See the sources referenced in this chapter.
21 See Chapter 1 in this book.
22 What this 'something' might be is discussed in Chapter 6.

5 Binary universality: Walzer, thinning the thick and fattening up the thin

1 Morgenthau also agrees with this.
2 The literature Walzer's work has generated is vast. A brief sample could include
   Karl-Otto Apel, 'Globalization and the Need for Universal Ethics', *European
   Journal of Social Theory* 3, no. 2 (2000); Veit Bader, 'Citizenship and Exclusion:
   Radical Democracy, Community, and Justice. Or, What Is Wrong with
   Communitarianism?', *Political Theory* 23, no. 2 (1995); Charles R. Beitz,
   'Nonintervention and Communal Integrity', *Philosophy and Public Affairs* 9,
   no. 4 (1980b); Alex J. Bellamy, 'Supreme Emergencies and the Protection of
   Non-Combatants in War', *International Affairs* 80, no. 5 (2004); Ken Booth, Tim
   Dunne, and Michael Cox, 'How Might We Live? Global Ethics in a New
   Century', *Review of International Studies* 26, no. 2 (2000); Chris Brown, 'Cultural
   Diversity and International Political Theory', *Review of International Studies* 26,
   no. 2 (2000); Hedley Bull, 'Recapturing the Just War for Political Theory', *World
   Politics* 31, no. 4 (1979); Anne Caldwell, 'Empire and Exception', *New Political
   Science* 28, no. 4 (2006); Martin L. Cook, 'Michael Walzer's Concept of
   "Supreme Emergency"', *Journal of Military Ethics* 6, no. 2 (2007); Omar
   Dahbour, 'Three Models of Global Community', *The Journal of Ethics* 9 (2005);
   Gerald Doppelt, 'Walzer's Theory of Morality in International Relations',
   Philosophy and Public Affairs 8, no. 1 (1978); James M. Dubik, 'Human Rights,
   Command Responsibility, and Walzer's Just War Theory', *Philosophy and
   Public Affairs* 11, no. 4 (1982); Jean Bethke Elshtain, 'Terrorism, Regime
   Change, and Just War: Reflections on Michael Walzer', *Journal of Military
   Ethics* 6, no. 2 (2007); W.B. Gallie, 'Wanted: A Philosophy of International
   Relations', *Political Studies* 37, no. 3 (1979); W.A. Galston, 'Community,
   Democracy, Philosophy: The Political Thought of Michael Walzer', *Political
   Theory* 17, no. 1 (1989); D. Lackey, 'A Modern Theory of Just War', *Ethics* 92
   (1982); Ernesto Laclau, 'The Death and Resurrection of the Theory of Ideology',
   Journal of Political Ideologies 1, no. 3 (1996); David Luban, 'The Romance of
   the Nation-State', *Philosophy and Public Affairs* 9, no. 4 (1980); Lionel K.
   McPherson, 'The Limits of the War Convention', *Philosophy and Social
   Criticism* 31, no. 2 (2005); Monica Mookherjee, 'Exclusion, Internalization,
   Harm: Towards a Case-Based Alternative to Walzer's Thin Minimalism',
   Ethnicities 3, no. 3 (2003); Brian Orend, *Michael Walzer on War and Justice*
   (Cardiff: University of Wales Press, 2000); Alan Revering, 'Eschatology in the
   Political Theory of Michael Walzer', *Journal of Religious Ethics* 33, no. 1 (2005);
   Richard Shapcott, 'Anti-Cosmopolitanism, Pluralism and the Cosmopolitan

Harm Principle', *Review of International Studies* 34 (2008); Daniel Statman, 'Supreme Emergencies Revisited', *Ethics* 117 (2006); Caroline Walsh, 'Rawls and Walzer on Non-Dometic Justice', *Contemporary Political Theory* 6 (2007).

3   Global politics for Walzer is international politics. That is to say the political relations between states within what he, following Hedley Bull, considers to be an international society. Hedley Bull, *The Anarchical Society: A Study of Order in World Politics* (London: Macmillan, 1977).

4   For Morgenthau, the accident is an alchemical one that leads him back into the jaws of totalitarianism and for Beitz, it is his accidental Houdini moment.

5   This is not to suggest that escape is ever possible. I am not proposing a grammatically emancipatory project. I am only suggesting that we read grammatically in order to trace where such seductions lead us – assembling reminders for a particular purpose. To do any more than that would be to find myself 'digging'.

6   I am aware that the implication of reading grammatically is to highlight how we may find ourselves seduced by the same pictures. See Chapter 1 of this book.

7   It is important to note that for Walzer, membership of a political community means membership of a state. As he says, 'Men and women without membership anywhere are stateless persons', Michael Walzer, *Spheres of Justice: A Defence of Pluralism and Equality* (Oxford: Blackwell, 1983), 31.

8   This is not to say that this is necessarily a weakness, only that this signals a *grammatical* feature of Walzer's language game. Indeed, all language games must accept something as 'given' otherwise they could never get off the ground. Thus, to criticise this as a weakness would be to misunderstand the point of a grammatical reading, since it is not the questioning of the truth and falsity of the assumptions that is at stake here.

9   Walzer is a committed public intellectual and takes seriously the view that he has a role to play as a social critic that should be engaged in the politics of his political community (the USA), not just theorising.

10   Walzer views the social critic as one 'who holds up a mirror to society'; Walzer, *Thick and Thin: Moral Argument at Home and Abroad*, 42.

11   I use naturalism to refer to the philosophical doctrine. See Martin Hollis, 'The Last Post?', in *International Theory: Postivism and Beyond*, ed. Steve Smith, Ken Booth, and Marysia Zalewski (Cambridge: Cambridge University Press, 1996). That is not to say that Walzer manages to avoid naturalism completely as his evocation of the rights to life and liberty grammatically demonstrate.

12   This makes objectivity possible for Descartes.

13   Walzer takes the phrase 'supreme emergency' from Winston Churchill. See Walzer, *Arguing About War* (New Haven, CT: Yale University Press, 2004), 33.

14   In everyday usage 'fat chance' means little or no hope of success. For example, someone says, 'This week I'm going to win the £3 million lottery jackpot' to which comes the reply 'Fat chance!'

15   The idea of 'fit' is really his original notion of contract in *Just and Unjust Wars*. In the case of a 'genuine contract', he says a state's 'territorial integrity and political sovereignty can be defended in exactly the same way as individual life and liberty' because those rights are simply the collective form of individual rights. Walzer, *Just and Unjust Wars: A Moral Argument with Historical Illustrations* (London: Allen Lane, 1977), 54.

16   Walzer talks of foreigners as strangers here. See Michael Walzer, 'The Moral Standing of States: A Response to Four Critics', in *International Ethics*, ed. Charles Beitz, *et al.*, *A Philosophy and Public Affairs Reader* (Princeton, NJ: Princeton University Press, 1985).

17   Walzer lists the 'sheer number of recent horrors' that fall under this category for him: Bosnia and Kosovo, Rwanda, the Sudan, Sierra Leone, the Congo, Liberia and East Timor. Walzer, *Arguing About War*, xii.

18 Walzer is quite clear that even in these cases, we cannot shy away from the fact that war itself may produce immoralities albeit justifiable *in extremis*. Ibid.

6 In defence of universality: (im)possible universalism Notes

1 Mick Jagger and Keith Richards, *You Can't Always Get What You Want* Performed by The Rolling Stones (Decca Records/ABKCO, 1968).
2 There is no implication that one is necessarily a good language learner or a good reader. There is the implication that one should learn as best one can though, if nothing else out of respect for the person's work whom you are reading.
3 See Chapter 1 for more detail on learning a language.
4 There is an issue of meaning, intention and authorship that arises at this point. Unfortunately, we can't explore it here but Wittgenstein's private language argument is very relevant. See Pin-Fat, '(Im)Possible Universalism: Reading Human Rights in World Politics', *Review of International Studies* 26, no. 4 (2000).; Wittgenstein, *Philosophical Investigations* (Oxford: Basil Blackwell, 1958).
5 For more on thinking producing ways of being in the world and therefore, it being an ethico-political act, see Véronique Pin-Fat, 'How Do We Begin to Think About the World?', in *Global Politics: A New Introduction*, ed. Jenny Edkins and Maja Zehfuss (London: Routledge, 2008).
6 Needless to say, a grammatical reading doesn't understand language this way. It seeks to stay on the surface of language (word–word relations) and resist the urge to dig. See Chapter 1.
7 See Chapter 1 and also Wittgenstein's private language argument that is an argument against the possibility of being subjective in this sense of the word. Being subjective relies on a Cartesian picture of the subject among other things. See also Pin-Fat, '(Im)Possible Universalism: Reading Human Rights in World Politics'.
8 There is absolutely no implication here that language games have only one grammar. It depends on which reminders one wants to assemble for which purpose that help one decide which grammatical feature of a language game to focus on.
9 For the biopolitical effects of inclusion by exclusion, see Georgio Agamben, *Homo Sacer: Sovereign Power and Bare Life*, trans. Daniel Heller-Roazen (Stanford, CA: Stanford University Press, 1998); Georgio Agamben, *Means without Ends: Notes on Politics*, trans. Vincenzo Binetti (Minneapolis: University of Minnesota Press, 2000); Jenny Edkins, 'Whatever Politics', in *Sovereignty and Life: Essays on Georgio Agamben*, ed. Matthew Carlarco and Seven DeCaroli (Stanford, CA: Stanford University Press, 2007); Jenny Edkins, Véronique Pin-Fat, and Michael J. Shapiro, eds, *Sovereign Lives: Power in Global Politics* (New York: Routledge,2004); Cristina Masters and Elizabeth Dauphinée, eds, *The Logics of Biopower and the War on Terror* (Basingstoke: Palgrave Macmillan,2007); V. Pin-Fat and M. Stern, 'The Scripting of Private Jessica Lynch: Biopolitics, Gender and the "Feminization" of the US Military', *Alternatives: Global, Local, Political* 30, (2005).
10 Thanks to Jenny Edkins for all the long-standing, still ongoing, conversations on whether drawing lines is unavoidable.
11 Jagger and Richards, *You Can't Always Get What You Want.*
12 Most pervasive in global politics are the language games that deploy universal human rights. For grammatical readings of some of them, see Pin-Fat, '(Im)Possible Universalism: Reading Human Rights in World Politics'; Robin Redhead, 'Imag(in)Ing Women's Agency', *International Feminist Journal of Politics* 9, no. 2 (2007).

13 I feel reasonably confident that this isn't the only aspect one could see so I'm not making any claims about this being the only conclusion that one could draw from reading universality grammatically. Much will depend on why someone wants to do a grammatical reading.

14 I should refrain from generalising and say, more accurately, that divine universalism, ideal universalism and binary universalism are leaky. More grammatical readings of universality would need to be done to say anything more.

15 All lines are like this, I suspect, when they are read grammatically.

16 Edkins and Pin-Fat, 'Life, Power, Resistance', in *Sovereign Lives: Power in Global Politics*, edited by Jenny Edkins, Véronique Pin-Fat and Michael J. Shapiro. New York: Routledge, 2004.; Edkins and Pin-Fat, 'Through the Wire: Relations of Power and Relations of Violence', *Millennium: Journal of International Studies* 34, no. 1 (2005).; Pin-Fat and Stern, 'The Scripting of Private Jessica Lynch: Biopolitics, Gender and the "Feminization" of the US Military'.

17 In *The Hunting of the Snark* saying something 'thrice' is significant. Lewis Carroll plays on its significance in the poem, just as I have been doing throughout this book. Carroll effectively exploits the idea that 'The proof is complete if only I've stated it thrice' only to conclude that 'much yet remains to be said'. I agree.

18 'Propositions are truth-functions of elementary propositions. (An elementary proposition is a truth-function of itself)' Ludwig Wittgenstein, *Tractatus Logico-Philosophicus*, trans. C.K. Ogden (London: Routledge & Kegan Paul, 1922), 5.0.

19 This isn't to suggest that only grammatical readings of universality could show this. I would like to think that grammatical readings of many things could achieve the same. See Jenny Edkins, Nalini Persram, and Véronique Pin-Fat, eds, *Sovereignty and Subjectivity*, Critical Perspectives on World Politics (Boulder, CO: Lynne Rienner, 1997); Edkins and Pin-Fat, 'Through the Wire: Relations of Power and Relations of Violence'; Pin-Fat and Stern, 'The Scripting of Private Jessica Lynch: Biopolitics, Gender and the "Feminization" of the US Military'; Redhead, 'Imag(in)Ing Women's Agency'.

20 The line between laughter and weeping is itself a precarious one. I have certainly experienced laughing one moment and then found myself crying in the next.

21 Lewis Carroll, *The Hunting of the Snark: An Agony in Eight Fits* (New York: Macmillan, 1891), Fit the Third, The Baker's Tale.

Bibliography

Ackerly, Brooke A., Maria Stern, and Jacqui True, eds. *Feminist Methodologies for International Relations.* Cambridge: Cambridge University Press, 2006.

Adams, Douglas. *Life, the Universe and Everything*: Houndsmills: Pan Macmillan, 1982.

Agamben, Georgio. *Homo Sacer: Sovereign Power and Bare Life.* Trans. Daniel Heller-Roazen. Stanford, CA: Stanford University Press, 1998.

— —. *Means without Ends: Notes on Politics.* Trans. Vincenzo Binetti. Minneapolis: University of Minnesota Press, 2000.

Amstutz, Mark R. *International Ethics: Concepts, Theories, and Cases in Global Politics.* Oxford: Rowman & Littlefield Publishers, 1999.

Apel, Karl-Otto. 'Globalization and the Need for Universal Ethics'. *European Journal of Social Theory* 3, no. 2 (2000): 137–55.

Aron, Raymond. 'Max Weber and Power Politics'. In *Max Weber and Sociology Today*, ed. O. Stammer. Oxford: Basil Blackwell, 1971.

Ayer, A.J. *Language, Truth and Logic.* London: Gollancz, 1936.

Bader, Veit. 'Citizenship and Exclusion: Radical Democracy, Community, and Justice. Or, What Is Wrong with Communitarianism?' *Political Theory* 23, no. 2 (1995): 211–46.

Bain, William. 'Deconfusing Morgenthau: Moral Inquiry and Classical Realism Reconsidered'. *Review of International Studies* 26, no. 3 (2000): 445–64.

Baker, Gordon. *Wittgenstein's Method: Neglected Aspects.* Oxford: Blackwell, 2004.

Baker, G.P., and P.M.S. Hacker. *Wittgenstein: Understanding and Meaning: An Analytical Commentary on the Philosophical Investigations.* Vol. 1. Oxford: Basil Blackwell, 1980.

— —. *Wittgenstein: Rules, Grammar and Necessity: An Analytical Commentary on the Philosophical Investigations.* Vol. 2. Oxford: Basil Blackwell, 1985.

— —. 'Malcolm on Language and Rules'. *Philosophy* 65 (1990): 167–79.

Baldwin, David, ed. *Neoliberalism and Neorealism: The Contemporary Debate.* New York: Columbia University Press, 1993.

Beitz, Charles R. *Political Theory and International Relations.* Princeton, NJ: Princeton University Press, 1979.

— —. 'Justice and International Relations'. In *John Rawls' Theory of Justice*, edited by G.H. Blocker. Athens, OH: Ohio University Press, 1980a.

— —. 'Nonintervention and Communal Integrity'. *Philosophy and Public Affairs* 9, no. 4 (1980b): 385–91.

— —. 'Cosmopolitan Ideals and National Sentiment'. *Journal of Philosophy* 80 (1983): 591–99.

— —. *Political Equality: An Essay in Democratic Theory*. Princeton, NJ: Princeton University Press, 1989.

— —. 'Sovereignty and Morality in International Affairs'. In *Political Theory Today*, edited by David Held. Cambridge: Cambridge University Press, 1991.

— —. *Political Theory and International Relations*. 2nd edn. Princeton, NJ: Princeton University Press, 1999.

— —. 'Rawls's Law of Peoples'. *Ethics* 110, no. 4 (2000): 669–96.

— —. 'Reflections'. *Review of International Studies* 31, no. 2 (2005): 409–23.

Beitz, Charles, Marshall Cohen, Thomas Scanlon, and A. John Simmons, eds. *International Ethics*. Princeton, NJ: Princeton University Press, 1985.

Bellamy, Alex J. 'Supreme Emergencies and the Protection of Non-Combatants in War'. *International Affairs* 80, no. 5 (2004): 829–50.

Bernstein, Richard J. *The Restructuring of Social and Political Theory*. London: Methuen, 1979.

— —. *Beyond Objectivism and Relativism*. Oxford: Basil Blackwell, 1989.

— —. *The New Constellation: The Ethical-Political Horizons of Modernity/Postmodernity*. Cambridge: Polity Press, 1991.

Binkley, Timothy. *Wittgenstein's Language*. The Hague: Martinus Nijhoff, 1973.

Bonanate, Luigi. *Ethics and International Politics*. Trans. John Irving. Cambridge: Polity Press, 1995.

Booth, Ken, Tim Dunne, and Michael Cox. 'How Might We Live? Global Ethics in a New Century'. *Review of International Studies* 26, no. 2 (2000): 1–28.

Booth, Ken, and Nicholas J. Wheeler. *The Security Dilemma: Fear, Cooperation, and Trust in World Politics*. Basingstoke: Palgrave Macmillan, 2008.

Boyle, Joseph. 'Just and Unjust Wars: Casuistry and the Boundaries of the Moral World'. *Ethics and International Affairs* 11 (1997): 83–98.

Brown, Chris. 'Ethics of Coexistence: The International Theory of Terry Nardin'. *Review of International Studies* 14 (1988): 213–22.

— —. 'Cosmopolitan Confusions: A Reply to Hoffman'. *Paradigms: The Kent Journal of International Relations* 2, no. 2 (1988/89): 102–11.

— —. *International Relations Theory: New Normative Approaches*. London: Harvester Wheatsheaf, 1992.

— —. 'Cultural Diversity and International Political Theory'. *Review of International Studies* 26, no. 2 (2000): 199–214.

— —. *Sovereignty, Rights and Justice: International Political Theory Today*. Cambridge: Polity, 2002.

— —. 'The House That Chuck Built: Twenty-Five Years of Reading Charles Beitz'. *Review of International Studies* 31, no. 2 (2005): 371–79.

Bull, Hedley. 'International Theory: The Case for a Classical Approach'. *World Politics* 18, no. 3 (1966).

— —. 'Order Vs. Justice in International Society'. *Political Studies* 19, no. 3 (1971).

— —. *The Anarchical Society: A Study of Order in World Politics*. London: Macmillan, 1977.

— —. 'Recapturing the Just War for Political Theory'. *World Politics* 31, no. 4 (1979): 588–99.

Caldwell, Anne. 'Empire and Exception'. *New Political Science* 28, no. 4 (2006): 489–506.

Campbell, David. *Politics without Principle: Sovereignty, Ethics, and the Narratives of the Gulf War*. Boulder, Co.: Lynne Rienner, 1993.

— —. *National Deconstruction: Violence, Identity and Justice in Bosnia*. Minneapolis: University of Minnesota Press, 1997.

Campbell, David, and Michael J. Shapiro, eds. *Moral Spaces: Rethinking Ethics and World Politics*. Minneapolis: Minnesota Press, 1999.

Caney, Simon. 'Global Interdependence and Distributive Justice'. *Review of International Studies* 31, no. 2 (2005): 389–99.

Cannell, John Clucas. *The Secrets of Houdini*. New York: Dover Publications Inc., 1973.

Carroll, Lewis. *The Hunting of the Snark: An Agony in Eight Fits*. New York: Macmillan, 1891.

Cavell, Stanley. *The Claim of Reason: Wittgenstein, Skepticism, Morality and Tragedy*. Oxford: Clarendon Press, 1979.

Cladis, Mark S. 'Wittgenstein, Rawls and Conservatism'. *Philosophy and Social Criticism* 20, no. 1/2 (1994): 13–37.

Cochran, Molly. *Normative Theory in International Relations: A Pragmatic Approach*. Cambridge: Cambridge University Press, 1999.

Collins Dictionary of the English Language, ed. Thomas Hill Long, London and Glasgow: Collins, 1979.

Conant, James. 'Throwing Away the Top of the Ladder'. *The Yale Review* 79 (1991): 328–64.

Cook, Martin L. 'Michael Walzer's Concept of "Supreme Emergency"'. *Journal of Military Ethics* 6, no. 2 (2007): 138–51.

Cozette, Murielle. 'Reclaiming the Critical Dimension of Realism: Hans J. Morgenthau on the Ethics of Scholarship'. *Review of International Studies* 34 (2008): 5–27.

Crary, Alice, and Rupert Read, eds. *The New Wittgenstein*. London: Routledge, 1999.

Dahbour, Omar. 'Three Models of Global Community'. *The Journal of Ethics* 9 (2005): 201–24.

Daniels, Norman, ed. *Reading Rawls: Critical Studies on Rawls' 'A Theory of Justice'*. New York: Basic Books, 1989.

Der Derian, James, and Michael J. Shapiro, eds. *International/Intertextual Relations: Postmodern Readings of World Politics*. Lexington, MA: Lexington Books, 1989.

Diamond, Cora. *The Realistic Spirit: Wittgenstein, Philosophy, and the Mind*. Cambridge, MA: The MIT Press, 1995.

Donnelly, Jack. 'Twentieth-Century Realism'. In *Traditions of International Ethics*, edited by Terry Nardin and David R. Mapel. Cambridge: Cambridge University Press, 1993.

Doppelt, Gerald. 'Walzer's Theory of Morality in International Relations'. *Philosophy and Public Affairs* 8, no. 1 (1978): 3–26.

Dower, Nigel. *World Ethics: The New Agenda*, Edinburgh Studies in World Ethics. Edinburgh: Edinburgh University Press, 1998.

Dubik, James M. 'Human Rights, Command Responsibility, and Walzer's Just War Theory'. *Philosophy and Public Affairs* 11, no. 4 (1982): 354–71.

Duffy, G., B. Frederking, and S. Tucker. 'Language Games: Dialogical Analysis of Inf Negotiations'. *International Studies Quarterly* 37, no. 3 (1998): 297–320.

Edkins, Jenny. *Poststructuralism and International Relations: Bringing the Political Back In*. Boulder, CO: Lynne Rienner Publishers, 1999.

— —. 'Whatever Politics'. In *Sovereignty and Life: Essays on Georgio Agamben*, edited by Matthew Carlarco and Seven DeCaroli. Stanford, CA: Stanford University Press, 2007.

Edkins, Jenny, Nalini Persram, and Véronique Pin-Fat, eds. *Sovereignty and Subjectivity*. Boulder, CO: Lynne Rienner, 1997.

Edkins, Jenny, and Véronique Pin-Fat. 'Jean Bethke Elshtain: Traversing the Terrain Between'. In *The Future of International Relations: Masters in the Making?*, edited by Iver Neumann and Ole Waever, pp. 290–315. London: Routledge, 1997a.

— —. 'The Subject of the Political'. In *Sovereignty and Subjectivity*, edited by Jenny Edkins, Nalini Persram and Véronique Pin-Fat, pp. 1–18. Boulder, CO: Lynne Rienner Publishers, 1997b.

— —. 'Life, Power, Resistance'. In *Sovereign Lives: Power in Global Politics*, edited by Jenny Edkins, Véronique Pin-Fat and Michael J. Shapiro. New York: Routledge, 2004.

— —. 'Through the Wire: Relations of Power and Relations of Violence'. *Millennium: Journal of International Studies* 34, no. 1 (2005): 1–24.

Edkins, Jenny, Véronique Pin-Fat, and Michael J. Shapiro, eds. *Sovereign Lives: Power in Global Politics*. New York: Routledge, 2004.

Edwards, James C. *Ethics without Philosophy: Wittgenstein and the Moral Life*. Tampa, FL: University Presses of Florida, 1982.

Elshtain, Jean Bethke. *Public Man, Private Woman: Women in Social and Political Thought*. Princeton, NJ: Princeton University Press, 1981.

— —. *Women and War*. New York: Basic Books, 1987.

— —. *Women and War*. With a new epilogue edn. Chicago: University of Chicago Press, 1995.

— —. *New Wine and Old Bottles: International Politics and Ethical Discourse*. Notre Dame, IN: University of Notre Dame Press, 1998.

— —. 'Terrorism, Regime Change, and Just War: Reflections on Michael Walzer'. *Journal of Military Ethics* 6, no. 2 (2007): 131–37.

Enloe, Cynthia. *Bananas, Beaches and Bases*. London: Pandora, 1989.

Feinberg, Joel. 'Duty and Obligation in the Non-Ideal World'. *Journal of Philosophy* 70, no. 9 (1973): 263–75.

— —. 'Rawls and Intuitionism'. In *Reading Rawls: Critical Studies on Rawls' 'A Theory of Justice'*, edited by Norman Daniels. Oxford: Basil Blackwell, 1975.

Feyerabend, Paul K. *Against Method: Outline of an Anarchistic Theory of Knowledge*. London: NLB, 1975.

Fierke, K.M. *Changing Games, Changing Strategies*. Manchester: Manchester University Press, 1998.

— —. 'Links across the Abyss: Language and Logic in International Relations'. *International Studies Quarterly* 46 (2002): 331–54.

Fierke, K.M., and K.E. Jorgensen, eds. *Constructing International Relations: The Next Generation*. Armonk, NY: M.E. Sharpe, 2001.

Finch, Henry Le Roy. *Wittgenstein*. Shaftesbury: Element, 1995.

Forde, Steven. 'Varieties of Realism – Thucydides and Machiavelli'. *Journal of Politics* 54, no. 2 (1992): 372–93.

— —. 'Classical Realism'. In *Traditions of International Ethics*, edited by Terry Nardin and David R. Mapel. Cambridge: Cambridge University Press, 1993.

Frost, Mervyn. *Towards a Normative Theory of International Relations*. Cambridge: Cambridge University Press, 1986.

— —. 'The Role of Normative Theory in IR'. *Millennium: Journal of International Studies* 23, no. 1 (1994): 109–18.

— —. *Ethics in International Relations: A Constitutive Theory*, Cambridge Studies in International Relations. Cambridge: Cambridge University Press, 1996.

Gallie, W.B. 'Wanted: A Philosophy of International Relations'. *Political Studies* 37, no. 3 (1979): 484–92.

Galston, W. A. 'Community, Democracy, Philosophy: The Political Thought of Michael Walzer'. *Political Theory* 17, no. 1 (1989): 119–30.

George, Jim. *Discourses of Global Politics: A Critical (Re)Introduction to International Relations*. Boulder, CO: Lynne Rienner Publishers, 1994.

Glock, Hans-Johann. *A Wittgenstein Dictionary*. Oxford: Blackwell, 1996.

Griffiths, Martin. *Realism, Idealism and International Politics: A Reinterpretation*. London: Routledge, 1992.

Hare, J.E., and C.B. Joynt. *Ethics and International Affairs*. London: Macmillan, 1982.

Held, Virginia, Sidney Morgenbesser, and Thomas Nagel, eds. *Philosophy, Morality, and International Affairs*. London: Oxford University Press, 1974.

Hendrickson, David C. 'In Defense of Realism: A Commentary on Just and Unjust Wars'. *Ethics and International Affairs* 11 (1997): 19–54.

Hobbes, Thomas. *Leviathan*. Edited by C.B. Macpherson. London: Penguin, 1968.

Hoffmann, Stanley. *Duties Beyond Borders: On the Limits and Possibilities of Ethical International Politics*. Syracuse: Syracuse University Press, 1981.

— —. *The Political Ethics of International Relations*. New York: Carnegie Council on Ethics and International Affairs, 1988.

Hollis, Martin. *The Philosophy of Social Science: An Introduction*. Cambridge: Cambridge University Press, 1994.

— —. 'The Last Post?' In *International Theory: Positivism and Beyond*, edited by Steve Smith, Ken Booth and Marysia Zalewski. Cambridge: Cambridge University Press, 1996.

Hollis, Martin, and Steve Smith. *Explaining and Understanding International Relations*. Oxford: Clarendon Press, 1991.

Hutchings, Kimberly. *International Political Theory: Rethinking Ethics in a Global Era*. London: SAGE, 1999.

Hutchinson, A.P.A. 'The Emotion of Shame in the Testimony of Holocaust Survivors'. PhD in progress, University of Manchester, 2005.

Hutchinson, Phil. *Shame and Philosophy: An Investigation in the Philosophy of Emotions and Ethics*. London: Palgrave, 2008.

Ignatieff, Michael. *The Lesser Evil: Political Ethics in an Age of Terror*. Edinburgh: Edinburgh University Press, 2004.

Johnston, Paul. *Wittgenstein and Moral Philosophy*. London: Routledge, 1991.

Kelly, John C. 'Wittgenstein, the Self, and Ethics'. *The Review of Metaphysics* 48, no. 3 (1995): 567.

Kenny, Anthony. *The Legacy of Wittgenstein*. Oxford: Basil Blackwell, 1984.

— —, ed. *The Wittgenstein Reader*. Oxford: Blackwell, 1994.

Keohane, Robert O., ed. *Neorealism and Its Critics*. New York: Columbia University Press, 1986.

Kipnis, K., and D.T. Meyers, eds. *Political Realism and International Morality: Ethics in the Nuclear Age*. London: Westview Press, 1987.

Kontos, Alkis. 'The World Disenchanted'. In *The Barbarism of Reason: Max Weber and the Twilight of Enlightenment*, edited by Asher Horowitz and Terry Maley. Toronto: University of Toronto Press, 1994.

Koontz, Theodore J. 'Noncombatant Immunity in Michael Walzer's Just and Unjust Wars'. *Ethics and International Affairs* 11 (1997): 55–82.

Kratochwil, F. V. *Rules, Norms and Decisions: On the Conditions of Practical and Legal Reasoning in International Relations and Domestic Affairs*. Cambridge: Cambridge University Press, 1989.

Kripke, Saul A. 'Wittgenstein on Rules and Private Language'. In *Perspectives on the Philosophy of Wittgenstein*, edited by Irving Block. Oxford: Basil Blackwell, 1981.

Kukathas, Chandran, and Philip Pettit. *Rawls: A Theory of Justice and Its Critics*. Oxford: Polity Press, 1990.

Lackey, D. 'A Modern Theory of Just War'. *Ethics* 92 (1982): 533–346.

Laclau, Ernesto. 'The Death and Resurrection of the Theory of Ideology'. *Journal of Political Ideologies* 1, no. 3 (1996): 201–20.

Lapid, Yosef. 'The Third Debate: On the Prospects of International Theory in a Post-Positivist Era'. *International Studies Quarterly* 33 (1989): 235–54.

Linklater, Andrew. *Men and Citizens in the Theory of International Relations*. London: Macmillan, 1990.

——. *The Transformation of Political Community: Ethical Foundations of the Post-Westphalian Era*. Oxford: Polity, 1998.

Lu, Catherine. 'Cosmopolitan Liberalism and the Faces of Injustice in International Relations'. *Review of International Studies* 31, no. 2 (2005): 401–8.

Luban, David. 'The Romance of the Nation-State'. *Philosophy and Public Affairs* 9, no. 4 (1980): 392–97.

Machiavelli, Niccolò. *The Prince*. Edited by Quentin Skinner and Russell Price. Cambridge: Cambridge University Press, 1988.

Malcolm, Norman. 'Wittgenstein's Philosophical Investigations'. In *The Philosophy of Mind*, edited by V.C. Chappell, 74–100. Englewood Cliffs, NJ: Prentice Hall, 1962.

——. *Nothing Is Hidden: Wittgenstein's Criticism of His Early Thought*. Oxford: Basil Blackwell, 1986.

Masters, Cristina, and Elizabeth Dauphinée, eds. *The Logics of Biopower and the War on Terror*. Basingstoke: Palgrave Macmillan, 2007.

McDonald, Henry. 'Crossroads of Skepticism: Wittgenstein, Derrida, and Ostensive Definition'. *The Philosophical Forum* 21, no. 3 (1990): 261–76.

McPherson, Lionel K. 'The Limits of the War Convention'. *Philosophy and Social Criticism* 31, no. 2 (2005): 147–63.

Miller, David. 'Justice and Inequality'. In *Inequality, Globalization, and World Politics*, edited by Andrew Hurrell and Ngaire Woods. Oxford: Oxford University Press, 1999.

——. *Citizenship and National Identity*. Cambridge: Polity Press, 2000.

——. 'Defending Political Autonomy: Discussion of Charles Beitz'. *Review of International Studies* 31, no. 2 (2005): 381–88.

Mookherjee, Monica. 'Exclusion, Internalization, Harm: Towards a Case-Based Alternative to Walzer's Thin Minimalism'. *Ethnicities* 3, no. 3 (2003): 345–68.

Morgenthau, Hans J. 'Positivism, Functionalism, and International Law'. *American Journal of International Law* 34 (1940): 260–84.

— —. *Scientific Man Vs. Power Politics*. Chicago: University of Chicago Press, 1946.

— —. *In Defense of the National Interest*. New York: Alfred Knopf, 1951.

— —. 'Another "Great Debate": The National Interest of the United States'. *The American Political Science Review* XLVI, no. 4 (1952): 961–88.

— —. 'The Nature and Limits of a Theory of International Relations'. In *Theoretical Aspects of International Relations*, edited by W.T.R. Fox. Notre Dame, IN: University of Notre Dame Press, 1959.

— —. 'The Intellectual and Moral Dilemma of History'. *Christianity and Crisis* (8th February 1960).

— —. *The Decline of Democratic Politics*. Vol. One, Politics in the Twentieth Century. Chicago: University of Chicago Press, 1962.

— —. *Politics among Nations: The Struggle for Power and Peace*. 3rd edn. New York: Alfred Knopf, 1964.

— —. *Truth and Power: Essays of a Decade, 1960–1970*. London: Pall Mall Press, 1970.

— —. 'Thought and Action in Politics'. *Social Research: An International Quarterly of the Social Sciences* 38, no. Winter (1971): 611–32.

— —. *Science: Servant or Master?* Edited by Ruth Nanda Anshen. New York: New American Library, 1972.

— —. ' Fragment of an Intellectual Autobiography'. In *Truth and Tragedy: A Tribute to Hans Morgenthau*, edited by Kenneth W. Thompson and Robert J. Myers. Washington, DC: The New Republic Book Company, Inc., 1977.

— —. 'The Sanctity of Moral Law'. *Christian Ethics Today: Journal of Christian Ethics* 3:4, no. 12 On-Line (1997).

Morrice, David. 'The Liberal-Communitarian Debate in Contemporary Political Philosophy and Its Significance for International Relations'. *Review of International Studies* 26, no. 2 (2000): 233–51.

Mulhall, Stephen. *Inheritance and Originality: Wittgenstein, Heidegger, Kierkegaard*. Oxford: Oxford University Press, 2001.

Mulhall, Stephen, and Adam Swift. *Liberals and Communitarians*. Oxford: Basil Blackwell, 1992.

Murray, A.J.H. 'The Moral Politics of Hans Morgenthau'. *Review of Politics* 58, no. Winter (1996): 81–107.

— —. *Reconstructing Realism: Between Power Politics and Cosmopolitan Ethics*. Keele: Keele University Press, 1997.

Myers, Robert J., ed. *International Ethics in the Nuclear Age*. Lanham, MD: University Press of America, 1987.

— —. 'Hans J. Morgenthau on Speaking Truth to Power: A Profile'. *Society* 29, no. 2 (1992): 65–71.

Nagel, Thomas. *The View from Nowhere*. Oxford: Oxford University Press, 1986.

Nardin, Terry. *Law, Morality and the Relations of States*. Princeton, NJ: Princeton University Press, 1983.

— —. 'The Problem of Relativism in International Ethics'. *Millennium: Journal of International Studies* 18, no. 2 (1989): 149–61.

— —. 'Just and Unjust Wars Revisited'. *Ethics and International Affairs* 11 (1997): 1.

Nardin, Terry, and David R. Mapel, eds. *Traditions of International Ethics*. Cambridge: Cambridge University Press, 1993.

Norman, Richard. *Ethics, Killing and War*. Cambridge: Cambridge University Press, 1995.

Onuf, Nicholas Greenwood. *World of Our Making: Rules and Rule in Social Theory and International Relations*. Columbia, SC: University of South Carolina Press, 1989.

Oppenheim, Felix E. *The Place of Morality in Foreign Policy*. Lexington, MA: Lexington Books, 1991.

Orend, Brian. *Michael Walzer on War and Justice*. Cardiff: University of Wales Press, 2000.

Peterson, Ulrik Enemark. 'Breathing Nietzsche's Air: New Reflections on Morgenthau's Concepts of Power and Nature'. *Alternatives* 24, no. 1 (1999): 83–113.

Pettman, Ralph, ed. *Moral Claims in World Affairs*. London: Croom Helm, 1979.

Pichler, Hans Karl. 'The Godfathers of "Truth": Max Weber and Carl Schmitt in Morgenthau's Theory of Power Politics'. *Review of International Studies* 24, no. 2 (1988).

Pin-Fat, Véronique. 'Ethics and the Limits of Language in International Relations Theory: A Grammatical Investigation'. PhD, University of Wales Aberystwyth, 1997a.

——. 'Why Aren't We Laughing?: Grammatical Investigations in World Politics'. *Politics* 17, no. 2 (1997b): 79–86.

——. '(Im)Possible Universalism: Reading Human Rights in World Politics'. *Review of International Studies* 26, no. 4 (2000): 663–74.

——. 'The Metaphysics of the National Interest and the "Mysticism" of the Nation State: Reading Hans J. Morgenthau'. *Review of International Studies* 31, no. 2 (2005): 217–36.

——. 'How Do We Begin to Think About the World?' In *Global Politics: A New Introduction*, edited by Jenny Edkins and Maja Zehfuss. London: Routledge, 2008.

Pin-Fat, Véronique, and Maria Stern. 'The Scripting of Private Jessica Lynch: Biopolitics, Gender and the "Feminization" of the US Military'. *Alternatives: Global, Local, Political* 30 (2005): 25–53.

Pitkin, Hanna. *Wittgenstein and Justice: On the Significance of Ludwig Wittgenstein for Social and Political Thought*. Berkeley: University of California Press, 1993.

Plato. 'Parmenides'. In *Plato: The Collected Dialogues Including the Letters*, edited by Edith Hamilton and Huntington Cairns. Princeton, NJ: Princeton University Press, 1961.

Pleasants, Nigel. *Wittgenstein and the Idea of a Critical Social Theory*. London: Routledge, 1999.

Rawls, John. *A Theory of Justice*. Cambridge, MA: Harvard University Press, 1971.

——. 'Kantian Constructivism in Moral Theory'. *Journal of Philosophy* 77, (1980): 515–72.

——. *The Law of Peoples*. Cambridge, MA: Harvard University Press, 1999.

Redhead, Robin. 'Imag(in)Ing Women's Agency'. *International Feminist Journal of Politics* 9, no. 2 (2007): 218–38.

Rengger, Nicholas. 'Reading Charles Beitz: Twenty-Five Years of *Political Theory and International Relations*'. *Review of International Studies* 31, no. 2 (2005): 361–69.

Revering, Alan. 'Eschatology in the Political Theory of Michael Walzer'. *Journal of Religious Ethics* 33, no. 1 (2005): 91–117.

Robinson, Fiona. *Globalising Care: Ethics, Feminist Theory, and International Relations*. Oxford: Westview, 1998.

Root, Michael. *Philosophy of Social Science: The Methods, Ideals, and Politics of Social Inquiry*. Oxford: Blackwell, 1993.

Rorty, Richard. *Philosophy and the Mirror of Nature*. Oxford: Basil Blackwell, 1980.

Rosenberg, Justin. 'What's the Matter with Realism?' *Review of International Studies* 16, no. 4 (1990): 285–303.

Rosenblum, N. L. 'Moral Membership in a Postliberal State'. *World Politics* 36, no. 4 (1984): 581–96.

Roth, Guenther, and W. Schluchter. *Max Weber's Vision of History*. Berkeley: University of California Press, 1979.

Russell, G. *Hans J. Morgenthau and the Ethics of American Statecraft*. London: Louisiana State University Press, 1990.

Shapcott, Richard. *Justice, Community and Dialogue in International Relations*. Cambridge: Cambridge University Press, 2001.

— —. 'Anti-Cosmopolitanism, Pluralism and the Cosmopolitan Harm Principle'. *Review of International Studies* 34, (2008): 185–205.

Smith, Michael Joseph. *Realist Thought from Weber to Kissinger*. Baton Rouge: Louisiana State University Press, 1986.

— —. 'Growing up with Just and Unjust Wars: An Appreciation'. *Ethics and International Affairs* 11, (1997): 3–18.

Smith, Steve. 'The Forty Years Detour: The Resurgence of Normative Theory in International Relations'. *Millennium: Journal of International Studies* 21, no. 3 (1992): 489–506.

Spegele, Roger D. 'Political Realism and the Remembrance of Relativism'. *Review of International Studies* 21, no. 3 (1995): 211–36.

Staten, Henry. *Wittgenstein and Derrida*. Oxford: Basil Blackwell, 1985.

— —. 'Wittgenstein and the Intricate Evasion Of "Is"'. *New Literary Theory* 19, no. 2 (1988): 281–300.

Statman, Daniel. 'Supreme Emergencies Revisited'. *Ethics* 117, (2006): 58–79.

Stern, Maria. *Naming Security – Constructing Identity: 'Mayan-Women' in Guatemala on the Eve of 'Peace'*. Manchester: Manchester University Press, 2005.

Sylvester, Christine. *Feminist International Relations: An Unfinished Journey*. Cambridge: Cambridge University Press, 2002.

Thompson, Janna. *Justice and World Order: A Philosophical Inquiry*. London and New York: Routledge, 1992.

Thompson, John B. *Critical Hermeneutics: A Study in the Thought of Paul Ricoeur and Jürgen Habermas*. Cambridge: Cambridge University Press, 1981.

Thompson, Kenneth W., ed. *Ethics and International Relations*, Ethics in Foreign Policy Volume 2. Oxford: Transaction Books, 1985a.

— —. 'Ethics and International Relations: The Problem'. In *Ethics and International Relations*, edited by Kenneth W. Thompson. Oxford: Transaction Books, 1985b.

Thompson, Kenneth W., and Robert J. Myers, eds. *Truth and Tragedy: A Tribute to Hans Morgenthau*. Washington, DC: The New Republic Book Company, Inc., 1977.

Tickner, J. Ann. 'Hans Morgenthau's Principles of Political Realism: A Feminist Reformulation'. *Millennium: Journal of International Studies* 17, no. 3 (1988): 429–40.

— —. *Gender in International Relations: Perspectives on Achieving Global Security*. New York: Columbia University Press, 1992.

Tooze, Roger. 'The Unwritten Preface: International Political Economy and Epistemology'. *Millennium: Journal of International Studies* 17, no. 2 (1988): 285–93.

Turner, S.P., and R.A. Factor. *Max Weber and the Dispute over Reason and Value: A Study in Philosophy, Ethics and Politics*. London: Routledge & Kegan Paul, 1984.

Valls, Andrew, ed. *Ethics in International Affairs: Theories and Cases*. Oxford: Rowman & Littlefield, 2000.

Vincent, R. John. *Human Rights and International Relations*. Cambridge: Cambridge University Press, 1986.

Walker, R.B.J. *Inside/Outside: International Relations as Political Theory*. Cambridge: Cambridge University Press, 1993.

Walsh, Caroline. 'Rawls and Walzer on Non-Dometic Justice'. *Contemporary Political Theory* 6, (2007): 419–36.

Waltz, Kenneth N. *Man, the State, and War: A Theoretical Analysis*. New York: Columbia University Press, 1959.

— —. *Theory of International Politics*. New York: McGraw-Hill Publishing Co., 1979.

Walzer, Michael. *Obligations: Essays on Disobedience, War, and Citizenship*. Cambridge, MA: Harvard University Press, 1970.

— —. *Just and Unjust Wars: A Moral Argument with Historical Illustrations*. London: Allen Lane, 1977.

— —. 'The Moral Standing of States: A Response to Four Critics'. *Philosophy and Public Affairs* 9, (1980): 209–29.

— —. 'The Distribution of Membership'. In *Boundaries: National Autonomy and Its Limits*, edited by Peter G. Brown and Henry Shue, 1–35. Totowa, NJ: Rowman and Littlefield, 1981.

— —. *Spheres of Justice: A Defence of Pluralism and Equality*. Oxford: Blackwell, 1983.

— —. 'Liberalism and the Art of Separation'. *Political Theory* 12, no. 3 (1984): 315–30.

— —. 'The Moral Standing of States: A Response to Four Critics'. In *International Ethics*, edited by Charles Beitz, Marshall Cohen, Thomas Scanlon and A. John Simmons, 217–37. Princeton, NJ: Princeton University Press, 1985.

— —. 'Friends and Enemies'. *New Republic* 197, no. 26 (1987a): 13–14.

— —. *Interpretation and Social Criticism*. Cambridge, MA: Harvard University Press, 1987b.

— —. 'Notes on Self-Criticism'. *Social Research* 54, no. 1 (1987c): 33–43.

— —. *The Company of Critics: Social Criticism and Political Commitment in the Twentieth Century*. London: Peter Halban, 1989a.

— —. 'The State of Political Theory'. *Dissent* 36, no. 3 (1989b): 337–37.

— —. 'A Critique of Philosophical Conversation'. *The Philosophical Forum* 21, no. 1–2 (1989–90): 182–96.

— —. 'The Communitarian Critique of Liberalism'. *Political Theory* 18, no. 1 (1990): 6–23.

— —. 'Moral Minimalism'. *Deutsche Zeitschrift für Philosophie* 42, no. 1 (1994a): 3–13.

— —. 'Multiculturalism and Individualism'. *Dissent* 41, no. 2 (1994b): 185–91.

— —. *Thick and Thin: Moral Argument at Home and Abroad*. Notre Dame: University of Notre Dame Press, 1994c.

— —. 'The Politics of Rescue'. *Social Research* 62, no. 1 (1995): 53–66.

— —. 'Spheres of Affection'. In *For Love of Country: Debating the Limits of Patriotism*, edited by Joshua Cohen, 125–27. Boston: Beacon Press, 1996.

— —. 'A Response'. *Ethics and International Affairs* 11, (1997a): 99–104.

— —. *On Toleration*. New Haven, CT: Yale University Press, 1997b.

— —. *Arguing About War*. New Haven, CT: Yale University Press, 2004a.

— —. *Politics and Passion: Toward a More Egalitarian Liberalism*. New Haven and London: Yale University Press, 2004b.

Weber, Max. 'Politics as a Vocation'. In *From Max Weber: Essays in Sociology*, edited by H.H. Gerth and C. Wright Mills. New York: Oxford University Press, 1971.

Wheeler, Nicholas J. *Saving Strangers*. Oxford: Oxford University Press, 2000.

Wight, Martin. *International Theory: The Three Traditions*. Edited by Gabriele Wight and Brian Porter. London: Leicester University Press, 1994.

Winch, Peter. *The Idea of a Social Science and Its Relation to Philosophy*. London: Routledge, 1958.

Wittgenstein, Ludwig. *Tractatus Logico-Philosophicus*. Trans. C.K. Ogden. London: Routledge & Kegan Paul, 1922.

— —. *Philosophical Investigations*. Trans. G.E.M. Anscombe. Edited by G.E.M. Anscombe and R. Rhees. 3rd edn. Oxford: Basil Blackwell, 1958a.

— —. *The Blue and Brown Books*. 2nd edn. Oxford: Basil Blackwell, 1958b.

— —. *On Certainty*. Trans. Paul Denis and G.E.M. Anscombe. Edited by G.E.M. Anscombe and G.H. von Wright. Oxford: Basil Blackwell, 1969.

— —. *Lectures and Conversations on Aesthetics, Psychology and Religious Beliefs*. Edited by C. Barrett. Oxford: Basil Blackwell, 1970.

— —. *Philosophical Grammar*. Trans. A.J.P. Kenny. Edited by R. Rhees. Oxford: Basil Blackwell, 1974.

— —. *Remarks on the Foundations of Mathematics*. Trans. G.E.M. Anscombe. Edited by G.H. von Wright, R. Rhees and G.E.M. Anscombe. Revised edn. Oxford: Basil Blackwell, 1978.

— —. *Culture and Value*. Trans. Peter Winch. Edited by G.H. von Wright and H. Nyman. Oxford: Basil Blackwell, 1980a.

— —. *Remarks on Colour*. Trans. L.L. McAlister and Margarete Schättle. Edited by G.E.M. Anscombe. Oxford: Basil Blackwell, 1980b.

— —. *Remarks on the Philosophy of Psychology*, Vol. 1. Trans. G.E.M. Anscombe. Edited by G.E.M. Anscombe and G.H. von Wright. Oxford: Basil Blackwell, 1980c.

— —. *Remarks on the Philosophy of Psychology*, Vol. 2. Trans. G.E.M. Anscombe. Edited by G.E.M. Anscombe and G.H. von Wright. Oxford: Basil Blackwell, 1980d.

— —. *Zettel*. Trans. G.E.M. Anscombe. Edited by G.E.M. Anscombe and G.H. von Wright. 2nd edn. Oxford: Basil Blackwell, 1981.

— —. *Philosophical Occasions*. Edited by J. Klagge and A. Nordmann. Indianapolis: Hackett, 1993.

Wong, Benjamin. 'Hans Morgenthau's Anti-Machiavellian Machiavellianism'. *Millennium: Journal of International Studies* 29, no. 2 (2000): 389–409.

Index

106, 108, 110; thin 101–3, 108, 110;
use in language games 112–13;
see also binary universality; divine
universality; ideal universality
universals: particulars vs 60
utilitarianism 53
utopianism: realism vs 55

value neutrality 35
values: facts vs 32–5
veil of ignorance 72–3, 74, 82, 127
verifiability 33
vita activa 41, 49, 60
vita comtemplativa 41, 42, 49, 51, 53

Walzer, Michael: communitarianism
85, 91, 104, 127; conjunctive failure
104, 108, 110; moral dilemma of
international politics 86–7, 104, 115;
as particularist 85; picture of ethico-
political space 96, 103–10; picture
of reason 98–103; picture of subject

91–8, 127; as pluralist 93; work 85–6;
see also binary universality
war: civil 107–8; just 94; morality of
85–6
Weber, Max 50, 53, 54, 136n16
will to know 49, 50, 51, 53
will to live 49, 50, 51
wisdom: as gift of intuition 55–6
Wittgenstein, Ludwig: conservatism
charges 16–17; on grammar 19–22;
on language games 10–12, 15–16; on
language and reality 5; mysticism
24, 26, 28, 124, 125; on pictures 19,
20; rejection of metaphysics 7–14,
28; 'spirit' of philosophy 6–7, 27;
Tractatus Logico-Philosophicus 6,
26–8, 123–5; work as therapeutic 27
wonderment *see* shock of wonderment
word–object relations 113
word–word relations 117
world disenchanted 50
world order: just 67